A COMPENDIUM OF STATE STATUTES AND INTERNATIONAL TREATIES IN TRUST AND ESTATE LAW

A Compendium of State Statutes and International Treaties in Trust and Estate Law

A Reference and Referral Guide for Practicing Attorneys

M. HENNER

Q

Quorum Books

Westport, Connecticut • London, England

Library of Congress Cataloging in Publication Data

Henner, M. (Murray)
A compendium of state statutes and international treaties in trust and estate law.

Bibliography: p.
Includes index.
1. Inheritance and succession—United States—States. 2. Wills—United States—States. 3. Inheritance and succession. 4. Wills. I. Title.
KF753.Z95H46 1985 346.7305'2 85-3354
ISBN 0-89930-076-6 (lib. bdg.) 347.30652

Library of Congress Catalog Card Number: 85-3354
ISBN: 0-89930-076-6

First published in 1985 by Quorum Books

Greenwood Press
A division of Congressional Information Service, Inc.
88 Post Road West, Westport, Connecticut 06881

Printed in the United States of America

10 9 8 7 6 5 4 3 2 1

For Marsha, Margot, and Sean

Contents

Preface

There is a great deal of validity to the old adage "the world is getting smaller." Modern technology has made for ease of movement around the globe, providing inhabitants of foreign countries the opportunity to establish several residences simultaneously. With the acquisition of more than one abode, complex legal questions have arisen that may and often do have substantial impact on the lifestyles of individuals and their plans for the future. External and/or internal variables, which derive from the legal system of a particular jurisdiction, determine crucial issues such as the manner in which families inherit personalty and/or realty. Often these variables result in undue taxation of an estate, resulting in the unfortunate depletion of assets that have taken a lifetime to accumulate. Matrimonial disputes between spouses residing in different geographic areas and disputes with regard to child support are frequently the products of this freedom of movement. Amplification and development of business transactions have resulted in practical and genuine problems involving immigration laws. Once a person is settled in a foreign land, the inevitable purchase or sale of property takes place.

There is no one exhaustive and conclusive source of information that could contain all of the laws affecting the potential problems posed by the above circumstances. Perhaps one of the most frustrating problems for a lawyer engaged in the general practice of law is how to manage a client's problem when it will require knowledge of the fundamental legal principles of a foreign jurisdiction. The breadth of knowledge and licensing requirements essential to handle matters outside a lawyer's home base would also be impossible for any lawyer to possess.

The aim of this book is to assist the general practitioner in managing such complex situations as they affect estates. It directs the lawyer to appropriate authoritative sources of information, people, and organizations, after acquiring a rudimentary familiarity with the laws of specific foreign jurisdictions and the several states. More importantly, however, it is my intention to provide certain tools for the attorney that will add to his or her understanding of the questions raised by the attorney's client, thus improving the basic attorney-client relationship.

This book has been divided into several specific areas of Estate practice. They are Estates (Testacy-Intestacy); Conflict of Laws; Gathering the Information; Foreign Taxation of Estates; Adopted, Illegitimate, and Posthumous Children; The Law of Intestacy; Western European Inheritance Laws; and Revocation of Wills. Also included are locations and telephone numbers of bar associations and referral services that provide the practitioner with easy access for referral purposes.

In the discussion of general estate matters, the laws of wills and intestate succession are addressed and examined. Treatment of a foreign beneficiary of a decedent in a host country; the rights of surviving spouses and adopted, illegitimate, and posthumous children; simultaneous death; proof of wills in probate; revocation of wills; and interaction with United States treaties are considered and summarized in subsequent chapters.

This book is not intended to be a definitive text on estate law; it is still all-important that competent, licensed attorneys are consulted and retained in any and all matters that require legal representation. Lay people are cautioned to consult licensed practitioners for in-depth or conclusive counseling on the law and its interpretations. Lawyers consulting this guide are also cautioned to refer to licensed counsel in foreign jurisdictions or on matters outside their field of legal expertise.

Acknowledgments

In writing this acknowledgment I am reminded of the many hours spent researching, writing, editing, and shepherdizing the material contained in this book. But more importantly, the special people who devoted their time and energies to the preparation of this book come to mind. It is these people that provided encouragement, expertise, moral support, and insight throughout this endeavor.

I want to extend a special note of gratitude to my two associates, Celeste P. Kaufman and Karen A. Weiner, for their unbounded efforts in compiling the material for this book. Despite the intrusion into their personal lives, these two attorneys spent numerous hours in law libraries throughout New York City researching and reviewing the statutes and cases contained in this book. At times I'm sure it must have seemed like an endless task but their diligence and patience were unbounded and to be much admired.

Thanks must also be offered to my colleagues, George Brenner, Dr. Volker Henckel, Suzanne McGrattan, Frederick Reisert, and Thomas R. Raleigh. Each provided considerable insights into the various laws contained in this book. Late nights and early mornings were spent with each comparing genealogical charts, client questionnaires, intestacy tables, and various other documents.

I am also indebted to my paralegal staff, namely, Lance Kramer and David Sobel. Together they spent many long days assembling the vast array of statutes and treatises given them. They provided order and sequence to material that at times appeared to be incapable of being organized. My secretarial staff was truly superb. Both Marion Abernathy and Shirley Zyrb spent countless hours typing without complaint and for that I thank them. Special thanks must also go to Dr. Robert Sobel for his aid in proofreading the manuscript. His expertise in this area was truly invaluable and was much relied upon.

The librarians and staff at the law libraries at Hofstra University School of Law, New York University School of Law, St. John's University Law School, The Association of the Bar of the City of New York and the Library of Congress in Washington, D.C. were immensely helpful in directing me to the correct aisles in the library or in helping me find misplaced and lost books. My thanks to them all.

Finally, I must give loving thanks to my wife, Marsha, my parents, Pauline and Martin Henner, as well as Melba, Harry, and Jonathan Goldstein and particularly Rebecca Kon, who continually provided me with emotional support, understanding, and great enthusiasm for this project.

How to Use This Guide

It is apparent to most general practitioners that the laws of respective jurisdictions can differ to such an extent that the outcome of a particular legal proceeding is often dependent upon the practitioner's practical skills as opposed to his or her expertise in legal concepts that may be pertinent. The above is true particularly with regard to the management of foreign estates by counsel retained outside of the practitioner's host jurisdiction. Communication with foreign counsel without a basic understanding of the legal tenets involved in that jurisdiction will certainly call for additional confusion and delay in the host jurisdiction because of the practitioner's inability to convey to a client exactly what is going on in the foreign locale. In each of the major substantive chapters in this book, tools or information have been included for facilitating the fact-gathering process, differentiating between various laws in the several jurisdictions, and directing counsel to other agencies and foreign infrastructures for further information.

Providing foreign counsel with all relevant data, that is, fact gathering involved in the host jurisdiction, can often effectuate expedient processing of a client's claim or objection and project a more competent, positive, and reassuring image to the client awaiting results. One should keep in mind however, and stress to one's client, that relatively, the judicial bureaucracy in certain jurisdictions moves at a snail's pace as opposed to the conquerable bureaucracy in the host jurisdiction. Foreign statutes requiring the passage of time to process a claim may also be alien to a client who has had no experience in dealing with the judicial system.

The organizational charts and information data sheets in this book have been most helpful to my firm in exposing and providing for all information in various proceedings that eventually is required by foreign counsel. Completing this information is a cumbersome task; however, it saves much time and energy, and, after all, time is money.

A COMPENDIUM OF STATE STATUTES AND INTERNATIONAL TREATIES IN TRUST AND ESTATE LAW

1 Estates

The primary focus of this chapter is to provide counsel with an overview of the inheritance system in the United States. Understanding the basic tenets underlying the systematic development of the law of estates is essential to provide your client with a rudimentary knowledge of probate and non-probate systems. Through this knowledge and understanding, a lay person will acknowledge many of the problems potentially encountered down the arduous road to receiving letters testamentary or letters of administration. An explanation and commentary on properly constructed testamentary instruments are provided for counsel, along with a general discussion of the legal ramifications encountered when one dies intestate. The historical perspective, short as it may appear, is essential for counsel to assimilate. The inheritance laws in the United States emerged out of necessity for the state to "provide" for the heirs of a domiciliary when a decedent did not so provide. Since legitimate forms of property ownership are as varied in legal results upon a decedent's death as there are state statutes, the extent of a testator's power to dispose of property interests by will is explored. In addition, a simplified explanation of probate's potentially advantageous qualities can convey to a client the need for affirmative review and action by counsel on a regular basis.

A basic knowledge of the complex differences between community property and common law jurisdictions will clearly establish a smoother flow of the required information and documentation from counsel to foreign counsel. For this reason, a commentary has been included in this area. I hope it will assist you in laying the proper foundation for further estate planning and in expeditious administration of a decedent's assets upon the client's subsequent demise. The proper method for preservation and maintenance of appropriate records along with a simplified net worth statement will assist you, before a decedent's death, in cataloging assets of your client.

THE INHERITANCE SYSTEM

Every Western society recognizes private ownership of property. This recognition is not without legal restrictions or limitations. The right to pass wealth in the form of personalty, real property, or mixed property at death is either a natural, statutory, or constitutional right in the United States, and some form of inheritance has been universally recognized in the ancient and modern worlds.

The inheritance system responds to a basic human desire to protect and provide for family and loved ones upon death. It can be viewed as a natural and proper expression and as a reinforcement of family ties that aids in the development of a healthy society. The system can also be viewed as an incentive for creativity, initiative, and productivity by encouraging those who are capable to make provisions for individuals who are or may become dependents. Estate planning can be an essential device for savings to ultimate beneficiaries of large amounts of wealth. The interplay between the laws of several jurisdictions often has a definitive impact on the amount a distributee or devisee eventually receives. The failure to provide for a competent estate plan can likewise result in the operation of the laws of intestacy. Thus a sovereign state in effect has the last word on a testator's intent in accordance with the statute governing such dispositions.

The estates of deceased persons are classified as testate and intestate.

> A person is said to die intestate when he dies without making a will, or dies without having anything to testify what his wishes were with respect to the disposal of his property after his death. The word is often used to signify the person himself. Thus in speaking of the property of a person who died intestate, it is common to say "the intestate's property," i.e., the property of the person dying in an intestate condition.[1]

The disposition of the property is controlled by a state or foreign country's intestate laws, which provide at certain junctures for the inheritance of an intestate's property, real and personal, by his or her heirs and distributees. Beyond these junctures, there are usually general provisions according to which an intestate's heirs and distributees are to be determined. However, there is no complete statutory scheme in any state that is detailed enough to provide specifically for every case that may arise under this area of the law. Frequently, these statutes must be construed and applied in cases in which there is no specific statutory provision that is directly on point with a factual situation in a particular case.

In cases in which there is no specific statutory provision, the issue of whether to construe the appropriate statute in accordance with the common law or the civil law arises. Since many, if not most, of the statutes embody a combination of principles from both the common law and the civil law, it is not surprising that there is a contrariety in the cases in construing the statutes of descent and distribution. In some of the cases, the courts have based their construction on the common law, and in others they have turned to the civil law. It appears that when the legislature has adopted some particular rule of either system of law, such as the method of computing next of kin, this does not necessarily indicate an intention that the particular system shall control in the matter of construction.

The statutes in the various states establish the order of priority in which the individuals who have claim to an estate shall inherit the property of an intestate. For example, in the various statutes, the children of an intestate or their representatives are granted priority over brothers and sisters of the intestate and grandparents. The statutes embody a policy of placing parents on equal ground with their children. Brothers and sisters are preferred to grandparents, and parents are preferred to brothers and sisters. Although this is the general scheme of intestate distribution in a majority of the states, each state statute should be carefully analyzed when dealing with this area of the law.

TESTACY AND INTESTACY

A person who dies leaving a valid will is said to have died testate. Generally, a *will* is a ''written instrument executed with the formalities required by statutes, whereby a person makes a disposition of his property to take effect after his death.''[2] When testacy prevails, the property of the decedent is distributed in accordance with the provisions of the will. It is conceivable that a will does not dispose of the entire estate or that certain dispositive provisions are invalid. In those instances, separate proceedings in the court of competent jurisdiction may be required. These proceedings are sometimes referred to as ''construction proceedings.'' At these proceedings, the court may interpret various articles of the will, particularly in the event of ambiguous or vague language. The testator's intent is usually all-important in these proceedings. Under other circumstances, that portion of the estate not disposed of by will may be distributed in accordance with the intestacy laws.

There is no law that mandates that an individual must have a will drafted, although every person may do so upon obtaining a certain age and upon fulfilling certain other requirements. The only role the law plays with regard to making a will is to prescribe certain formalities to insure that the document will be accepted as a will in the appropriate jurisdictions.

The decision to make a will means that one can control who will receive one's property, in what proportions, at what time, and upon what conditions, as well as who shall settle one's estate. Society also has a claim upon a person to make a will, because it is entitled to have its members exercise their best judgment in providing for their dependents through their estates. The state is within its rights when it expects its citizens to provide for their families. In addition, one's will is often the only permanent record of oneself that is left behind. The will becomes a matter of public record that can be read by anyone for as long as it remains legible. Therefore, although there are statutory provisions that encompass the administration of an estate of one dying without a will, the making of a will is a privilege and a duty that should be exercised by all.

The requirements of testamentary validity are as varied as the number of jurisdictions provided by statute for said requirements.

Speaking broadly, nothing more is needed than a legible writing, a signature by the maker of the will, testamentary capacity, and formal attestation by the number of competent witnesses specified by the laws of the governing jurisdiction. By statute in a number of states a will valid by the law of the jurisdiction where it was executed is valid under the law of the domicile of the maker at the time of his death, even though it would fail to meet the requirements of the latter jurisdiction at the time of its execution or later.[3]

A form of the Uniform Wills Act has been adopted in many states. ''Thus, the body of law surrounding the preparation of wills is benign; yet it is well understood among estate planners that a failure to meet the few legal requirements is a serious matter, for the invalidity of a will means distribution of the property in a way rigidly prescribed by statutes of descent and distribution regardless of the testator's actual intent.''[4]

HISTORICAL PERSPECTIVE

As is true of the law in general, the law of inheritance in the United States derives much of its content from English law. In medieval England, personal property was of little importance. Real property was significant, because it was the basis of wealth and the foundation of the social system. The possession of land was a reflection of a man himself. Originally, an interest in land was severely restricted, because the *Statute of Uses* (1535) virtually destroyed the right to devise lands in England. The demand for the right was so great that the *Statute of Wills* was enacted in 1540, during the reign of Henry VIII, recognizing the devise of lands. The only specific requirement as to the manner of execution was that the devise be in writing. The document did not have to be made by or signed by the testator. Wills of personal property, drawn as testaments, were not required to be in writing to be valid. The opportunity for the perpetration of fraud, however, was a strong factor that led to the enactment of the *Statute of Frauds* in 1676. This statute required devises to be in writing and signed by the testator or by some person in the testator's presence and at his or her express direction. The execution of the document required the presence of witnesses.

Until 1837 testaments were the province of the church courts under English law. Subsequently, probate and administration were handled by Courts of Probate. Gradually, as the feudal system of land law came to an end, the law of wills and the law of testaments became one.

The principles of law that were based upon feudalism were never a part of the general jurisprudence of the United States. There are statutes in every state regulating the substantive and procedural law of wills, and the two English statutes are models for most of the substantive law in the United States. The old traditions in this area have left many traces on inheritance terminology. Land still "descends" to an "heir," and goods and money are "distributed" to a "next of kin." This formality of language is fading, however.

In contrast, it should be noted that the French settlements, in what is now Louisiana, were governed by French law, which was largely based upon Roman law.[5]

WHAT MAY PASS BY WILL

The terms *property* and *estate* usually signify to the lay person possession of concrete, tangible objects, such as automobiles and jewelry. They do not recognize the legal understanding of property, which encompasses not only tangible items but the intangible relationship embraced that deals with the relationship of people to the property itself. The law, therefore, provides a more expansive meaning and views property interests as a bundle of rights.

Property interests that may pass by will include many objects and overlap many areas of substantive law. For example, in many jurisdictions, one who has entered into a contract may dispose of his or her rights under the contract by will. Generally, most states permit every kind of property interest, both real and personal, whether or not it is related to tangible or intangible objects, to pass by will as long as the interest does not expire upon death and it is not subject to an inter vivos (lifetime) conveyance or arrangement that has created in someone else the right to take property by operation of law other than succession.

All property that a testator owned upon his or her death can be disposed of by will, and it is usually immaterial from what source the testator had originally acquired the property. However, the testator can convey only property that he or she owns or has a legal interest in. Therefore, unless the testator had a valid power, he or she cannot devise or bequeath property to which the testator does not have title. In other words, a legatee's rights to specific property would not vest when, without the will, the property would not become part of the decedent's estate.

The fact that the testator has title to property that he or she does not possess, either at the time of the execution of the will or upon the testator's death, does not render the property inalienable by a will. However, if delivery of certain property is essential to establishing title in the testator, failure of delivery will prevent the property from passing under a will.

The law that governs the determination of what property may be passed by will usually depends on the nature of the transferred property. The extent of the power of the testator to dispose of real property is usually determined by the law of the situs. Disposition of personal property is governed by the domiciliary state of the testator regardless of the location of the personalty.

TYPES OF PROPERTY INTERESTS AND GENERAL CAVEATS

1. Restriction on power to alienate—such a restriction on the testator's power to sell or dispose of the property does not make it inalienable by his or her will.

2. Undivided interest—the owner of an undivided interest cannot bequeath or devise the entire property to a third person. The owner can, however, bequeath or devise his or her own interest.

3. Under some state statutes, property that is exempt from execution by judgment creditors, such as life insurance and homesteads, cannot be devised or bequeathed. It can be bequeathed only if the intention of the testator is indisputable. Usually, interests such as life insurance pass by operation of law to the last recorded beneficiary with the carrier or institution insuring the life of the decedent.

4. A legatee who dies before the testator cannot devise or bequeath property that the legatee would have taken under the will of such testator if he or she had survived the testator.

5. One who has acquired a lien upon property cannot devise the property itself. The lien intertest can be passed by will along with the indebtedness it secures.

6. An executor cannot bequeath as his or her own property that which the executor holds in a representative capacity.

7. A tenant in common may devise or bequeath his or her undivided interest in property. A tenant cannot devise a specific part of such realty in severalty.

8. An attempted devise of property held in joint tenancy is ineffective, and the property passes by operation of law pursuant to the surviving joint tenant's right of survivorship.

9. After it is acquired, personal property may pass by will.

10. The prevailing view is that property disposed of after execution of a will and then again acquired may pass by will, although much common law has held the will inoperative as to that real estate.

11. A change in the form of property will not prevent its passing under a general devise or bequest, although it may in some instances prevent its passing under a specific devise or bequest.

12. An equitable interest may be devisable unless it is by its nature inalienable and the sole owner of corporate stock has an equitable interest in the corporate property that is devisable.

13. The interest of the vendor and the purchaser under a contract for the sale of property are each subject to devise.

14. The unpaid portion of the purchase price for land deeded to another may be disposed of by the grantor by will.

15. The interest conferred by a land warrant or certificate for the purchase of public lands is devisable.

16. Rights of action that do not cease with the death of the owner may be disposed of by will.

17. Reversionary remainders and estates may be devised or bequeathed.

18. In general, contingent estates are devisable if the person to take is ascertained and only the event is uncertain. Whether a contingent estate is devisable when the person to take is uncertain depends upon applicable state statutes.

19. In general, a testator may dispose of by will the proceeds of life insurance payable to his or her estate or representatives or assigns.

20. A spouse may devise property as he or she wishes, but the property or the rights of the other spouse cannot be disposed of as imparted. Land owned by the entirety cannot be devised by either spouse.

21. In general, either spouse may dispose of his or her community property by will, but neither has the right to dispose of the interest of the other in community property.

22. Property payable or transferable to others at the death of the testator, as when the testator has a life estate, may not be disposed of by will.

23. Authorities differ about whether one can dispose of one's own dead body by will.

The right to take property disposed of by will is not a natural, inalienable constitutional right in the United States. Indeed, in virtually every state, there are statutes that relate directly to this right as numerous common law doctrines that disable certain persons from taking property by will. However, as a general rule, testamentary dispositions are usually required to be enforced as long as they do not violate public policy, state statutes, or settled principles of law.

One who has testamentary capacity may dispose of one's property in any manner and to any person one desires who is capable of taking. This is subject to certain rights that, for example, a surviving spouse may have. Generally, in the absence of some special disability declared by statute, any person can be a legatee or devisee. In some jurisdictions, testamentary dispositions in favor of a person deemed incapable of receiving property will be null and void.

The capacity of a devisee or a legatee to take a present vested interest is to be determined at the time of the testator's death and must exist at that time. Generally, capacity at the date of the testator's death is not affected or destroyed by a prior or subsequent incapacity. Similarly, an incapacity existing between the date of execution of a will and the testator's death is irrelevant as long as capacity has been restored by the date of the testator's demise. However, when the interest given is conditional and not intended to vest until a time subsequent to the testator's death, the date of the actual vesting of the interest is the time for the determination of the devisee's or legatee's capacity, subject to the Rule against Perpetuities.

THE TESTAMENTARY DISPOSITION

In general, to be able to take by will, the donee or beneficiary must be in existence either at the time of the testator's death or when the gift would vest under the will. A child ''in vitre sa mire'' is incapable of taking a devise. The devise to such a child is valid even though his or her birth occurs after the death of the testator.

In general, restrictions on testamentary dispositions of realty and the capacity to take such testamentary gifts are governed by the law of the state where the realty is situated. However, when a gift of personal property is at issue, some jurisdictions mandate that the law of the state of testator's domicile is controlling, and other jurisdictions use the law of the legatee's domicile.

Husbands and wives may make any testamentary disposition of their property as they see fit to the exclusion of each other. This right is subject to dower and curtesy and statutory rights and limitations. Therefore, under varying statutes, a husband's testamentary disposition of his estate may exclude his wife from taking any portion, and a wife may deprive her husband by will of any interest whatsoever in her estate (but see the directory of state statutes regarding rights of election in chapter 6 of this book). However, by virtue of express or implied prohibition, the right to defeat a surviving spouse's right to a share of the property of a deceased spouse by testamentary disposition has been denied when the attempted disposition is made by a husband and, in some jurisdictions, when made by a wife. This denial has been made with respect to a husband's defeat of his wife's taking a share of his personal or real property and a wife's defeat of her husband's right to take a share of her personal or real property. It has been recognized that a husband may not dispose of by will personal property items that under statute are to be given to the surviving widow.

In general, a spouse may freely make testamentary dispositions of the amount of his or her property in excess of the statutory share to which the surviving spouse is entitled as a right. A married woman's will that purports to give her husband less than his statutory share is usually not invalid. It is however, subject to the right of the husband to demand and receive his share. The fact that the will of the wife does not provide for her husband and the fact that the husband does not consent to the will does not operate to void the will entirely. It will simply be nullified to the extent of the husband's legal rights.

The right of a spouse to a bequeathed legacy from the other spouse is not affected by their separation and subsequent divorce. Statutory provisions that bar either party to a divorce from any claim to the property of the other apply to claims that arise by reason of the marriage relation. They do not act to prevent a divorced spouse from claiming property bequeathed to such spouse by the other.

LINEAL DESCENDANTS

The meaning to be attached to the phrase ''lineal descendants,'' when used in a will designating intended beneficiaries, gives rise to the assumption that the testator used these words in their natural and ordinary context. Lineal descendants encompass all persons in the direct line of descent from the ancestor. The phrase embraces all of those persons, even to the remotest generation, who by consanguinity trace their lineage to the person named.

However, if the testator's intention is clear, he or she can limit the phrase, for example, to include children only. Factors such as testator's intention at the time the will is made, as ascertained from the contents of the will itself, or from the circumstances surrounding its execution can be determinative.

PROBATE AND NON-PROBATE DISTRIBUTIONS

A will does not necessarily have to be a complex legal instrument consisting of pages upon pages of legal jargon. President Calvin Coolidge squeezed his entire will into one sentence by stating, "I leave my entire estate to my wife, Grace, and request that she be appointed executrix without bond."[6] Although a will can be as simple as the above, ordinarily an individual has more than one beneficiary in mind and may also want to provide for certain contingencies such as common disasters or successor fiduciaries. Under these circumstances, more thought and care must be given in the preparation of the will.

Many clients have already arranged for their assets to pass by operation of law, outside of probate, and question the need for a will. The answer to that question may be one that involves tax ramifications of their present disposition or contrary provisions under a jurisdiction's intestacy laws. The jurisdiction may also intercede in the distribution of one's estate by appointing an administrator of the court's choosing. If there are minor or orphan children, a guardian would probably be appointed to manage either the children's person or property or both. That guardian is not necessarily a relative or friend of the decedent or his or her family. The intestacy laws provided in this book are an ideal source of initial discussion with the client, who may be a potential beneficiary under a foreign jurisdiction's statute. The right-of-election statutes provided herein also provide the practitioner with the statutory rights a spouse or child may have as against a testamentary instrument.

COMMON LAW AND COMMUNITY PROPERTY

The question of property ownership can also be a complex area to explain to a lay person. Some states have a community-property system, and others allow the common law system of ownership. In community-property states in the United States, such as Arizona, California, Idaho, Louisiana, Nevada, New Mexico, Texas, and Washington, the general assumption is that a husband and a wife each own half of all property that was acquired after the marriage, with the exception of inherited property and gifts acquired from third parties. Since these laws vary from state to state, it is imperative to consult with a local attorney in the community-property state in question, preferably, one who is familiar with Estate practice. A contact with the local bar association in which the decedent had his or her domicile, or where real property is located, is a far better method of selection of counsel than rummaging through voluminous directories in search of an attorney in the geographic area in question.

In all other states, the common law system is applicable. Therefore, a husband and wife separately own whatever they have independently purchased from their own funds. It is usually assured that a party is the owner of all property acquired during the marriage if the other spouse does not receive any income therefrom.

Ownership may also be dependent upon whose name appears on the deed or title to property. If there is more than one name, the property is usually deemed to be "jointly owned." There are two main forms of joint ownership: joint tenancy and tenancy in common. *Joint tenancy* is also known as joint tenancy with a right of survivorship, but in either case the survivor automatically acquires the property when one owner dies. However, there may be state estate taxes to be paid on said property because of its inclusion in the gross estate of the decedent. Therefore, tax considerations must also be researched thoroughly to determine the liquidity of the estate for these purposes and the source from which said tax liabilities will be paid. Property held in joint tenancy should not be included in a will and is not subject to probate procedures, because the property automatically passes by operation of law. However, the same result may be effected in a number of ways by inclusion in an individual's will. Perhaps there is a need to change the form of property ownership when creating the estate plan. One reason for inclusion in a testamentary instrument may be a testator's desire to provide for contingent beneficiaries.

With respect to property held as a *tenancy in common*, each owner's share passes to his or her heirs instead of to the surviving owner or owners. *Tenancy by the entirety* is a third form of ownership, which operates similarly to a joint tenancy. However, it is applicable only to real estate owned by a husband and wife. When one spouse dies, the survivor automatically acquires the property.

It is of the utmost importance to keep careful and meticulous records of the manner in which jointly owned property is acquired. Without proof that the co-owner(s) furnished a portion of the purchase price or acquired his or her share as a gift or as an inheritance, the Internal Revenue Service will insure that the entire value of jointly owned property should be included in the estate of the co-owner who dies first.

The following are some examples of how the forms of ownership will affect the entries made on a net worth statement such as the simplified form shown in this chapter:

Community property: If you are married and live in a community-property state, your list of assets should include one-half of the value of each item of property you have acquired during the marriage. Similarly, if there is a mortgage or some other form of debt connected with a particular piece of property owned in a community-property state, only one-half of the unpaid balance should be included under liabilities. All items separately owned should be recorded at full value.

A Simplified Client Net Worth Statement

Assets		Liabilities	
Liquid Currency	______	Mortgages and Liens	______
Total Savings Account	______	Outstanding Loans	______
Total Checking Account	______	Charge Account	______
Bonds	______	Arrears in Taxes	______
Municipals	______	Other Bills	______
Certificates of Deposit	______	TOTAL LIABILITIES	______
Stocks	______		
Foreign Real Property	______		
Foreign Personalty	______		
Notes Payable	______		
Actual Cash Value Life Insurance	______		
Real Property	______		
Business Valuation	______		
Collections	______		
Cars and RVs	______		
Household Furnishing	______		
Fine Art	______		
Jewelry, Coins, Furs	______		
Miscellaneous	______		
TOTAL ASSETS	______		

ASSETS LESS LIABILITIES EQUALS NET WORTH ______

Joint ownership of inherited property: Only the share you received as an inheritance or gift should be included.

Joint ownership of property bought by you and other owners: The amount recorded should be in proportion to the amount originally furnished to buy the property.

2 Conflict of Laws

The true worth of any reference book on the law can often be valued in terms of the amount of practical information it provides and the ultimate time saved by counsel in research hours away from the office. The primary purpose of this chapter is to familiarize counsel with the basic tenets of the substantive area of law known as "Conflicts" as it relates to Estate practice. An appreciation of this field of law commences with a review of the historical development of the major schools of thought in the area and the application of the determining governing law in host and foreign jurisdictions.

The rights, duties, and powers of estate fiduciaries are addressed and examined in this chapter as well. Queries involving potential difficulties arising out of basic general rules are raised and examined. This commentary is designed to afford counsel with a clearer understanding of the common situations encountered by host and foreign administrators in the course of managing an estate. Recognition of these problems will expedite the collection of foreign assets, while insuring that the estate is not burdened with unnecessary expense.

A knowledge of the authority of receivers is often useful and effective in the expeditious management and settlement of an estate. This chapter explores the ability of the foreign administrator to act and significant exceptions to any vested authority granted to him or her pursuant to statute.

HISTORICAL ANALYSIS

Ordinarily, a court is convened to decide a case in which the operative facts upon which a judgment will be based occurred within the jurisdictional limits of the court. Often, however, part of the operative facts occurred within a different jurisdiction. The forum court must then determine what effect is to be given to the "foreign" law. The branch of the law that deals with the effect of foreign law at the forum state is known as Conflict of Laws.

Before the nineteenth century, Conflict of Laws was of little importance in England. Conflict of Laws is a relatively new concept to Anglo-American law;

however, its European history dates from the Middle Ages, when law was territorial. Law in Europe, with the exception of England, was local customary law rather than national law until the inception of the Napoleonic Codes. This complex structure of relatively small territorial areas rapidly gave rise to problems of conflict of laws. Three successive schools of thought developed and are identified by the names of the countries in which their complete development was attained.

The *Italian school* flourished throughout the fourteenth century and focused on the diverse local laws of the cities of Lombardy as well as with the relationship of those laws to the general legislation of the then German Empire of which Lombardy was a part. The principal characteristic of this school of thought was its division of the problems into various legal categories, such as property, contracts, and so on, and then devising resolutions accordingly.

The *French school* developed throughout the sixteenth, seventeenth, and eighteenth centuries. The distinctive characteristic of this ideology is the bipartite division of laws into areas that are real and those that are personal. *Real laws* were defined as those that affect tangible items, whereas *personal laws* covered individuals and their rights. In addition, it was assumed that only personal laws were entitled to extraterritorial effect. The result was that, in most situations, the conflict-of-laws problem was to be determined in accordance with the local laws of the forum territory. Only in cases in which exceptional circumstances existed would the conflict be resolved in accordance with external law. Laws that could be categorized as either real or personal were given the same strict territorial effect as real laws. Territoriality was the general rule, and extraterritoriality was the exception. The rationale behind this was the general requirements of justice or that, due to necessity, personal legal relations could only be appropriately governed by the law of the persons concerned. The eighteenth-century exponents of the French school did little, unfortunately, but engage in dissertations on the division of laws according to their nature and categorize particular types of law as either real or personal.

The *Dutch school* expanded upon the basic principles of the French theorists but focused on a different justification for applying foreign law in their own courts. It is these theories that supposedly form the present thought in England and in the United States.

"The first systematic treatment of Conflict of Laws in English was that by Story, whose treatise was published in 1834. Story drew largely from the writings of the Dutch jurists, particularly from Huberus' short discussion."[7] Before 1834 there was no complete English work addressing Conflict of Laws. There were relatively few decided cases on the subject both in England and the United States. The reason for the lack of interest in this area can be attributed to the fact that English law was no longer local and had become national under the driving force of the king's judges relatively soon after the Norman conquest. In addition, most of the intercourse with other countries was conducted by merchants for trade, and their transactions were governed by the general body of Law Merchant during the Middle Ages. However, in the United States, the states were separate legal entities and reproduced a situation that was analogous to France before codification. In addition, England became a nation of trade with increasing interests abroad after the Napoleonic Wars. It is against this background that Joseph Story published his treatise on Conflict of Laws in 1834. Story used the works of continental jurists, particularly, from the Dutch school, such as Huberus and Johann Voet. Anglo-American courts long regarded Story's treatise as authoritative, and it was largely because of his treatise that his writings were introduced to the territoriality comity theories as articulated by Voet.

The proper approach to the solution of problems with Conflict of Laws has become a subject of much controversy. Modern scholars do not think that the comity rationale is a satisfactory explanation for the forum state to apply foreign law. In addition, if it is assumed that law is territorial and can have no operative effect beyond the territorial limits of the domain of the sovereign from whom the particular law emanates, then to apply foreign law in their own courts as such upon any theory is in itself inconsistent. These scholars make the assumption that all law is territorial (and can never have effect beyond the territorial boundaries of its own state).

At the same time, due to the existence of given facts, legal rules create legal rights, duties, relations, and so on, and legal relations are created at the place where the facts have the proper connection. Therefore, when a case is brought to a foreign court, the court gives effect to a legal right created by foreign law and not the law of the forum.

If the assumption is accepted that a court dealing with a problem that involves foreign law enforces a foreign-created right, there must be some element that permits the foreign state to create that right. In other words, the foreign state must be vested with jurisdiction to have the power. Therefore, there must be bases for jurisdiction that vary in accordance with the type of case.

A number of authorities have rejected the territoriality theories of enforcement of foreign-created rights. For example, Walter Wheeler Cook asserted that there is no reason why any state or country should not be able to determine the legal consequences that will attach to any given set of facts that is presented to its courts for resolution.[8]

It is, therefore, conceivable that Anglo-American courts may attach to a given foreign set of facts the same legal consequences that would attach to purely domestic facts. Those cases to which the legal consequences would not attach are those in which the foreign facts are not subject to the same considerations as domestic cases.

ESTATE ADMINISTRATION

In the absence of statutory mandates, the general rule is that upon the death of a property owner, testate or intestate, succession of movable property is governed by the law of the situs. However, an estate cannot be administered until all of the assets are realized and the debts are extinguished. Administration is generally conducted through the intermediary of a probate-court-appointed fiduciary. If the will designates an executor, administration of the estate is conducted by that individual, if that person so qualifies before the court. If a will is silent on this issue or an individual dies intestate, an administrator is appointed. In the area of Conflict of Laws, this distinction is of little importance; therefore, unless otherwise distinguished, the term *administrator* includes executor. The American legal system is structured so that administration in several states is treated as a separate process in each of the states involved.

The question may arise as to the proper place at which to probate a will when a decedent dies testate. The probate of a will disposing of movable property generally takes place at the decedent's domicile. Probate of a will can occur in any state where there are assets; however, there is some conflict regarding movable property as to the circumstances under which there can be probate without prior probate at the domicile. In the absence of extraordinary circumstances, probate courts generally await the outcome of probate proceedings at the domicile before they take action.

EFFECT OF PROBATE ON CONFLICT OF LAWS

The difficult question arises as to the effect of probate proceedings in one state or other states involved. In a strict sense, an adjudication regarding the validity of a will is binding on only the parties before the court and property located within the jurisdiction of the probate court. In the absence of a governing statute, it is generally held that a will's validity in the disposition of movables is governed by the law of the decedent's domicile at the time of death, and it would appear in the interest of expediency that an adjudication at the domicile should be accorded recognition elsewhere. This position is delineated in the Restatement, as well as in court decisions.

It is possible for a will to be admitted to probate before probate at the domicile or even without probate taking place there. It has been held that a foreign adjudication is ineffective at the domicile, but it is conclusive as to property that is located within the jurisdiction of a foreign court.

THE ADMINISTRATOR

The law of the state in which the administrator is appointed and the administrator's ability to obtain jurisdiction of the defendant or of property belonging to the defendant determines the administrator's ability to sue in that state. The situation is different, however, when an action is commenced in another state. In theory, the administrator is not vested with authority to act outside the state of his or her appointment. It follows, therefore, that absent a statutory mandate, the administrator cannot sue outside the state of his or her appointment on claims that belonged to the decedent. However, if a judgment is obtained against a debtor of the estate in the state of the administrator's appointment, the claim is merged in the judgment and becomes an asset for which the administrator becomes responsible. He or she can enforce the judgment and sue on it in another state. Suits by other administrators become barred by the judgment. However, if judgment in the original action is in favor of the defendant, the obligor may nevertheless be sued again by another administrator.

Exceptions to the rule that an administrator may not sue or be sued outside the state of his or her appointment arise when the claims are personal to the administrator. Theoretically, an administrator possesses the claim that is merged in the judgment, which has allowed the administrator to sue upon a judgment in his or her favor. An administrator is entitled to sue anywhere upon any contract he or she has made, and after the administrator is appointed, he or she may sue upon a claim for a tort to the estate. Although these claims seem personal, an administrator may still have to account to the probate court that appointed him or her. Additionally, an administrator's agreements on torts may be sued upon outside of the state in which the administrator was appointed.

Attempts have been made to sue an administrator who has wrongfully, or rightfully, removed assets from the state of appointment and then converted them. The U.S. Supreme Court ruled in *Michigan Trust Company v. Ferry*[9] that an administrator who was out of the state of his or her appointment was still subject to the jurisdiction of that state's courts until there was a final accounting. This kept the administrator accountable to the state of his or her appointment even if the administrator was no longer amenable to process. Additionally, an administrator may, in some cases, be sued in a state where he or she had taken assets and wrongfully dealt with them.

An administrator who deals with assets, actually or theoretically, located in a state other than the one where the administrator was appointed acts with questionable authority. However, when dealing with chattels within the state of his or her appointment, the administrator's authority is clear. These chattels can be taken possession of and/or recovered if they are removed to another state without the administrator's authority. To recover chattels, an administrator in one state need not qualify as one in another, because the administrator is suing to recover property that is now his or hers. Although administrators have been granted authority over chattels temporarily located within a state for purposes of administration, this power has also been denied. The local administration of negotiable paper, bonds, and shares of stock depends "Upon the view which is to be kept as to the nature of the tangible evidence of these allegations."[10] Mercantile practice generally dictates that evidence of the obligation is treated as the rest. *Sometimes* the note, bill, bond, or certificate is viewed as being only evidence of an obligation, which is usually treated as an asset in the debtor's state of domicile. With this view, an administrator in possession of the evidence is in the same position as any other administrator with respect to an ordinary debt, but the obligation could be administered only by an administrator from the same domicile as the debtor.

As an asset, an obligation not evidenced by transferable paper will, for administrative purposes, be located at the debtor's domicile. This is true even though the local administrator may sue the debtor in any other state in which he or she becomes amenable to process. The debtor would be relieved of liability upon payment to an administrator at the debtor's domicile.

If a debtor actually enters another state and pays a local administrator there, "this should operate as quittance."[11] Furthermore, the debtor's presence exposes him or her to suit and being compelled to pay. This same result can also occur if the debtor has property within the state that can be subject to judicial seizure. If a debtor should pay an administrator when not subject to a suit, this payment is made to a person who is authorized to receive it; accordingly, if a local administrator is appointed, the debtor will become liable to that person.

A foreign administrator's possession of the title to the obligation is not enough to justify payment to him or her. In a case in which there is more than one administrator, only one can possess title. If the domiciliary administrator has title, but is in a poor position to sue out of his or her state of appointment, another administrator, even if not domiciliary, has the ability to sue locally and obtain a judgment giving that administrator ownership of the asset.

Under the present system, a debtor many times will find it impossible to ascertain whether there are local creditors and difficult to determine if a local administrator has been appointed. Local creditors may file their claims at some other place where there is administration so that they are not greatly prejudiced by the system, even if a foreign administrator receives payment. Since the validity of a payment depends on the chance of the existence of local creditors or local administrators, debtors fearing a future local administrator might refuse to pay a foreign administrator. This refusal would probably force a local administration, which, although not benefiting the creditors, would bring unnecessary expense to the estate.

For the most part, only a local administrator has the power to deal with chattels that are located in a state in which no one has been granted a letter of administration. In the case that there is no local administrator, a foreign administrator might be presented to take possession and administer the property. It is important to note, though, that if an inheritance tax is imposed by the state of their location, unless it is paid, it is unlikely that the state will acquiesce in the removal of chattels to another state.

In the absence of a statute, a foreign administrator is not permitted to administer land. Common law holds that a decedent's land will descend to the heir. Therefore, absent a court order for its sale, a personal representative has no authority to administer it. A local representative must administer it, even if statute has changed the common law rule to make land an asset. However, many courts have held that a personal representative need not qualify as a local administrator to sell land if his or her authority to do so comes from the will.

"The process of administration is a matter of local law, but it is probable that in administering the assets of decedents a state may not under the Constitution of the United States prefer its own citizens over those of other states.''[12] As long as this requirement is met, the law of the place where the claim is filed will determine priorities, the time for proof, the manner of making proof, and other related matters. When there is a solvent estate, each administration will occur independently. After paying all of the filed claims, any surplus will usually be transmitted to the domicile. However, probate courts have also used their discretion in retaining assets for local distribution. When the entire estate is insolvent, the two administrations take place in conjunction with each other. An illustration of this occurred in *In re Hanredday's Estate*,[13] when the deceased died domiciled in Illinois. His widow was appointed administratrix in both Illinois and Wisconsin. Although the estate was insolvent, the assets in Wisconsin were sufficient to pay the creditors in that state, and the lower Wisconsin court ordered them to be paid and the surplus sent to Illinois. The Supreme Court of Wisconsin reversed the decision, ruling that ``where the entire assets of the deceased are insufficient to pay all his just obligations, there is such an interdependence between the various jurisdictions as to require the application of the old maxim that equality is equity.''[14] The court then held that the percentage of assets retained in Wisconsin should not exceed the percentage transmitted to creditors elsewhere.

In the state of his or her appointment, an administrator must account not only for assets obtained in that state but for any assets received as a court-authorized administrator.

RECEIVERSHIP

Receivers derive their authority from the state in which they were appointed. This authority extends only as far as the state border accordingly. A receiver's authority in another state will only come into existence if that state consents. It is possible for a receiver to gain title to the assets located within the state of his or her appointment, which will be valid elsewhere. Furthermore, if a receiver sues within the state of his or her appointment, any resulting judgment against a debtor of the estate is entitled to full faith and credit. Further proceedings on the claim by that or any other receiver will also be barred.

Although the general rule is that a foreign receiver can not act locally, there are several exceptions to this rule. Once a receiver gains title to a chattel, the receiver may sue wherever necessary to recover the chattel or damages if it is injured. Contracts made by a receiver in an official capacity also entitle him or her to sue out of the state of the receiver's appointment.

If it is allowed by the law of the place of incorporation, a receiver may also sue out of his or her state of appointment to enforce the personal liability of shareholders. Furthermore, the law of the place of incorporation will often allow receivers appointed there to enforce the liability of stockholders located in other states regardless of their local policy about foreign receivers.

The doctrine of statutory succession also permits a receiver appointed at a corporation's domicile to sue and to reduce to his or her possession assets located in another state.[15] If a statute in the state of incorporation provides for the doctrine of statutory succession upon the dissolution of a corporation, the receiver or some state official will become the successor of the property. States other than the one where the receiver was appointed will recognize his or her authority, because the receiver as quasi-trustee theoretically succeeds to the title of the corporation. This recognition of authority of a foreign receiver is in reality done as a matter of convenience, because one state cannot confer authority in another without that state's consent. In this case, the courts have found statutory succession to be a convenient way for a foreign receiver to deal with local assets.

A court may order a local receiver to transmit assets collected in that state to another without local administration. However, when the assets are retained, there will be local administration. Even though a court might prefer to favor local creditors by not letting a foreign receiver gain control of local assets, this obligation is imposed upon them by the Supreme Court of the United States. This obligation, however, extends only to creditors who are natural persons and citizens of another state, since foreign corporations are not protected by the interstate-privileges clause.

Furthermore, assets that are deposited as corporation funds to benefit local claimants may be preferred upon its distribution. In accordance with the aforementioned restraints, local law will govern matters such as proof of claim and priorities and procedure.

3 Gathering the Information

The gathering of information in an accurate and expeditious manner is an essential tool of lawyers that is of particular significance in the substantive area of law dealing with wills, trusts, and estates. The nature of the subject matter necessitates a thorough methodology when questions of ancestry, descendancy, heirship, and family lineage are ever present.

Sharp interviewing skills are mandatory as is knowing how to retrieve relevant information from various institutions and agencies. This chapter will assist you in conducting the actual interview and provide further useful practices for dealing with domestic and foreign public agencies and institutions. Such information should facilitate a fluid administration of any estate. Also provided are a compilation of the many government and private agencies with direct contacts and detailed client-interview questionnaires.

As any estate-planning practitioner will tell you, a sound estate plan is often based upon the factual data that a client elicits at the preliminary conferences conducted in his or her office. This information can be just as significant subsequent to a decedent's death, for it will enable foreign counsel to prepare all relevant documents with greater speed and efficiency.

The Estate Analysis Questionnaire included in this chapter is lengthy. It anticipates questions that may never arise within the context of any particular estate proceeding. However, its meticulous completion will assist you or a foreign practitioner in narrowing legal issues to be determined and can assist in the expeditious processing of a legal claim.

Very often, foreign counsel will ask you to prepare affidavits of heirship indicating in very specific terms what your client's relationship was to the decedent. To this end various items are necessary. Purchase a three-ring binder (looseleaf style). This binder will hold charts such as the Ancestry Chart illustrated in this chapter, and keep biographical data you collect regarding a client's ancestry in good order. Information concerning each branch of your client's family should be placed in a separate manila file folder and appropriately labeled. All correspondence and miscellaneous material can be kept in that folder.

Estate Questionnaire

Our File No.: ______________________ Date of Interview: ______________________

Attorney: ______________________ Telephone (client): (B) ______________________

Referred by: ______________________ Telephone: (H) ______________________

Personal Data

CLIENT	SPOUSE
Legal Name	
______________________	______________________
Aliases	
______________________	______________________
Domicile	
______________________	______________________
Employer's Name	
______________________	______________________
Employer's Address	
______________________	______________________
Other Residences	
______________________	______________________
Citizenship	
______________________	______________________
Present Occupation	
______________________	______________________
Former Occupations	
______________________	______________________
Place of Birth	
______________________	______________________
Date of Birth	
______________________	______________________
Where Do You Vote?	
______________________	______________________
Former Spouse Name	
______________________	______________________
Former Marriage Terminated by	
______________________	______________________
Date of Termination and Court	
______________________	______________________
Where Married to Present Spouse	
______________________	______________________
Date of Present Marriage	
______________________	______________________
Military Service	
______________________	______________________

Social Security Number

Place and Date of Adoption

General Health

Family Physician and Address

Annual Income

Education

Present Occupation

Other Dependents, Names, Addresses, Relationship

Children

Any Adopted Children?

Names of Adopted Children

Adopted Children Issue of

Names of Natural Children

Aliases

Date of Birth of All Children

Address of Children

Present Occupation of Children

Any Children Handicapped or under Disability?

General Health of Children

Issue of Children (Grandchildren)

Name

Aliases

Address

Date of Birth and (Death)

Place of Birth and (Death)

Name

Aliases

Address

Date of Birth and (Death)

Place of Birth and (Death)

Name

Aliases

Address

Date of Birth and (Death)

Place of Birth and (Death)

Name

Aliases

Address

Date of Birth and (Death)

Place of Birth and (Death)

Name

Aliases

Address

Date of Birth and (Death)

Place of Birth and (Death)

Client's Parents

FATHER MOTHER

Name

Aliases

Address

Date of Birth and (Death)

Place of Birth and (Death)

Client's Spouse's Parents

FATHER MOTHER

Name

Aliases

Address

Date of Birth and (Death)

Place of Birth and (Death)

Siblings

CLIENT'S SPOUSE'S

Name

Aliases

Address

Date of Birth and (Death)

Place of Birth and (Death)

Name

Aliases

Address

Date of Birth and (Death)

Place of Birth and (Death)

Name

Aliases

Address

Date of Birth and (Death)

Place of Birth and (Death)

Name

Aliases

Address

Date of Birth and (Death)

Place of Birth and (Death)

Nephews and Nieces

CLIENT'S	SPOUSE'S

Name

Aliases

Address

Date of Birth and (Death)

Place of Birth and (Death)

Name

Aliases

Address

Date of Birth and (Death)

Place of Birth and (Death)

Name

Aliases

Address

Date of Birth and (Death)

Place of Birth and (Death)

Name

Aliases

Address

Date of Birth and (Death)

Place of Birth and (Death)

Name

Aliases

Address

Date of Birth and (Death)

Place of Birth and (Death)

Name

Aliases

Address

Date of Birth and (Death)

Place of Birth and (Death)

Family Tree of Client (Draft Here)

Family Tree of Client's Spouse (Draft Here)

Two types of charts must be constructed to trace a client's ancestry in the proper fashion. The first is known as a *direct ancestry chart*, which indicates the names of the client, client's parents, and his or her grandparents and great-grandparents. The second is a series of *descendant's charts*, which are made for each branch of the client's family. This chart should begin with the most ancient ancestor in each branch and indicate his or her children, grandchildren, great-grandchildren, and so on. Forms for these charts can be purchased from genealogical societies, genealogy departments of libraries, and some bookstores.

Locating the client's close and distant relatives.

The best source of information regarding a client's ancestors is the pool of living relatives. Although older relatives may not recall dates and ages, they will probably be helpful with names, places, and circumstances that could confirm or refine the information subsequently found in documents. Older relatives are usually eager to talk about the past, and although their memories may be clouded regarding current events, they are usually remarkably clear regarding events that took place years ago.

Ancestry Chart

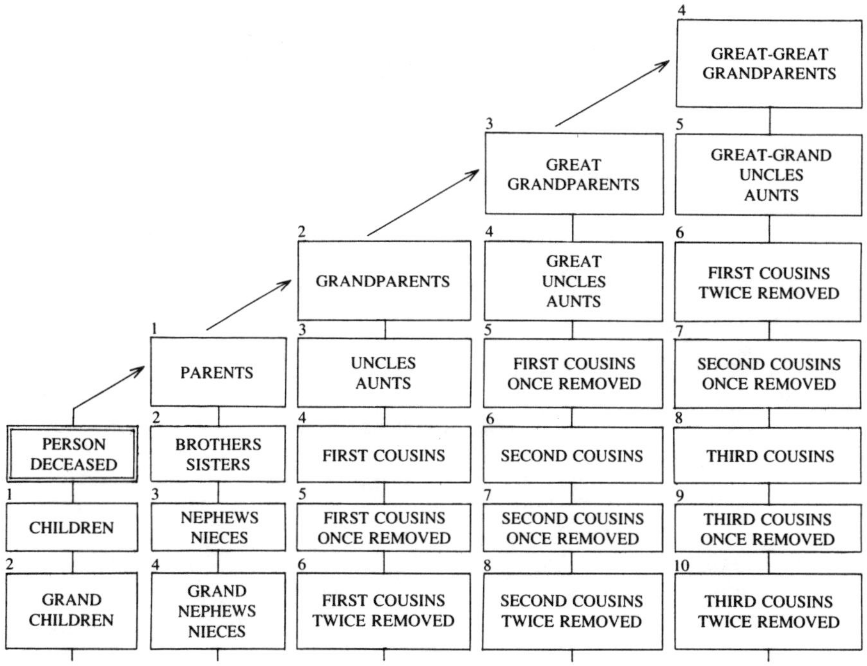

Writing to relatives, making telephone calls, or visiting relatives.

Once you have located relatives who might be able to help you in filling in the gaps, set up a meeting with them to ask specific questions. It should be noted that this method is not the most reliable and will have to be confirmed through official records and documents.

PUBLIC RECORDS IN THE UNITED STATES

There are a wide variety of public records in the United States that may be accessible to you in a search for your client's ancestors. Death certificates, birth certificates, marriage records, census records, wills, administration and probate records, immigration and naturalization records, newspaper obituaries, church records, and baptismal certificates will assist you in procedurally and substantively providing foreign counsel with the requested information.

Direct Ancestry Chart

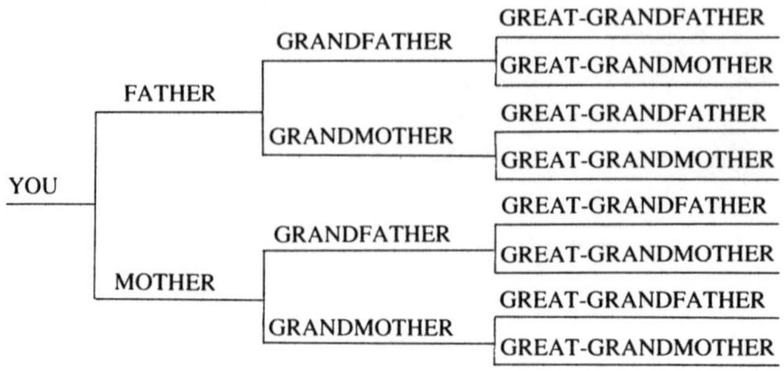

Sample Descendant's Chart

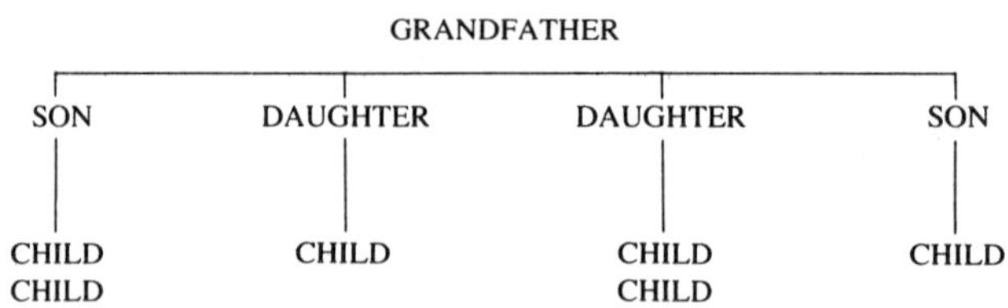

Death certificates.

Information varies from state to state; however, the following can usually be located: date and hour of death, cause of death, place of death, address of deceased, age of deceased, birthdate, birthplace, if married, name of spouse, name of father and maiden name of mother, social security number, funeral home, cemetery where deceased was buried, party furnishing information for death certificate and attending physician at death. If the date of death and place are known, a photocopy can usually be obtained. Fees are minimal. If a relative died in a major city, the death certificate probably has an index number. Annual indexes provide such information. For example, in New York, the local History and Genealogy Division of the New York Public Library has such indexes dating from August 1888. In some other states, all birth, death, and marriage records are kept in the state capital or the country where the event took place. For more information, obtain the following for your law-office files: "Where to Write for Birth and Death Records" (Department HEW Pub. No. HRA 75-1142), "Where to Write for Marriage Records'' (Department HEW Pub. No. HSM 72-1144), ''Where to Write for Divorce Records'' (Department HEW Pub. No. HSM 73-1145). Each of these booklets costs thirty-five cents and can be obtained by writing to the Superintendent of Documents, United States Government Printing Office, Washington, D.C. 20402. *How to Trace Your Family Tree*, by the American Genealogical Research Institute, is also an excellent source of information for state-by-state information.

When you are requesting a copy of a certificate, be certain to provide as much information as you can about the person whose record is being requested. State that you are the attorney for whomever you represent and the reason you are requesting the document.

FEDERAL CENSUS RECORDS

The National Archives can assist you in your search through the mails. Ask for GSA Form 7029, ''Order for Copies—Census Records,'' to make your requests. The mailing address is National Archives and Records Service, NNC, Washington, D.C. 20408. The National Archives also handles mail requests for copies of 1900 census returns, but they must be applied for on Federal Form GSA 7163, ''1900 Census Application.'' The National Archives building is at Eighth Street and Pennsylvania Avenue, N.W., Washington, D.C. 20408. Branch offices often contain census and other records for particular regions. There are eleven branches as follows:

380 Trapelo Road, Waltham, Massachusetts 02154
Military Ocean Terminal, Building 22, Bayonne, New Jersey 07002
5000 Wissahickon Avenue, Philadelphia, Pennsylvania 19144
1557 St. Joseph Avenue, East Point, Georgia 30044
7358 S. Pulaski Road, Chicago, Illinois 60629
2306 E. Bannister Road, Kansas City, Missouri 64131
4900 Hemphill Street, Ft. Worth, Texas 76115
Building 48, Denver Federal Center, Denver, Colorado 80225
1000 Commodore Drive, San Bruno, California 92677
6125 Sand Point Way, Seattle, Washington 98115
24000 Avila Road, Laguna Niguel, California 92677

SHIP LISTS

Passenger lists of almost every ship that ever arrived in an American port since 1820 can be found at the National Archives. If you have the name of the ship and date of arrival, it is relatively easy to find the microfilm roll at the National Archives. These lists often contain the age, occupation, and former residence of the party in question. *Locating Your Immigrant Ancestor*, by James and Lila Neagles, can be a helpful research tool. If the exact date of arrival or the name of the ship is unavailable, consult the *Morton Allan Directory of European Passenger Steamship Arrivals*, available at the National Archives and most major libraries.

NATURALIZATION RECORDS

On September 26, 1906 the naturalization procedures were standardized. Naturalization records are on file after that date in the United States and are available at the Immigration and Naturalization Service, Washington, D.C. 20536. Form G-641 explains how to get information from the service. These records contain information on the citizen's spouse, children, and date and place of arrival. Naturalization records before September 26, 1906 might be held in any federal, state, or local court where naturalization took place.

PROBATE RECORDS

The will is a good source of tracing a client's relations, because most people bequeath their property to relatives. All wills are available for public inspection once they are filed after a person's death. Probate laws vary from state to state; however, most wills can be found at the local courthouse in the Surrogate's Court. The same is true for administration proceedings.

RECORDS IN EUROPE

Austria.

For birth, death, or marriage records, write for assistance to:
Heraldisch-Genealogische Gesellschaft
"Adler" Haarhof 41, A-1010, Vienna

United States Information Center
Karntnerstrasse 38, A-1010, Vienna

The Austrian National Library
Osterreichische Nationalbibliothek
Josefplatz, A-1014, Vienna

Belgium.

The address of the National Archives is: Archives Generales du Ruyaume, 78 Galerie Ravensteen, Brussels. For recent birth, marriage, and death records, write to: Officier de l'Etat Civil, (Name of Town), Belgium. A genealogical society is the Service de Centralisation des Etudes Genealogiques et Demographiques de Belgique, 26 Rue aux Laines, Brussels.

Britain.

Birth, death, and marriage records are at: Somerset House, London, W.C. 2 London.

Denmark.

Birth, death, and marriage records are at: Public Record Office, Copenhagen, Vibary, Aabenraa, or Odense.

State archives are at: Rigsarkivet, Rigsdagsgarden 9, 1218 Copenhagen. The Royal Library in Copenhagen may also help: Det Kongelige Bibliothek, Christians Brygge 8, 1219, Copenhagen, as well as the Danish Embassy, 3200 Whitehaven Street, N.W., Washington, D.C. 20008.

France.

French Public Sources are:
Paris, National Archives (twelfth-eighteenth centuries); National Library (thirteenth-nineteenth centuries)

Municipal Archives, Avignon, Bayonne, Bordeaux, Carpentras, Chambery, Colmar, Dijon, Grenoble, Marseilles, Metz, Strasbourg, and Troyes

Archives Nationales de France, 60 rue des Frances-Bourgeois, Paris 3
French Consulate, New York, tel. 212-535-0100
La Mairie (Town Hall) of place where event occurred.

Germany.

Records are kept in the Civil Registry where the event occurred. Write to: Standesamt (Civil Registry Office), (Name of Town), Germany. For ship lists departing from Germany (Hamburg) write to: Staatsarchiv, Rathaus Market I, 2000 Hamburg, Federal Republic of Germany.

Italy.

For birth, death, or marriages in Rome, write to: Instituto Centrale di Statistica, Via Cesare Balbo 16, Rome, Italy. For civil records from other communities, write to: Ufficio di Stato Civil, (Name of Town), Italy. The National Archives is located at: Archivio Centrale della Stato, Corso Rinnascimento 40, Rome, Italy.

NEWSPAPER OBITUARIES

Most public libraries have back issues on file in the microfilm department. It is possible that the death of a client's ancestor was published in the obituaries by other relatives. A great deal of information may be contained in these obituaries. For example, you may find names of descendants, the funeral home, and the cemetery. The notice often contains a list of remaining living relatives of the deceased, which may aid in locating heirs. You can always use the obituaries to confirm information you already have as well.

If a relative lived in New York or was a prominent figure, the *New York Times Obituary Index* can be of some help in locating the date of death. There is a cumulative index of obituary articles from 1858 through 1966. The American Antiquarian Society in Worcester, Massachusetts, has compiled an extensive unpublished index of newspaper obituaries since 1800 and will furnish you references on request. The California State Library in Sacramento, California, has valuable indexes to obituaries of even minor people in the news in California. Also consult the *American Newspapers, 1821–1936: A List Available in the United States and Canada*, by Winfred Herould.

CITY DIRECTORIES

Directories are still published for most cities, although not in New York. Old editions of these directories can be found, either as originals or on microfilm, in most municipal libraries and historical societies. The Library of Congress and the National Archives in Washington, D.C. have a huge collection of old city directories.

BAR ASSOCIATIONS

The following list of bar associations will enable the practitioner to contact a local attorney within each state who is familiar with that state's inheritance laws and who is a member of the state's Trust and Estates Committee.

National Bar Association

American Bar Association
1155 East 60th Street
Chicago, Illinois 60637
312–493–0533

State Bar Associations

Alabama State Bar
205–269–1515

Alaska Bar Association
907–272–9431

State Bar of Arizona
602–252–4804

Arkansas Bar Association
501–375–4605

State Bar of California
415–922–1440

Colorado Bar Association
303–222–9421

Connecticut Bar Association
203–249–9141

Delaware State Bar
302–658–5278

The District of Columbia Bar
202–638–1500

The Florida Bar
904–222–5286

State Bar of Georgia
404–522–6255

Hawaii State Bar Association
808–537–1868

Idaho State Bar
208–342–8958

Illinois State Bar Association
217–525–1760

Indiana State Bar Association
317–639–5465

Iowa State Bar Association
515–243–3179

Kansas Bar Association
913–234–5696

Kentucky Bar Association
502–564–3795

Louisiana State Bar Association
504–566–1600

Maine State Bar Association
207–622–7523

Maryland State Bar Association, Inc.
301–685–7878

Massachusetts Bar Association
617–523–4529

State Bar of Michigan
517–372–9030

Minnesota State Bar Association
612–335–1183

Mississippi State Bar
314–635–4128

The Missouri Bar
314–635–4128

State Bar of Montana
406–442–7660

Nebraska State Bar Association
402–475–7091

State Bar of Nevada
702–323–0338

New Hampshire Bar Association
603–669–4869

New Jersey State Bar Association
609–394–1101

State Bar of New Mexico
505–842–3901

New York State Bar Association
518–445–1211

The North Carolina State Bar
919–828–4620

State Bar Association of North Dakota
701–255–1404

Ohio State Bar Association
614–421–2121

Oklahoma Bar Association
405–524–2365

Oregon State Bar
503–229–5788

Pennsylvania Bar Association
717–238–6715

The Bar Association of Puerto Rico
809–724–3358

Rhode Island Bar Association
401–421–5740

The South Carolina Bar
803–799–6653

State Bar of South Dakota
605–224–7554

Tennessee Bar Association
615–329–1601

State Bar of Texas
512–475–4200

Utah State Bar
801–322–1015

Vermont Bar Association
802–223–2020

The Virginia Bar Association
804–977–1396

Virginia State Bar
804–786–2061

Washington State Bar Association
206–622–6054

The West Virginia Bar Association
304–342–1474

The West Virginia State Bar
304–348–2456

State Bar of Wisconsin
608–257–3838

Wyoming State Bar
307–632–9061

Additional Associations

American Academy of Matrimonial Lawyers
President: William H. Dasilva
585 Stewart Avenue
Garden City, New York 11530
516–222–0700

Association of Immigration and Nationality Lawyers
Chairman: Seymour Rosenberg
11 West 42nd Street
New York, New York 10036
212–736–7251

Bankruptcy Lawyers Bar Association
President: Nathan B. Fogelson
2 Park Avenue
New York, New York 10016
212–686–3838

Customs and International Trade Bar Association
President: Harvey A. Isaacs
1 Whitehall Street
New York, New York 10004
212–425–0060

The Federal Bar Association
President: Donald Paley
Empire State Chapter
GPO Box 2
New York, New York 10001

Federal Bar Council
President: Robert B. Fiske, Jr.
370 Lexington Avenue
New York, New York 10017

French-American Bar Association, Inc.
Secretary: Pierre Lorsy
170 Broadway
New York, New York 10038

4 Foreign Taxation of Estates

The estate practitioner has always been called upon to review taxation issues that are complex and varied but nonetheless of crucial importance in the settlement of an estate. Understanding the fundamentals of tax law are essential. However, the intent of this chapter is not to provide you with that education but to point out how the field of estate law is interwoven with general taxation concepts. Proper estate planning and management have a direct impact on the ultimate distribution received by an heir or donee. Attention to the most minute details of all relevant statutes is required.

This chapter further addresses and examines the foreign tax statutes and issues of non-residency and alienage in the United States and abroad. Attention is called to the foreign tax treaties and their interrelationship with the federal law of estate taxation in the United States.

ALIENS AND NON-RESIDENT ALIENS

Generally, non-resident aliens are subject to the United States estate taxes (federal) at lower rates than citizens on property located in the United States at the time of a decedent's death. This tax is different from the estate tax on citizens and residents. In addition, the marital deduction is not available to non-resident aliens unless a treaty between the United States and the foreign country provides for the marital deduction. The following treaties have been abbreviated in general format; however, the substance is basically self-explanatory.

For a non-resident alien to receive special estate tax treatment, he or she must be a non-citizen. The provisions of the Immigration and Nationality Act determine, for estate tax purposes, citizenship. In addition, residence is equivalent to domicile for estate tax purposes. The requirement of physical presence combined with an actual intent to remain in the country indefinitely is needed. Therefore, the taxable estate of an illegal alien dying in the United States is subject to federal estate tax under Section 2001 of the Internal Revenue Code.[16]

In general, the situs of a non-resident alien's property is determined by rules contained in the Internal Revenue Code and relevant treaties. Real estate situated in the United States is included in a non-resident alien's gross estate as is tangible personal property located physically in the United States.

A non-resident alien's estate may also be subject to multiple death taxes on United States situs property when his domicile imposes death taxes on a world-wide basis, but these individuals are not entitled to a credit for foreign death taxes. Multiple taxation is avoided when the foreign country permits a credit against its foreign death tax for United States estate tax paid by the non-resident alien on his or her United States property. (Also see individual treaties entered into between the United States and the particular foreign country.)

The United States Federal Estate tax Return (Form 706) must be filed within nine months of a decedent's death, unless an extension is granted. For decedents dying in 1982, a return must be filed if the gross estate is $225,000.00 or more reduced by the sum of post-1976 taxable gifts and specific exemptions (gift tax) for gifts made between September 8, 1976 and January 1, 1977. For decedents dying in 1983 the corresponding gross estate is $275,000.00; for 1984, $325,000.00; for 1985, $400,000.00; for 1986, $500,000.00; and for 1987 and thereafter, $600,000.00. For non-resident aliens, a return must be filed if the gross estate in the United States is greater than $60,000.00 (also reduced by post-1976 taxable gifts and exemptions).

The following treaties are not conclusive in their application. Lay people and lawyers are cautioned to research the actual treaty for supplements and the actual statement of the law. The relevant portions of the following treaties have been included for the sole purpose of providing information on the interrelationship between the foreign country and the United States for estate tax purposes.

BELGIAN ESTATE TAX TREATY

An estate tax convention between the United States and Belgium for the prevention of fiscal evasion in regard to taxes on estates and successions and for the avoidance of double taxation was signed on May 27, 1954, and the Senate asserted to its ratification on February 25, 1955. Upon the exchange of the instruments of ratification, the convention will be put into effect in regard to estates or successions of persons expiring on or after that date. The treaty contains the following provisions:

ARTICLE I: Taxes covered—The convention affects the United States estate tax and the Belgium succession duty and the duty on transfer by death.

ARTICLE II: Treaty terms defined—The laws of each contracting estate are applied in ascertaining whether a decedent at the time of death was a national or domiciliary of that country.

ARTICLE III: Situs of property—The following rules are to be exclusively applied in the determination of the situs of property or property rights.

(a) The location of the real property is its situs.

(b) Tangible personal property, as well as currency and various forms of money recognized as legal tender in the place where it was issued, has a taxable situs at the place of its physical location. If it is in transit, its situs is the point of destination.

(c) Debts (which include indemnities, insurance, and bonds but not negotiable promissory notes, checks, and bills of exchange) are situated at the debtor's place of residence. In the case of corporations, the situs is the place of creation or organization.

(d) The place of the drawer's residence acts as the situs for bills of exchange and checks. Promissory notes are situated at the place of the maker's residence.

(e) The taxable situs of shares of stock in a corporation is the place where the corporation was created or organized.

(f) Ships, aircraft, and shares thereof have a taxable situs at the place of documentation or registration.

(g) Goodwill as an asset is situated at the place where the trade, business, or profession to which it pertains is conducted.

(h) The designation of the situs of patents, trademarks, and designs is the place where they are registered or used, if they are not registered.

(i) Copyrights, franchises, rights, or licenses to use artistic and scientific works, copyrighted material, patents, trademarks, or designs have a taxable situs at the place where the rights arising therefrom are exercisable.

(j) The designation of taxable situs for rights or causes of action ex delicto surviving for the benefit of an estate of a decedent is the place where such rights or causes of action arose.

(k) All other property has a taxable situs at the place where the decedent was domiciled at the time of demise.

ARTICLE IV: Elimination of extraterritorial taxation. Exemptions—The state imposing a tax on a non-domiciliary decedent must allow a "specific exemption in an amount not less than the proportion thereof which the property value subjected to its tax bears to the property value which would have been subjected to its tax if the decedent had been domiciled in such state" (p. 762).

ARTICLE V: Credits. Avoidance of double taxation—when a tax is imposed on property by the United States on the basis of domicile or citizenship, and Belgium also taxes the same property because the decedent was an inhabitant of Belgium at the time of death, each country will allow a tax credit for the tax imposed by the other with respect to the property and included for tax purposes by both.

A further credit is available if property is situated outside or inside of both countries. However, the decedent must have been a United States citizen and inhabitant of Belgium, or the United States regards the decedent as a domiciliary of the country, and Belgium regards the decedent as an inhabitant. The allowable credit must equal the tax imposed with respect to such property by the country imposing the smaller tax.

The computation of this credit is to be made after the allowance for other credits against the tax.

Any claims for credit or refund arising under the above provisions must be applied within six years after the date of the decedent's death. Interest does not accrue on the credit or refund, and the final allowance of credit will not be made until the tax of the other country has been satisfied.

ARTICLE VI, VII, & VIII: Administrative-assistance provisions.

ARTICLE IX: Extension of treaty provisions.[17]

FRENCH ESTATE TAX TREATY

The estate tax convention between the United States and France was signed on October 18, 1946. The convention became effective upon the exchange of instruments of ratification on October 17, 1949, and it applies to estates of decedent's dying on or after that date. A protocol signed on May 17, 1948 also became effective on October 17, 1949. On November 24, 1978, a new estate and gift tax treaty was entered into, and on August 22, 1980 the instruments of ratification were exchanged between representatives of the United States and France. The treaty, which became effective on October 1, 1980, includes these provisions:

TITLE I: TAXES ON ESTATES AND INHERITANCES

ARTICLE I: Taxes covered—The convention covers the United States Federal estate tax and the French tax on inheritances.

ARTICLE II: Treaty terms defined—

1. In this title, unless otherwise required:

(a) "United States" means the United States of America, and when used in a geographical sense includes only the states, the territories of Alaska and Hawaii, and the District of Columbia.

(b) "France," when used in a geographical sense, includes only metropolitan France, excluding Algeria and the Colonies.

(c) "Tax" means the United States federal estate tax or the French inheritance tax.

2. Any terms not otherwise defined shall, unless otherwise required, have the meaning as defined under the laws of the contracting state relating to the taxes that are the subject of this Title.

ARTICLE III: Domicile. Situs of property—In determining whether a decedent was a domiciliary of the territory of a contracting state at the time of death, the law in force in such country will apply.

The taxable situs of any rights or interests is to be determined in accordance with the following rules:

(a) The situs of real property is the place of its location. Real property includes leases of more than eighteen years duration, but mortgages and other liens as security are excluded.

(b) Corporeal movable property, bank notes, and any other kind of moneys recognized as legal tender in the place where it was issued has a taxable situs at the place of its physical location at the time of the decedent's death.

(c) Ships and aircraft have a taxable situs at the place of registration or documentation.

(d) Goodwill as an asset has a taxable situs at the place where the business is carried on or the profession practiced.

(e) The taxable situs of patents, trademarks, and designs is the place of registration.

(f) The taxable situs of copyrights and rights or licenses to use any copyrighted material, patent, trademark, or design is at the place where the rights arising therefrom are exercisable.

(g) Shares in a corporation have a situs at the place where the company is incorporated. This is also applicable to property held by a nominee for the decedent's benefit.

(h) Checks and bills of exchange have a taxable situs at the place of the drawer's residence. The taxable situs for negotiable promissory notes is the place of the maker's residence.

(i) All other property, other than the above mentioned, has a taxable situs at the place where the decedent was domiciled at the time of his death.

ARTICLE IV: Allowance of exemptions—"A contracting state imposing taxes on a decedent not domiciled at the time of his death in its territory but domiciled in the territory of the other state must allow every abatement, exemption, deduction, or credit applicable under its law had the decedent been domiciled in its territory, in an amount not less than the proportion thereof which the value of the property situated in such state, according to Article III, bears to the value of the property which would have been subject to the tax of such state if the decedent had been domiciled in its territory" (p. 2858). The contracting state imposing such taxes may not take account of property situated according to Article III outside its territory in determining the amount or rate of tax. Article IV provisions do not apply to the tax imposed by the United States in the case of a deceased citizen of the United States.

ARTICLE V: Credit provisions—Credit is provided against the tax of a contracting state imposing tax in the case of a deceased person who was a domiciliary in such state at the time of death. The credit is in the amount of the tax imposed by the other contracting state on property situated in its territory and included for tax purposes by both states. The credit amount may not exceed the portion of tax imposed by the former state that is attributable to such property.

In addition to the above authorized credit, in cases where each contracting state regards the decedent as being domiciled in its own territory, each state shall allow against its tax a ''credit for the part of the tax imposed by the other state with respect to property included for tax purposes by both states and with a situs in the territory of both states or outside of both territories. The total of these additional credits will be equal to the amount of tax imposed on such property by the state imposing the smaller tax. These credits are divided between the 2 states in proportion to the amount of tax imposed by each of the countries with respect to such property'' (p. 2858).

For these purposes, the amount of the tax of each contracting state attributable to any designated property will be ascertained after taking into account any applicable abatement, credit, remittance, diminution, or increase, as provided by its law, other than any credit authorized by Article V.

ARTICLE VI: Claims for credit for credit or refund—Any claims for credit or refund arising under the above provision must be applied for within five years of the date of the decedent's death. No interest is allowed on any amount refunded.

TITLE III: ADMINISTRATIVE AND FISCAL ASSISTANCE PROVISIONS

TITLE IV: GENERAL PROVISIONS PROTOCOL

ARTICLE I: Determination of domicile—''The determination of whether a citizen of the United States acquired a domicile in France will, for purposes of the French tax or inheritance, be made in conformity with Article 103 of the French Civil Code as in effect on May 17, 1948.

''Likewise, the determination of whether a citizen of France acquired a domicile in the United States, will for the purposes of Federal estate taxes, be made in conformity with Section 81 of the United States Estate Tax Regulations in effect on May 18, 1948 (p. 2858).[18]

WEST GERMAN ESTATE TAX TREATY

On December 3, 1980 the estate and gift tax treaty with West Germany was signed, and it was transmitted to the United States Senate for its advice and consent to ratification on January 15, 1981.[19] The Senate approved the treaty on November 18, 1981, subject to the understanding that certain congressional committees, as well as the General Accounting Office, be afforded access to information that is exchanged between the United States and Germany pursuant to Article 14 (Exchange of Information of the Convention).

The treaty modified the countries' jurisdictional rules to avoid double taxation on estates of United States citizens and domiciliaries of German domiciliaries. In addition, gifts made or received by such persons is also covered. The following two modifications were made:

1. "[A]n individual's country of domicile will have primary tax jurisdiction over the estates and gifts of its domiciliaries. However, real property and business property located in the other country will be subject to primary taxation in that country" (p. 3049–2).

2. "[I]n situations where both the Unites States and Germany, under their own domestic laws, consider an individual to be a domiciliary, that individual will be treated as having only one country of domicile for purposes of the taxes covered by the convention" (p. 3049–2). Several criteria are established in the treaty for determining which of the two countries is the domicile state.

The following articles represent the highlights of the West German Estate Tax Treaty:

ARTICLE I: Scope—The convention's provisions apply to the estate of any person who was a domiciliary of either Germany or the United States or of both countries at the time of death. The treaty is also applicable to all gifts made by donors who were domiciliaries of either country or both countries at the time the gifts were made.

ARTICLE II: Taxes covered—The convention covers the United States estate and gift taxes and the tax on generation-skipping transfers. The treaty applies to the German inheritance and gift taxes. As with other United States tax treaties, gift or death taxes that are imposed by state or local governments are not included within the treaty's provisions.

ARTICLE III: General definitions—The standard definitions generally found in most existing United States estate and gift tax treaties are contained within this convention.

ARTICLE IV: Fiscal domicile—other than property subject to situs taxation, the domiciliary's country has primary tax jurisdiction over all property. Determination of the country of domicile is analyzed according to the domestic laws of the United States and Germany. In the case of the United States estate and gift tax law, the domicile is determined under the regulations. With regard to Germany, if a person has a domicile or habitual abode in Germany or is considered to be subject to unlimited tax liability for the purpose of the German inheritance or gift tax, he or she will be treated as a domiciliary of Germany When both the United States and Germany treat an individual as domiciliary of each country, special rules apply for the purposes of this convention.

ARTICLE V: Immovable property—The laws of the country in which property is located will control the determination of whether such property is immovable. Ships and aircraft are not included within the definition of immovable property, and for the purposes of the United States immovable property is considered to mean real property.

ARTICLE VI: Business property—''Business assets that are owned by a non-domiciliary's permanent establishment which is located in the situs country and the assets of a fixed base of such a person which is situated in that country and is used for the performance of independent personal services'' is subject to the primary taxation of the situs country (p. 3049–3). A person is considered to have a permanent establishment in a country if he or she has an agent in that country who has habitually exercised a general contracting authority in that country.

ARTICLE VII: Ships and Aircraft—Ships, aircraft, and movable property in relation thereto that are involved in international traffic and belong to an enterprise that composes part of the estate or gift of a domiciliary of one country may only be subject to tax in that country of domicile.

ARTICLE VIII: Interests in partnerships—If an interest in a partnership forms part of the estate or gift of a person domiciled in one of the countries, and the partnership owns immovable or business property in the other contracting country, that other country may tax the partnership interest. However, the extent of the tax can only be the value of the interest that is attributable to such property.

ARTICLE IX: Property not expressly mentioned—Property, other than the above mentioned, which is not located within the domiciliary's country, may only be taxed in the decedent's or donor's country of domicile. However, this provision is not applicable to a United States citizen who is also a domiciliary of Germany, and it does not prevent Germany from taxing an heir, dower, or other beneficiary who was domiciled in Germany at the time the decedent died as the gift was made.

ARTICLE X: Deductions and exemptions—Deductions or reductions in the taxable value of immovable property, business assets, and interests in partnerships for debts incurred on such property is allowable under the provisions of the treaty. In addition, contributions made to charitable or public organizations in one country are generally exempt from tax in the other country. Private and public pensions, annuities, and other similar payments made by a governmental body as resident of one country are exempt from taxation by the other country to the extent that they would be exempt from tax in the first country if they were paid to a domiciliary of that country. In addition, property that passes to the spouse of a United States or German domiciliary and that is subject to situs country taxation is only subject to tax in that country to the extent that the value of the property exceeds 50 percent of the property that is subject to taxation in that country. The amount of this exemption may not exceed the German marital deduction or result in a United States tax lower than that which would otherwise occur using rates applicable to a United States domicile.

ARTICLE XI: Credits—When a person's property is taxed by both the United States and Germany, the treaty contains rules that are to be used in the determination of the amount of credits against estate gift and inheritance taxes allowable by each country. According to the first credit rule, the country of which the person was a domiciliary or a citizen will allow a credit for taxes imposed by the other country or property situated in that other country. When both countries tax the property of an individual on a worldwide basis because the person was a citizen of one country and a domiciliary of the other country, a second rule provides for an additional tax credit. The amount of the allowable credit cannot exceed the amount of tax imposed, computed before the credit is given. Additionally, the period of limitations during which claims for credit or refunds of taxes may be made, in some cases, may be longer than that allowed under the Internal Revenue Code.

ARTICLE XII: Estates & Trusts—In regard to property placed in trust, there exists a difference in the timing of taxable events between the United States and Germany. Therefore, the convention permits a credit for United States tax that could otherwise be lost under German law. German law mandates that a credit for foreign taxes is not allowed if the foreign tax was paid more than five years before the payment of the German tax. Since the United States imposes a tax upon the transfer of property to a trust, and Germany does not impose a tax until a beneficiary receives a distribution from the trust, a time lapse of more than five years can occur, which would result in a loss of credit. However, the convention allows a credit under such circumstances.

ARTICLES XIII & XIV: Administrative provisions.

ARTICLE XV: Members of diplomatic missions or consular posts.

ARTICLE XVI: Land Berlin—The convention is applicable to Land Berlin unless a contrary declaration is made to the United States by Germany within three months following the effective date of this treaty.

ARTICLE XVII: Entry into force—The treaty enters into force upon the exchange of instruments of ratification and will be applicable to the estates of persons dying and to gifts made on or after January 1, 1979. However, with regard to estates of decedents dying on or after January 1, 1974 and before January 1, 1979, the treaty provides that the competent authorities of the United States and Germany may agree to eliminate double taxation by allowing taxes on one country to be credited against the taxes of the other country, notwithstanding the difference in each country's internal rules regarding situs and standing domicile.

ARTICLE XVIII: Termination—The treaty was designed to continue indefinitely. However, the United States or Germany may terminate the convention after it has been effective for three years if at least six months prior notice has been given. Upon termination, "the treaty is applicable only to the estates of persons dying after or gifts made after the December 31 next following the expiration of the six months' period'' (p. 3049.5).[19]

ITALIAN ESTATE TAX TREATY

An estate tax convention between the United States and Italy was signed on March 30, 1955, and the convention became effective on October 26, 1956. The convention applies to estates and inheritances of persons dying on or after October 26, 1956. Ratification of the convention was consented to by the United States on July 29, 1955. The United States law is effective in the absence of specific treaty provisions. Highlights of Articles I to X follow:

ARTICLE I: Taxes covered—The convention covers the federal estate tax of the United States and the Italian tax on estates and inheritances.

ARTICLE II: Treaty terms defined—

1. As used in this convention:

(a) ''United States'' means the United States of America and when used in a geographical sense includes only the states, the territories of Alaska and Hawaii, and the District of Columbia.

(b) ''Italy'' means the Italian Republic.

(c) ''Tax'' means the United States federal estate tax or the Italian estate or inheritance tax.

(d) ''Competent authority'' for the United States means the commissioner of the Internal Revenue Service as authorized by the secretary of the Treasury. In regard to Italy, it applies to the Ministry of Finance, General Directorship of Indirect Taxes on Business.

2. Any terms not otherwise defined shall, unless otherwise required, have the meaning as defined under the laws of the contracting state.

ARTICLE III: Situs of property—In ascertaining whether a decedent was a national of or domiciled in one of the contracting states, or whether a debtor established residence therein, the laws in force in that country shall apply.

The determination of the situs of property or property rights is to be exclusively analyzed in accordance with the following rules:

(a) The location of the real property is its taxable situs.

(b) Tangible personal property, as well as bank currency and various forms of moneys recognized as legal tender in the place where it was issued, has a taxable situs at the place of its physical location. If such property is in transit, its taxable situs is the point of its destination.

(c) The debtor's residence acts as the situs for secured or unsecured debts. Corporate debts have a situs in the country where the corporation was created or organized.

(d) The taxable situs of shares of stock in a corporation including that held by a nominee is the place where the corporation was created or organized.

(e) Ships, aircraft, and shares thereof have a taxable situs at the place of registration.

(f) Goodwill as an asset has a taxable situs at the place where the business is carried on or the profession practiced.

(g) The designation of the taxable situs of patents, trademarks, and designs is the place where they are registered or used.

(h) Copyrights, franchises, rights to artistic and scientific works, and rights to use any copyrighted material, artistic and scientific works, patents, trademarks, or designs have a taxable situs at the place where the rights arising therefrom are exercisable.

(i) All other property, other than the above mentioned, has a taxable situs at the place where the decedent was domiciled at the time of death.

ARTICLE IV: Elimination of extraterritorial taxation. Exemptions—"In the case of non-domiciliary decedents, the state imposing the tax must allow a specific exemption in an amount not less than the proportion thereof which the value of the property subjected to its tax bears to the value of the property which would have been subjected to its tax if the decedent had been domiciled in such state" (p. 4362). No account may be taken of property located outside the contracting state when determining the amount or rate of the tax.

ARTICLE V: Credits. Avoidance of double taxation—The convention has no effect on the allowance of credits as authorized by Code Section 2011 for estate, inheritance, legacy, or succession taxes paid to the states, the District of Columbia, or the territories or possessions of the United States.

In the case of a decedent who was a domiciliary or national of one of the contracting countries at the time of death, a credit is allowed by that country for the tax imposed by the other country on, or in respect of, property situated in the latter country and included by both countries in their respective tax computations. The amount of this credit cannot exceed the portion of the tax imposed by the former state that is attributable to such property.[20]

ARTICLES VI through X: Administrative provisions.

FINNISH ESTATE TAX TREATY

An estate tax convention between the United States and Finland was signed on March 3, 1952, and the United States Senate consented to its ratification without amendment on July 4, 1952. The instruments of ratification were exchanged on December 18, 1952. The convention is applicable to the estates or inheritances of persons dying on or after December 18, 1952. United States law is applicable in those situations where the convention is silent. The following provisions are highlights of the treaty:

ARTICLE 1: Taxes covered—The convention covers the United States federal estate tax and the Finnish inheritance tax; the communal tax on inheritances, bequests, or devises; and the "poors percentage."

ARTICLE II: Treaty terms defined—

1. "As used in this convention:

(a) "The term 'United States' means the United States of America, and when used in a geographical sense, includes only the States, the Territories of Alaska and Hawaii, and the District of Columbia."

(b) "The term 'Finland' means the Republic of Finland."

(c) "The term 'tax' means the Federal estate tax imposed in the United States or the inheritance tax, the communal tax on inheritances, bequests or devises or the 'poors percentage,' imposed in Finland, as the context requires."

(d) "The term 'competent authorities' means, in the case of the United States, the Commissioner of Internal Revenue, as authorized by the Secretary of the Treasury, and in the case of Finland, the Taxation Department of the Ministry of Finance."

2. "In the application of the provisions of the present Convention by one of the contracting States, any term not otherwise defined shall, unless the context otherwise requires, have the meaning which such term has under the tax laws of that state" (p. 2763).

ARTICLE III: Situs of property—The question whether a decedent was a domiciliary or a citizen of the territory of the United States or a resident of Finland at the time of death is determined in accordance with the laws in force in such country. The following rules are to be used exclusively in the determination of situs of property or property rights:

(a) The taxable situs of real property is the place where it is located.

(b) "Tangible moveable property, bank or currency notes, and other forms of currency recognized as legal tender in the place of issue have a taxable situs at the place where they are located at the time of death. If [they are] in transit, the taxable situs is at the place of destination" (p. 2761).

(c) The taxable situs of debts, bonds, promissory notes, bills of exchange, and insurance is the place where the debtor resides. If the debtor is a corporation, the situs is the place in or under the laws of which such corporation was created or organized.

(d) Shares of corporate stock, including those held by a nominee, have a taxable situs at the place in or under the laws of which such corporation was created or organized.

(e) "Ships and aircraft have a taxable situs at the place of registration or documentation" (p. 2761).

(f) The taxable situs of the business or professional asset of goodwill is the place where the business is carried on or the profession is practiced.

(g) The taxable situs of patents, trademarks, and designs is the place where they are registered or used.

(h) "Copyrights, franchises, rights to artistic and scientific works and rights or licenses to use any copyrighted material, artistic and scientific works, patents, trademarks or designs have a taxable situs at the place where the rights arising therefrom are exercisable" (p. 2762).

(i) Property, other than the above mentioned, is deemed to be situated in accordance with the laws of the contracting state imposing the tax on the basis of situs of property within that state. If neither of the contracting states imposes the tax on the basis of situs of property therein, all such property is deemed to be situated where the deceased person was a domiciliary at the time of death.

ARTICLE IV: Specific exemptions. Estates of non-resident alien decedents—A specific exemption is allowed in respect to estates of non-resident alien decedents. "In the application of this article to the United States estate tax, the exemption in the case of a decedent resident of Finland at the time of death may not be less than that proportion of the exemption allowable in the case of a decedent domiciled in the United States which the value of the property situated in the United States bears to the entire gross estate—that is, the value of the property which would have been subject to the tax if the decedent had been domiciled in the United States.

"The country imposing the tax on the basis of the situs of the property may not, in determining the amount or rate of tax, take into account property situated outside that country" (p. 2762).

ARTICLE V: Credits. Avoidance of double taxation—"In the case of a deceased person who was domiciled in, or was a citizen of, the United States or a resident of Finland at the time of death, a credit is allowed by either country for the tax imposed by the other on or in respect of property situated in the latter country and included by both countries in the respective computations for tax purposes. The amount of the credit cannot exceed the portion of the tax imposed by the former country which is attributable to such property.

"If taxes are imposed in one of the contracting states by reason of the decedent's domicile therein or citizenship thereof and in the other contracting state by reason of the decedent's or beneficiary's residence therein, each country will allow a credit against its tax in accordance with a specifed formula" (p. 2762).

ARTICLE VI: Claims for credit or refund—Under the provisions of the convention, claims for credit or refund must be made within six years from the date of death of the decedent. Interest does not accrue on any such refunds.

ARTICLES VII, VIII, IX, X, and XII: Administrative assistance provisions.

ARTICLE XIII: Ratification and effective date.[21]

IRISH ESTATE TAX TREATY

An estate tax convention between the United States and Ireland was signed on September 13, 1949. The exchange of the instruments of ratification took place on December 20, 1951, and the convention became effective then in regard to the estates of decedents dying on or after that date. The convention may also be effective in regard to the estate of any person dying before December 20, 1951 at the option of the personal representative of the decedent. Highlights of the treaty follow:

ARTICLE I: Taxes covered—The United States federal estate tax and the Irish estate tax duty are covered.

ARTICLE II: Treaty terms defined—

1. ''In the present convention, unless the context otherwise requires:''

(a) ''The term 'United States' means the United States of America, and when used in a geographical sense means the States, the Territories of Alaska and of Hawaii, and the District of Columbia.''

(c) ''The term 'Ireland' means the Republic of Ireland.''

(b) ''The term 'territory' when used in relation to one or the other Contracting Party means the United States or Ireland, as the context requires.''

2. ''In the application of the provisions of the present Convention by one of the Contracting Parties, any term not otherwise defined shall, unless the context otherwise requires, have the meaning which it has under the laws of that Contracting Party relating to the taxes which are the subject of the present Convention'' (p. 4163).

ARTICLE III: Situs of property—The question of whether a decedent was a domiciliary of the territory of one of the contracting states is to be determined in accordance with the laws in force in that country.

The situs of any legal or equitable rights or interests is to be determined exclusively in accordance with the following rules:

(a) The taxable situs of immovable property is the place of its location.

(b) ''Tangible movable property, bank or currency notes, other currency recognized as legal tender is the place where issued, negotiable bills of exchange, and negotiable promissory notes have a taxable situs at the place where they are located at the time of the decedent's death'' (p. 4161). If the above mentioned are in transit at such time, the place of destination acts as the taxable situs.

(c) The taxable situs of secured or unsecured debts is the place where the decedent was domiciled at the time of death.

(d) Shares or stock in a corporation, other than municipal or governmental shares but including shares held by a nominee, have a taxable situs at the place or under the laws in which the corporation was created or organized.

(e) The taxable situs of money payable in accordance with an insurance policy is the place where the decedent was domiciled at the time of death.

(f) ''Ships and aircraft have a taxable situs at the place of registration or documentation'' (p. 4161).

(g) The taxable situs of the business or professional asset of goodwill is the place where the business is carried on or the profession is practiced.

(h) The taxable situs of patents, trademarks, and designs is the place where they are registered.

(i) ''Copyrights, franchises, and rights or licenses to use any copyrighted material, patent, trademark or design have a taxable situs at the place where the rights arising therefrom are exercisable'' (p. 4162).

(j) ''Rights or causes of action *ex delicta* surviving for the benefit of an estate are situated at the place where such rights or causes of action arose'' (p. 4162).

(k) ''Judgment debts are situated at the place where the judgment is recorded'' (p. 4162).

ARTICLE IV: Elimination of extraterritorial taxation—The contracting state that imposes a tax on property situated within that country may not take into consideration property located in other countries when determining the amount or rate of tax. This is not applicable, however, with respect to tax imposed in the United States in the case of a United States citizen who died a domiciliary of any part of Ireland. It also does not apply in regard to tax imposed in Ireland in the case of property passing under a disposition governed by Irish law.

ARTICLE V: Credits. Avoidance of double taxation—In the case of a decedent who was a domiciliary or national of one of the countries at the time of death, ''a credit is allowed by that country for the tax imposed by the other country on, or in respect of, property situated in the latter country and included by both countries in their respective computation for tax purposes.

''Where both countries consider that the decedent was domiciled in their respective territories at the time of death, in addition to the credit mentioned above, each country will, in respect of any property situated or deemed to be situated in both countries or in either country, allow a credit which bears the same proportion to the amount of its tax so attributable as to the amount of the other country's tax attributable to the same property, whichever is less, as the former amount bears to the sum of both amounts.

''An Irish duty on property pasing under a disposition governed by Irish law is the subject of a similar credit.

''The credit allowed by the convention is computed after taking into account other credits or allowances against the tax. Not affected, then, is the allowance of credits such as those authorized by Code Section 813(b) for inheritance, legacy, or succession taxes paid to states, the District of Columbia, or the territories or possessions of the United States, or those authorized by Code Section 813(a) and 936(b) for gift taxes'' (p. 4162).

ARTICLE VI: Claims for credit or refund—Claims for credit or refunds made in accordance with the provisions of the convention must be made within 6 years of the date of the decedent's death ''or within 6 years from the date on which a reversionary interest falls into possession. Interest is not paid on the amount so refunded when the tax was paid'' (p. 4162).

ARTICLES VII and IX: Administrative provisions.

ARTICLE VIII: Effective date.[22]

AUSTRIAN ESTATE AND GIFT TAX TREATY

An estate and gift tax convention between the United States and the Republic of Austria was signed in Vienna on June 21, 1982. The instruments of ratification were exchanged in Washington, D.C. on April 13, 1983 following the United States consent to ratification. The convention entered into force on July 1, 1983, and it is applicable to transfers of estates, gifts, and generation-skipping transfers occurring on or after that date. The following provisions are highlights of the treaty:

ARTICLE 1: Scope—The treaty is applicable to the estate of a decedent who was a domiciliary of either or both countries at the time of death. The treaty also applies to all gifts and generation-skipping transfers made by individuals who were domiciled in either the United States or Austria or in both countries. The treaty has no effect on the fiscal benefits accorded by the internal law of either country.

ARTICLE 2: Taxes covered—The convention is applicable to the Austrian inheritance and gift tax. The treaty is applicable to the United States federal estate tax, the federal gift tax, and the federal tax on generation-skipping transfers. The treaty is also applicable to any similiar taxes imposed by either country after the date of signature, which was June 21, 1982.

ARTICLE 3: General definitions—

1. "For the purpose of this Convention:

(a) "the term 'United States' means the United States of America, but does not include Puerto Rico, the Virgin Islands, Guam, or any other United States possession or territory;

(b) "the term 'Austria' means the Republic of Austria;

(c) "the term 'Contracting State' and 'the other Contracting State' mean the United States or Austria, as the context requires;

(d) "the term 'competent authority' means:

[i] "in the United States: the Secretary of the Treasury, or his delegate, and

[ii] "in Austria: the Federal Minister of Finance."

2. "As regards to the application of this Convention by a Contracting State, any term not defined therein shall, unless the context otherwise requires and subject to the provisions of Article 11, have the meaning which it has under the laws of that State concerning the taxes to which this convention applies" (pp. 653–54).

ARTICLE 4: Fiscal domicile—For purposes of this convention, rules have been established for determining an individual's domicile and for resolving cases of dual domicile. Initially, domicile is to be determined in accordance with the laws in force in each country. Therefore, an individual who is a resident of the United States is a domiciliary of that country, and an individual is domiciled in Austria if he or she is a resident of Austria.

ARTICLE 5: Real property—Real property has a taxable situs at the place of its location. "The term 'real property' includes property accessory to real property, livestock, equipment used in agriculture and forestry, and rights to payment for the working of mineral deposits and other natural resources. However, ships, boats, and aircraft are not considered real property" (pp. 651–53).

ARTICLE 6: Business property of a permanent establishment and assets pertaining to a fixed base used for the performance of independent personal services—"The business assets of a permanent establishment and assets pertaining to a fixed base, which are used for the performance of independent personal service, are taxed to the situs country. Any fixed place of business through which a person engages in a trade or business is considered a permanent establishment" (pp. 651–53).

ARTICLE 7: Property not expressly mentioned—Primary taxing jurisdiction over transfers of property made by a country's domiciliaries is with the country of domicile, other than for property specifically reserved for situs country taxation.

ARTICLE 8: Deductions and exemptions—"Deductions for debt are allocated between the situs country and the country of domicile as the basis of the relationship or lack thereof between the debt and the specific property. A taxpayer may use either the treaty rules or the Code rules for deductions, but not both. The treaty does not provide for the deduction of charitable gifts or a marital deduction" (pp. 651–53).

ARTICLE 9: Methods for elimination of double taxation—The United States rule of worldwide taxation of its citizens and residents is preserved in the convention. Double taxation is not an issue, because the United States allows credit for a tax paid to Austria or property subject to Austrian situs taxation and because Austria exempts from taxation property that is subject to situs taxation by the United States. A period of limitations is provided for within which credit or refunds of taxes may be made. Refunds based on provisions of the convention do not accrue interest.

ARTICLE 10: Nondiscrimination—Under similar circumstances, neither country can impose more burdensome taxes or requirements related thereto on citizens of the other country than it imposes on its own citizens. In addition, neither country may impose more burdensome taxation on a corporation wholly or partially owned by individual residents of the other country than it would impose if those owners were its residents.

ARTICLE 11: Mutual-agreement procedure—The competent authorities of the United States and Austria are authorized to consult together to attempt to alleviate individual cases of double taxation in accordance with the terms of the convention. The competent authorities are also directed to resolve any difficulties or doubts arising from its application and to communicate and meet with one another for purposes of carrying out the intent of the convention.

ARTICLE 12: Exchange of information—The convention provides for both spontaneous and requested exchanges of tax-related information between the two countries. "However, a country is not required to carry out administrative measures that are contrary to its own laws, to supply particulars not obtainable under its own laws, or to supply information that would disclose a trade secret or that would not be in the public interest. Nothing in the convention prohibits the use of the mails to deliver documents to private parties in the other country" (pp. 651–53).

ARTICLE 13: Diplomatic agents and consular officials—Diplomats and consular officials are specifically exempt from the application of the treaty provisions.

ARTICLE 14: Entry into force—The treaty enters into force on the first day of the third month following the month in which instruments of ratification have been exchanged, and it will apply to estates of persons dying, gifts made, and generation-skipping transfers deemed made on or after that date.

ARTICLE 15: Termination—If at least six months prior notice is given, either country may terminate the convention after it has been in force for five years. The treaty then will not apply to estates of persons dying, gifts made, or generation-skipping transfers deemed made after the December 31st next following the date of termination specified in the notice of termination.[23]

NORWEGIAN ESTATE TAX TREATY

An estate tax convention between the United States and Norway was signed on June 13, 1949. The convention became effective on December 11, 1951, when the instruments of ratification were exchanged. The convention covers the estates of decedents dying after that date. Provisions of the treaty follow:

ARTICLE 1: Taxes covered—The United States federal estate tax and the Norwegian tax on inheritances, including death gifts, are covered.

ARTICLE 2: Treaty terms defined—

1. As used in this convention:

(a) "The term 'United States' means the United States of America, and when used in a geographical sense means the States, and the District of Columbia.

(b) "The term 'Norway' means the Kingdom of Norway; the provisions of the Convention shall not, however, extend to Svabard and Jan Mayer, nor do they apply to the Norwegian dependencies outside Europe.

(c) "The term 'competent authorities' means, in the case of the United

States, the Commissioner of Internal Revenue or his authorized representatives; and in the case of Norway, the Ministry of Finance & Customs.''

2. ''In the application of the provisions of the present Convention by one of the contracting States, any term not otherwise defined shall, unless the context otherwise requires, have the meaning which such term has under its own laws'' (p. 6153).

ARTICLE 3: Situs of the property—In determining whether a decedent was domiciled in the territory of one of the contracting states at the time of demise, the laws in force in such country will apply. The following rules are to be used exclusively in determining the situs of particular property or property rights.

(a) The taxable situs of real property is the place where it is located.

(b) The taxable situs of tangible movable property, bank or currency notes, and other forms of currency recognized as legal tender in the place where it was issued is the place where they are located at the time of the person's death. If such property is in transit, the taxable situs is at the place of destination.

(c) The debtor's place of residence is the taxable situs for debts, including insurance. If the debtor is a corporation the situs is at the place in or under the laws of which such corporation was created or organized.

(d) Bonds, promissory notes, and bills of exchange are deemed to be situated in accordance with the laws of the contracting state imposing the tax on the basis of the situs of property. If neither state imposes the tax on the basis of situs, they are deemed to be situated at the place of the decedent's domicile.

(e) The taxable situs of shares of stock in a corporation, including that held by a nominee, is deemed to be at the place or under the laws of which such corporation was created or organized.

(f) Ships and aircraft have a taxable situs at the place of registration or documentation.

(g) The taxable situs of the business or professional asset of goodwill is the place where the business is carried on or the profession is practiced.

(h) Patents, trademarks, and designs have a taxable situs where they are registered or used.

(i) Copyrights, franchises, rights to artistic and scientific works, and rights or licenses to use any copyrighted natural, artistic, and scientific works; patents; trademarks; or designs have taxable situs at the place where the rights arising therefrom are exercisable.

(j) The taxable situs for property other than the above mentioned is the country where the deceased person was domiciled at the time of death.

ARTICLE 4: Specific exemptions. Estates of non-resident alien decedents—In regard to the estates of non-resident alien decedents, a specific exemption is allowed. ''In the application of this article to the United States estate tax, the exemption in the case of a decedent domiciled in Norway at the time of death, may not be less than that proportion of the exemption allowable in the case of a decedent domiciled in the United States which the value of the property situated in the United States bears to the entire gross estate—that is, the value of the property which would have been subject to the tax if the decedent had been domiciled in the United States.

"The country imposing the tax on the basis of the situs of the property may not, in determining the amount or rate of tax, take into account property situated outside that country" (p. 6152).

ARTICLE 5: Credits. Avoidance of double taxation—"In the case of a deceased person who was domiciled in or was a citizen of one of the countries at the time of death, a credit is allowed by that country for the tax imposed by the other country on or in respect of property situated in the other country and included by both countries in the respective computations for tax purposes. The amount of the credit cannot exceed the portion of the tax imposed by the former country which is attributable to such property.

"If the decedent is considered by each country as being domiciled therein or a citizen thereof at the time of death, in addition to the credit mentioned above, each country will, in respect of any property situated or deemed to be situated in both countries as in neither country, allow a credit which bears the same proportion to the amount of its tax so attributable or to the amount of the other country's tax attributable to the same property, whichever is less, as the former amount bears to the sum of both amounts.

"The credit allowed by each country is computed after taking into account any abatement, credit, remission, diminution, or increase, provided by its law, other than any credit authorized by the convention. Not affected, then, is the allowance of credits such as those authorized by Code Section 813(b) for inheritance, legacy, or succession taxes paid to states, the District of Columbia, or the territories or possessions of the United States, or those authorized by Code Sections 813(a) and 936(b)for gift taxes." (p. 6152).

ARTICLE 6: Claims for credit or refund—Claims must be made within six years from the decedent's death and interest does not accrue on any funds

ARTICLES 7 through 12: Administrative cooperation provisions

ARTICLE 13: Limitations on the convention—The convention does not affect the right of diplomatic and consular officers to other or additional exemptions. Nothing in the convention restricts any exemption, deduction, credit, or other allowance accorded by either of the states in the determination of its taxes.

ARTICLE 14: Effective date.[24]

Swiss Estate Tax Treaty

An estate tax convention between the United States and Switzerland was signed on July 9, 1951, and on July 4, 1952, the United States Senate consented to its ratification without amendment. The instruments of ratification were exchanged on September 17, 1952. The convention covers the estates or inheritances of persons who die on or after that date. Highlights of the treaty follow:

ARTICLE I: Taxes covered—The United States federal estate tax and the Swiss estate and inheritance taxes imposed by the cantons and political subdivision thereof are covered.

ARTICLE II: Treaty terms defined—

1. "As used in this convention:

(a) "The term 'United States' means the United States of America, and when used in a geographical sense means the States, the Territories of Alaska and Hawaii, and the District of Columbia.

(b) "The term 'Switzerland' means the Swiss Confederation.

(c) "The term 'tax' means the Federal estate tax imposed by the United States, or the inheritance or estate taxes imposed in Switzerland, as the context requires.

(d) "The term 'competent authorities' means, in the case of the United States, the Commissioner of Internal Revenue as authorized by the Secretary of the Treasury; and in the case of Switzerland, the Director of the Federal Tax Administration, as authorized by the Federal Department of Finances & Customs."

2. "In the application of the provisions of the present Convention by one of the contracting States any terms not otherwise defined, have the meaning which such term has under its own laws."

3. "For the purposes of the present Convention, each contracting state may determine whether the decedent was at the time of death domiciled therein or a citizen thereof" (p. 7463).

ARTICLE III: Specific exemption. Estates of non-resident alien decedents—"A specific exemption is allowed in the case of estates of nonresident alien decedents. In the application of this article to the United States estate tax, the exemption in the case of a decedent citizen of or domiciled in Switzerland at the time of death may not be less than that proportion of the exemption allowable in the case of a decedent domiciled in the United States which the value of the property situated in the United States bears to the entire gross estate—that is, the value of the property which would have been subject to the tax if the decedent had been domiciled in the United States. If a death duty should be imposed in Switzerland on the basis of the situs of movable property therein, the Swiss tax authorities will allow a similiar prorated specific exemption for estates of decedents who were citizens of or domiciled in the United States at the time of death" (p. 7461).

ARTICLE IV: Credits. Avoidance of double taxation—"In the case of a decedent who, at the time of his death, was a United States citizen domiciled in Switzerland, or in the case of a person not a United States citizen but regarded by the Federal government as domiciled in the United States and also regarded by the Swiss authorities as domiciled within their jurisdiction, the tax authorities of each country will allow a credit for tax paid in the other country with respect to property situated in such other country. The credit provisions do not apply in regard to property situated outside both of the countries and subject to tax by both countries.

"The property referred to above is as follows (these catagories are not described in the form of situs rules, but the effect is much the same)" (p. 7461):

(a) Corporate shares of stock, including that held by a nominee, which is created or organized under the laws of the other country or a political subdivision thereof

(b) Debts, as well as bonds, promissory notes, bills of exchange, and insurance, if the debtor resides in or, if it is a corporation, is created or organized in the other state

(c) "Corporeal movable property, including bank or currency notes and other forms of legal tender recognized as such is the place of issue, physically located in such other state at the time of the decedent's death" (p. 7462)

(d) Property that the competent authorities deem as property situated in such other state.

The credit that is allowable under the provisions of the convention is to be computed after other credits have been taken against the tax. The credits authorized by Code Section 813(b) and the credit authorized by Code Sections 813(a) and 936 (b) are not affected.

The tax for which credit may be authorized must be fully paid in the other country.

ARTICLE V: Claims for credit or refund—Claims for tax credit or refunds under the terms of the convention must be made within five years from the date of the decedent's death. Interest does not accrue on any refunds.

ARTICLES VI & VII: Administrative provisions.

ARTICLE VIII: Effective date.[25]

United Kingdom Estate Tax Treaty

The estate tax convention between the United States and the United Kingdom became effective upon the exchange of instruments of ratification on July 25, 1946. The convention is applicable to the estates of persons dying on or after that date. Upon the election of a personal representative, the convention will apply to the estate of any person dying before July 25, 1946 and after December 31, 1944.

On October 19, 1978, a new estate and gift tax treaty was signed, which replaced the estate tax treaty. The new treaty enters into force on November 11, 1979. It will have effect in the United States in regard to estates of individuals dying and transfer taking effect after that date. In the United Kingdom, it will take effect in regard to property for which there is a change in tax that arises after that date.

ARTICLE I: Taxes covered—The United States federal estate tax is covered. The convention covers the estate duty imposed in Great Britain.

ARTICLE II: Treaty terms defined—

1. Unless the context indicates otherwise, the following definitions are applicable to the convention:

(a) "United States" means the United States of America. When used in a geographical sense, it means the states, the territories of Alaska and Hawaii, and the District of Columbia.

(b) "Great Britain" means England, Wales, and Scotland and does not include the Channel Islands or the Isle of Man.

(c) "Territory," when used in relation to one of the contracting parties means the United States or Great Britain, as the context requires.

(d) "Tax" means the estate duty imposed in Great Britain or the United States federal estate tax, as the context requires.

2. Any term not otherwise defined shall, unless the context requires otherwise, have the meaning that it has under the laws of that contracting party relating to the taxes that are the subject of the present convention.

ARTICLE III: Situs of property—The determination of whether a decedent was a domiciliary in the territory of one of the contracting states at the time of death is determined in accordance with the laws in force in such country.

The following rules should be used in the determination of any of the following rights or interest, legal or equitable. The situs of rights or interests not within the following rules is determined in accordance with the law of the state other than the one in which the decedent was a domiciliary.

(a) The taxable situs of immovable property is the place where it is located.

(b) The taxable situs of the following is the place where they are located at the time of decedent's death:

1. Rights or interests in tangible movable property
2. Bank or currency notes
3. Other currency recognized as legal tender
4. Negotiable bills of exchange
5. Negotiable promissory notes

If the above mentioned was in transit, the taxable situs is the place of destination.

(c) The place where the decedent was domiciled at the time of death acts as the taxable situs for secured and unsecured debts.

(d) Shares of stock in a corporation, other than municipal or governmental, and including that held by a nominee, have a taxable situs at the place or under the laws of which such corporation was created or organized.

(e) The decedent's place of domicile at the time of demise acts as the taxable situs for money that is payable under an insurance policy.

(f) Ships, aircraft, or shares thereof have a taxable situs at the place of registration or documentation.

(g) The taxable situs of a business or professional asset of goodwill is the place where the business is carried on or the profession is practiced.

(h) Patents, trademarks, and designs have a taxable situs at the place of registration.

(i) Copyrights, franchises, and rights or licenses to use any copyrighted material, patent, trademark, or design have a taxable situs at the place where the rights arising therefrom are exercisable.

(j) Rights or causes of action *ex delicta* surviving for the benefit of an estate are situated at the place where such rights or causes of action arose.

(k) The taxable situs of judgment debts is the place where the judgment is recorded.

ARTICLE IV: Allowance of deductions—Determination of tax rates—Deductions, as authorized under the law of the taxing country, are allowed.

In fixing its tax rate on the estate of a non-resident of one of the contracting countries, only property situated within the taxing country may be taken into account. This is not applicable, however, with regard to tax imposed in the United States in the case of a United States citizen dying when domiciled in any part of Great Britain. In addition, this provision is not applicable to tax imposed in Great Britain in the case of property passing under a disposition governed by British law.

ARTICLE V: Credit provisions—Two rules have been provided with regard to credit allowable by one country against its estate tax or estate duty, as the case may be, for estate duty or tax imposed by the other country.

Therefore, in regard to the first rule, "the United States will allow against its estate tax in the case of a decedent domiciled in, or a citizen of, the United States a credit for United Kingdom estate duty imposed upon the decedent's property situated within the United Kingdom. No credit, then, will be allowed for tax imposed with respect to property not subjected to tax by the crediting country. The credit cannot exceed the portion of the tax imposed by the crediting country which is attributable to the property subjected to tax by the country in which the property is situated" (p. 8202).

Under the second rule, each country will be allowed, with regard to property situated in both countries, or deemed situated in either of the contracting countries, "a credit against its tax of that portion of the smaller of the two taxes—before the credit—attributable to such property which such tax of the crediting country bears to the sum of such taxes of both countries" (p. 8202).

Computation of the credit is made after taking into account any other credit, allowance or relief, or remission or reduction of tax. The allowance of credits such as those authorized by Code Section 813(b) for inheritance, legacy, or succession taxes paid to states, the District of Columbia, or the territories or possessions of the United States or those authorized by Code Sections 813(a) and 936(b) for gift taxes is not affected.

ARTICLE VII: Administrative provisions.

ARTICLE VIII: Basis for application of convention to colonies, overseas territories, and certain other areas over which authority is exercised by the respective governments.

ARTICLE IX: Application of convention to Northern Ireland.

ARTICLES X & XI: Effective date and ratification—The convention affects the estate of any person dying on or after July 25, 1946, the date of the exchange of instruments of ratification. Upon the election of a personal representative, the convention is effective as to the estate of any person dying before July 25, 1946 and after December 31, 1944. Article XI contains the provisions for the termination of the convention.[26]

5 Adopted, Illegitimate, and Posthumous Children

This chapter presents an overview and analysis of the interrelationship between inheritance substantive law and the law governing adopted, illegitimate, and afterborn or posthumous children. There has been a significant evolution in the law regarding the inheritance rights of these heirs in each of the several states, and, therefore, particular attention must be directed to each respective state statute. The spectrum of what a child may inherit ranges from nothing at all to all of the realty and personalty of a deceased parent.

We live in an age and society where it is virtually commonplace for a child to be born out of wedlock. In addition, parties are having children in their later years of life. Adoption rates have increased, and constant mobility of families is a reality. As such, knowledge of the law in your jurisdiction and sister states' jurisdictions is absolutely essential.

RIGHTS OF ADOPTED, ILLEGITIMATE, AND POSTHUMOUS CHILDREN

Most modern statutes afford an adopted child the right to inherit from and through the adopting parents. However, it should be noted that "unless a statutory authority is found, adopted children do not inherit from the adopting parent."[27] Statutes exist in almost every jurisdiction in the United States that have built into the adoption proceeding a process by which the adoptee gains the status of a natural child. When these statutes are found, a child will inherit the adoptive parent's intestate property.

Courts generally hold that an adopted child falls within the category of "children" found in the descent and distribution statutes. Furthermore, courts do not generally limit the word *issue* to mean natural children, since they believe that the word is used to include the "child" or "children" of the descendant.

A few states will not automatically confer inheritance rights to the adoptee during adoption proceedings. The rights will be conveyed only at this time if the petition for adoption provides that the child should acquire the rights of heirship. Furthermore, if only one adoptive parent executes the petition, and the petition makes the child heir of that parent only, the child may not inherit from that parent's spouse.

Posthumous children have the same rights of inheritance as the other children of the parent in most of the United States when that parent dies intestate. Furthermore, many statutes generally provide that "after born children take as if their parent had died intestate, even where the statute in terms provides for children whom the testator leaves 'at his death' unprovided for."[28]

Early common law dictated that illegitimate children were to be treated as "filuis nullvis—a child of no one and thus unable to inherit."[29] This severe rule has since been modified to afford an illegitimate child the same status as a legitimate child, at least as far as the mother's estate is concerned, in most states. Generally, these statutes, which allow an illegitimate child to inherit from his or her mother, will insure this right even if the mother has a legitimate child.

The rights of an illegitimate child to inherit from his or her father is limited when compared to the mother-child relationship. Some states will deny illegitimate children the right to inherit from their fathers by not including illegitimate children within the definition of "children" of a male descendant.[30] Still, most states recognize that words such as *child* and *issue* do not exclusively refer to children born in lawful wedlock. Furthermore, there are other states that have statutes enabling a bastard automatically to inherit when his or her father dies intestate. As far as community property is concerned, the courts are evenly divided on whether an illegitimate child may inherit.

The state statutes that follow should be researched thoroughly at the time an issue is presented with regard to adopted, illegitimate, posthumous, or pretermitted children and heirs. The following statutes are not totally conclusive on the subject matter involved, and attorneys and lay persons are cautioned to consult with local counsel for supplements and advice. The omission of a particular section that may be pertnient should not be interpreted as a lack of statutory law on the subject matter.

ALABAMA: WILLS AND DECEDENTS' ESTATES

Section 43-4-3. Relationship of adopted person to adopter and children of adopter; rights of inheritance of adopted person and descendants; right of inheritance from natural parents not barred.

For the purposes of inheritance of property under the laws of descent and distribution, an adopted person shall bear the same relation to his adopter and the natural and adopted children of the adopter as if he were the natural child of such adopting person. It is intended hereby to give an adopted person all right of inheritance from the person who adopts him and through him from his natural and adopted children and to give to the adopting person and his natural and adopted kindred all rights of inheritance from the adopted person and his descendants, including adopted children, the same as if such adopted person were born to the adopting person as a legitimate child. An adopted person's surviving spouse and descendants, including adopted children, shall inherit through such adopted person from the adopting person in lawful wedlock. Where an adopter is the spouse of a natural parent of an adopted child, such natural and adopted parent and kindred shall inherit from the adopted child the same as natural parents and kindred unless otherwise specifically provided in the final decree of adoption. Nothing in this chapter shall be construed as debarring a legally adopted person from inheriting property from his natural parents or other kin.

Section 43-8-48. Parent and child relationship.

If, for purposes of intestate succession, a relationship of parent and child must be established to determine succession by, through, or from a person:

(1) An adopted person is the child of an adopting parent and not of the natural parents except that adoption of a child by the spouse of a natural parent has no effect on the right of the child to inherit from or through either natural parent;

(2) In cases not covered by subdivision (1) of this section, a person born out of wedlock is a child of the mother. That person is also a child of the father, if:

a. The natural parents participated in a marriage ceremony before or after the birth of the child, even though the attempted marriage is void; or

b. The paternity is established by an adjudication before the death of the father or is established thereafter by clear and convincing proof, but the paternity established under this paragraph is ineffective to qualify the father or his kindred to inherit from or through the child unless the father has openly treated the child as his and has not refused to support the child.

Section 43-8-91. Pretermitted children.

(a) If a testator fails to provide in his will for any of his children born or adopted after the execution of his will, the omitted child receives a share in the estate equal in value to that which he would have received if the testator had died intestate unless:

(1) It appears from the will that the omission was intentional;

(2) When the will was executed the testator had one or more children and devised substantially all his estate to the other parent of the omitted child; or

(3) The testator provided for the child by transfer outside the will and the intent that the transfer be in lieu of a testamentary provision be reasonably proven.

(b) If at the time of the execution of the will the testator fails to provide in his will for a living child solely because he believes the child to be dead, the child receives a share in the estate equal in value to that which he would have received if the testator had died intestate.

(c) In satisfying a share provided by this section, the devisees made by the will abate as provided in Section 43-8-76.[31]

ALASKA STATUTES: DECEDENTS' ESTATES, GUARDIANSHIPS, ETC.

Section 13.11.020. Requirement that heir survive decedent for 120 hours.

Any person who fails to survive the decedent by 120 hours is considered to have predeceased the decedent for purposes of homestead allowance, exempt property, and intestate succession, and the decedent's heirs are determined accordingly. If the time of death of the decedent or of the person who would otherwise be an heir, or the times of death of both, cannot be determined, and it cannot be established that the person who would otherwise be an heir has survived the decedent by 120 hours, it is considered that the person failed to survive for the required period. This section is not to be applied where its application would result in a taking of intestate estate by the state under Section 25 of this chapter.

Section 13.11.045. Meaning of "child" and related terms.

If, for the purposes of intestate succession, a relationship of parent and child must be established to determine succession by, through, or from a person,

(1) an adopted person is the child of an adopting parent and not of the natural parents except that an adopted child and his issue have the rights of inheritance from the natural parents and their respective kin unless the decree of adoption specifically provides for termination of those rights of inheritance and except that adoption of a child by the spouse of a natural parent has no effect on the relationship between the child and that natural parent;

(2) in cases not covered by (1) of this section, a person born out of wedlock is a child of the mother; that person is also a child of the father, if:

(A) the natural parents participated in a marriage ceremony before or after the birth of the child, even though the attempted marriage is void; or

(B) the paternity is established by an adjudication before the death of the father or is established thereafter by clear and convincing proof, except that the paternity established under this subparagraph is ineffective to qualify the father or his kindred to inherit from or through the child unless the father has openly treated the child as his and has not refused to support the child.

Section 13.11.115. Pretermitted children.

(a) If a testator fails to provide in his will for any of his children born or adopted after the execution of his will, the omitted child receives a share in the estate equal in value to that which he would have received if the testator had died intestate unless:

(1) it appears from the will that the omission was intentional;

(2) when the will was executed the testator had one or more children and devised substantially all his estate to the other parent of the omitted child; or

(3) the testator provided for the child by transfer outside the will and the intent that the transfer be in place of a testamentary provision is shown by statements of the testator or from the amount of the transfer or other evidence.

(b) If at the time of execution of the will the testator fails to provide in his will for a living child solely because he believes the child to be dead, the child receives a share in the estate equal in value to that which he would have received if the testator had died intestate.

(c) In satisfying a share provided by this section, the devises made by the will abate as provided in AS 13.16.540.[32]

ARIZONA: DECEDENTS' ESTATES, ETC.— TRUSTS

Section 14-2109. Meaning of child and related terms.

If, for purposes of intestate succession, a relationship of parent and child must be established to determine succession by, through, or from a person:

1. An adopted person is the child of an adopting parent and not of the natural parents except that adoption of a child by the spouse of a natural parent has no effect on the relationship between the child and that natural parent.

2. In cases not covered by paragraph 1, a person born out of wedlock is a child of the mother. That person is also a child of the father, if either:

(a) The natural parents participated in a marriage ceremony before or after the birth of the child, even though the attempted marriage is void.

(b) The paternity is established by an adjudication before the death of the father or is established thereafter by clear and convincing proof, except that the paternity established under this subdivision is ineffective to qualify the father or his kindred to inherit from or through the child unless the father has openly treated the child as his and has not refused to support the child.

Section 14-2302. Pretermitted children.

A. If a testator fails to provide in his will for any of his children born or adopted after the execution of his will, the omitted child receives a share in the estate equal in value to that which he would have received if the testator had died intestate unless:

1. It appears from the will that the omission was intentional.

2. When the will was executed the testator had one or more children and devised substantially all his estate to the other parent of the omitted child.

3. The testator provided for the child by transfer outside the will and the intent that the transfer be in lieu of a testamentary provision is shown by statements of the testator or from the amount of the transfer or other evidence.

B. If at the time of execution of the will the testator fails to provide in his will for a living child solely because he believes the child to be dead, the child receives a share in the estate equal in value to that which he would have received if the testator had died intestate.

C. In satisfying a share provided by this section, the devises made by the will abate as provided in Section 14-3902.

Section 14-2601. Requirement that devisee survive testator by one hundred twenty hours.

A. A devisee who does not survive the testator by one-hundred twenty hours is treated as if he predeceased the testator, unless the will of decedent contains some language dealing explicitly with simultaneous deaths or deaths in a common disaster, or requiring that the devisee survive the testator or survive the testator for a stated period in order to take under the will.

B. If at the time of death of the testator, the devisee or both cannot be determined and it cannot be established that the devisee has survived the testator by one hundred twenty hours, it is deemed that the devisee has failed to survive for the required period.[33]

ARKANSAS: WILLS—DESCENT AND DISTRIBUTION

61-141. Illegitimate children.

Concerning the effect of illegitimacy on intestate succession:

(a) If the parents of a child shall have lived together as man and wife and, before the birth of their child, shall have participated in a marriage ceremony in apparent compliance with the law of the state where a marriage ceremony was performed, though the attempted marriage be void, their child is deemed to be the legitimate child of both parents for all purposes of intestate succession. A child born or conceived during a marriage is presumed to be the legitimate child of both spouses for the same purposes.

(b) If a man have a child or children by a woman, and afterward shall intermarry with her, and shall recognize such child or children to be his, such child or children shall be deemed and considered as legitimate.

(c) Any child conceived following artificial insemination of a married woman with the consent of her husband shall be treated as their child for all purposes of intestate succession; consent of the husband is presumed unless the contrary is shown by clear and convincing evidence.

(d) An illegitimate child or his descendants may inherit real or personal property in the same manner as a legitimate child from such child's mother or her blood kindred; but such child may not inherit real or personal property from his father or from his father's blood kindred.

(e) Property of an illegitimate person passes in accordance with the usual rules of intestate succession to his mother and his kindred of her blood; but the father of such person, or the blood kindred of such father, may not inherit from the illegitimate child (or his descendants) either real or personal property.

61-142. Posthumous heirs—Rights of inheritance.

Posthumous descendants of the intestate conceived before his death but born thereafter shall inherit in like manner as if born in the lifetime of the intestate, but no right of inheritance shall accrue to any person other than a lineal descendant of the intestate, unless such person be born at the time of the intestate's death.

61-147. Adopted children.

Where a child has been lawfully adopted:

(a) Such child (and his descendants) will inherit real and personal property from his adoptive parents and from the lineal ascendants, lineal descendants, and collateral kindred of such adoptive parents to the same extent and with the same rights as if he were the natural child of such adoptive parents; and in matters of such inheritance the natural child of the adoptive parents shall enjoy no priorities or preferences over adopted children. Where the intestate, an adoptive parent, has acquired real or personal property by gift, devise, or descent from one [1] of the intestate's parents, or some blood relative of such parent, the adopted child (or his descendants) shall not be excluded from the inheritance of such property on the ground that he lacks the blood of the parent from whom, or from whose blood relative, the property came to the intestate.

(b) The adoptive parents and their kindred will inherit real and personal property from the adoptive child (or his descendants) to the same extent and with the same rights as if the adopted child were the natural child of such adoptive parents.

(c) For all purposes of intestate succession, a child who has been adopted more than once shall be treated as a child of the parents who have most recently adopted him and shall cease to be treated as a child of his previous adopted parents.

(d) An adopted child may inherit from his natural parents and from their lineal and collateral kindred.

(e) A natural parent of a child who has been adopted may never inherit from or through such adopted child except in the following situation: If the natural parent shall marry, or remarry, and the child is adopted by the stepfather or stepmother who, by virtue of such marriage or remarriage, has become the spouse of the natural parent, then the natural parent and his kindred may inherit from such adopted child.

(f) An adopted child, if not mentioned by name or by reference to a class in the will of an adoptive parent, will inherit from that parent as a pretermitted child.

(g) Nothing in this act [Section 61-131 to 61-155] is intended to alter the application of Section 60-140, Arkansas Statutes (1947) Annotated, 1967 Replacement, to adopted children in cases where a testamentary beneficiary predeceased the testator.

(h) Where a child was adopted in another state or nation, the adoption will be recognized in Arkansas for the application of the rules of intestate succession set out in this section, if the adoption was effected in a court of competent jurisdiction through judicial proceedings which effectually separated the child from his natural parents and inducted the child into the family of the adopting parents; and, where such an adoption has been effected, then as to real estate situated in Arkansas, and also as to personal property where the domicile of the intestate was within this state at the time of his death, the devolution of such realty and personalty will be controlled by this section and not by the inheritance laws of the state in which the adoption was effected.

(i) A child is deemed to be adopted within the meaning of this section when:

[1] a final decree of adoption, or

[2] an interlocutory decree of adoption, which under the law of the jurisdiction wherein the proceeding was instituted has become final through lapse of time, has been entered by a court of competent jurisdiction of this state or of any other state or government.[34]

California: Wills and Succession

Section 90. Omitted children and grandchildren.

When a testator omits to provide in his will for any of his children, or for the issue of any deceased child, whether born before or after the making of the will or before or after the death of the testator, and such child or issue is unprovided for by any settlement and has not had an equal proportion of the testator's property bestowed on him by way of advancement, unless it appears from the will that such omission was intentional, such child or issue succeeds to the same share in the estate of the testator as if he had died intestate.

Illegitimate.

Where illegitimate child was unintentionally omitted from the will of her mother, such child was entitled to share in the estate as if she were legitimate. In re *Wardell's Estate (1881) 57 C. 484, 7 P.C.L.J. 431*; In re *Wardell's Estate (1877) Myr. 224.*

Evidence was insufficient to support judgment denying probate of holographic will of which beneficiary was son of person with whom testatrix committed suicide following execution of will, on ground of fraud or undue influence, where testatrix' heirs at law were two aunts, except for pretermitted illegitimate daughter whose rights would be assured by her appearance to claim them. In re *Muller's Estate (1936) 57 P. 2d 579, 217 C. 763.*

Whether testator publicly acknowledged that he was father of petitioner, who alleged that she was testator's illegitimate daughter and claimed share of his estate as pretermitted heir, was for jury. In re *Flood's Estate (1933) 21 P.2d 579, 217 C. 763.*

Acts and declarations of testator and his wife were competent to prove paternity of alleged illegitimate daughter of testator claiming share of estate as pretermitted heir. *Id.*

Within Civ.C., former Section 1307, giving right of inheritance to children not provided for by will, unless the omission appears intentional, illegitimate children, having right of inheritance under Civ.C. Section 1387 (repealed 1931.

See Sections 220-229, 231), provided for by provision for any persons claiming to be "heirs." In re *Lindsay's Estate (1917) 168 P.113, 176 C. 238.*

Section 250. Right of representation defined; posthumous child.

Inheritance or succession "by right of representation" takes place when the descendants of a deceased person take the same share or right in the estate of another that such deceased person would have taken as an heir if living. A posthumous child is considered as living at the death of the parent.

Section 255. Illegitimate children; inheritance rights; limitations.

Every illegitimate child is an heir of his mother, and also of the person who, in writing, signed in the presence of a competent witness, acknowledges himself to be the father, and inherits his or her estate, in whole or in part, as the case may be, in the same manner as if he had been born in lawful wedlock; but he does not represent his father by inheriting any part of the estate of the father's kindred, either lineal or collateral, unless, before his death, his parents shall have intermarried, and his father, after such marriage, acknowledges him as his child, or adopts him into his family; in which case such child is deemed legitimate for all purposes of succession. An illegitimate child may represent his mother and may inherit any part of the estate of the mother's kindred, either lineal or collateral.

Section 256. Illegitimate children; succession to estate.

The estate of an illegitimate child, who, having title to any estate not otherwise limited by marriage contract, dies without disposing thereof by will, is succeeded to as if he had been born in lawful wedlock, if he has been legitimated by a subsequent marriage of his parents or adopted by his father as provided by the Civil Code; otherwise, it is succeeded to as if he had been born in lawful wedlock and had survived his father and all persons related to him only through his father.

Section 257. Adopted children; inheritance rights; restriction.

An adopted child shall be deemed a descendant of one who has adopted him, the same as a natural child, for all purposes of succession by, from, or through the adopting parent the same as a natural parent. An adopted child does not succeed to the estate of a natural parent when the relationship between them has been severed by adoption, nor does such natural parent succeed to the estate of such adopted child, nor does such adopted child succeed to the estate of a relative of the natural parent, nor does any relative of the natural parent succeed to the estate of an adopted child.[35]

COLORADO: INTESTATE SUCCESSION AND WILLS

15-11-107. Kindred of half blood.

Relatives of the half blood inherit the same share they would inherit if they were of the whole blood.

15-11-108. After-born heirs.
Relatives of the decedent conceived before his death but born thereafter inherit as if they had been born in the lifetime of the decedent.

15-11-109. Meaning of child and related terms.
If, for purposes of intestate succession, a relationship of parent and child must be established to determine succession by, through, or from a person:

(a) An adopted person is the child of an adopting parent and of the adopted person's natural parents insofar as the rights of all persons to inherit from or through the adopted person and the right of the adopted person to inherit from or through any person are concerned, except to the extent that inheritance rights have been divested by a final order of relinquishment, a final decree of adoption, or an order terminating the parent-child relationship under the laws of this state or of any other jurisdiction.

(b) In cases not covered by paragraph (a) a person born out of wedlock is a child of the mother. That person is also a child of the father, if:

(I) The natural parents participated in a marriage ceremony before or after the birth of the child, even though the attempted marriage is void; or

(II) The paternity is established by an adjudication before the death of the father or is established thereafter by a preponderance of the evidence; except that the paternity so established is ineffective to qualify the father or his kindred to inherit from or through the child unless the father has openly treated the child as his and has not refused to support the child.[36]

CONNECTICUT: WILLS—ESTATE DISTRIBUTION, ADOPTION

Section 45-274. Distribution to spouse and children.
Children born out of wedlock may inherit.

(a) After distribution has been made to the husband or wife of the intestate of such portion or share of the estate of the intestate as such husband or wife is entitled by law, all the residue of the real and personal estate shall be distributed in equal proportions, according to its value at the time of distribution, among the children and the legal representatives of any of them who may be dead, except that children or other descendants who receive estate by advancement of the intestate in his lifetime shall themselves or their representatives have only so much of the estate as will, together with such advancement, make their share equal to what they would have been entitled to receive had no such advancement been made.

(b) [1] Children born before marriage whose parents afterwards intermarry shall be deemed legitimate and inherit equally with other children. [2] A child born out of wedlock shall inherit from (A) his or her mother and (B) his or her father, provided such father [i] has been adjudicated the father of such child by a court of competent jurisdiction, or [ii] has acknowledged under oath in writing to be the father of such child.

(c) For the purposes of this section [1] issue shall include children born out of wedlock and any of such issue qualify for inheritance under this section; [2] legal representatives shall include legal representatives of children born out of wedlock, provided both the child born out of wedlock through whom such legal representatives inherit and the legal representatives qualify for inheritance under this section.

Section 45-287. Simultaneous death; disposition of property.

(a) When no sufficient evidence of survivorship. When the title to property or the devolution thereof depends upon priority of death and there is no sufficient evidence that the persons have died otherwise than simultaneously, the property of each person shall be disposed of as if he had survived, except as provided otherwise in this section.

(b) Successive beneficiaries. When two or more beneficiaries are designated to take successively by reason of survivorship under another person's disposition of property and there is no sufficient evidence that such beneficiaries have died otherwise than simultaneously, the property thus disposed of shall be divided into as many equal portions as there are successive beneficiaries and such portions shall be distributed respectively to those who would have taken in the event that each designated beneficiary had survived.

(c) Joint tenants. When there is no sufficient evidence that two joint tenants have died otherwise than simultaneously, the property so held shall be distributed one-half as if one had survived and one-half as if the other had survived. If there are more than two joint tenants and all of them have so died, the property thus divided shall be in the proportion that one bears to the whole number of joint tenants.

(d) Life or accident insurance. When the insured and the beneficiary in a policy of life or accident insurance have died and there is no sufficient evidence that they have died otherwise than simultaneously, the proceeds of the policy shall be distributed as if the insured had survived the beneficiary.

(e) Applicability. This section shall not apply to the distribution of the property of a person who died before October 1, 1943, and shall not apply in the case of wills, living trusts, deeds, or contracts of insurance wherein provision had been made for distribution of property otherwise than as provided by this section.

Section 45-64a. Effects of final decree of adoption; surviving rights.

A final decree of adoption, whether issued by a court of this state or a court of any other jurisdiction, shall have the following effect in this state:

(1) All rights, duties, and other legal consequences of the genetic relation of the child and parent shall thereafter exist between the adopted person and the adopting parent and his relatives. Such adopted person shall be treated as if he were the genetic child of the adopting parent, for all purposes including the

applicability of statutes which do not expressly exclude an adopted person in their operation or effect;

(2) The adopting parent and the adopted person shall have rights of inheritance from and through each other and the genetic and adopted relatives of the adopting parent. The right of inheritance of an adopted person extends to the heirs of such adopted person, and such heirs shall be the same as if such adopted person were the genetic child of the adopting parent;

(3) The adopted person and the genetic children and other adopted children of the adopting parent shall be treated, unless otherwise provided by statute, as siblings, having rights of inheritance from and through each other. Such rights of inheritance extend to the heirs of such adopted person and the genetic children and other adopted children, and such heirs shall be the same as if each adopted person were the genetic child of the adopting parent;

(4) The adopted person shall, except as hereinafter provided, be treated as if he were the genetic child of the adopted parent for purposes of applicability of all documents and instruments, whether executed before or after the adoption decree is issued, which do not expressly exclude an adopted person in their operation or effect. The words ''child,'' ''children,'' ''issue,'' ''descendant,'' ''descendants,'' ''heir,'' ''heirs,'' ''lawful heirs,'' ''grandchild,'' and ''grandchildren,'' when used in any will or trust instrument, shall include legally adopted persons unless such document clearly indicates a contrary intention. Nothing in this section shall be construed to alter or modify the provisions of Section 45-162 regarding children born through A.I.D.;

(5) The legal relationship between the adopted person and his genetic parent or parents and the relatives of such genetic parent or parents is terminated for all purposes, including the applicability of statutes which do not expressly include such an adopted person in their operation and effect. The genetic parent or parents of the adopted person is relieved of all parental rights and responsibilities;

(6) The genetic parent or parents and their relatives shall have no rights of inheritance from or through the adopted person, nor shall the adopted person have any rights of inheritance from or through his genetic parent or parents and their relatives, except as provided in this section;

(7) The legal relationship between the adopted person and his genetic parent or parents and the relatives of such genetic parent or parents is terminated for purposes of the construction of documents and instruments, whether executed before or after the adoption decree is issued, which do not expressly include the individual by name or by some designation not based on a parent and child or blood relationship, except as provided in this section;

(8) Notwithstanding the provisions of subdivisions (1) to (7), inclusive, when one of the genetic parents of a minor child has died and the surviving parent has remarried subsequent to such parent's death, adoption of such child by the person with whom such remarriage is contracted shall not affect the rights of such child to inherit from or through the deceased parent and his relatives;

(9) Nothing in this section shall deprive an adopted person who is the genetic

child of a veteran who served in time of war as defined in Section 27-103 of aid under the provisions of Section 27-140 or deprive a child receiving benefits under the Social Security Act, 42 U.S.C. Sec. 301 et seq., as amended from time to time, from continued receipts of benefits authorized under said act;

(10) The provisions of law in force prior to October 1, 1959, affected by the provisions of this section shall apply to the estates or wills of persons dying prior to said date and to inter vivos instruments executed prior to said date and which on said date were not subject to the grantor's power to revoke or amend.[37]

DELAWARE: DECEDENTS' ESTATES; FIDUCIARY RELATIONS

Section 310. Posthumous children.

Posthumous children or children in the mother's womb, if born alive, are within the foregoing provisions respecting after-born children. Such children shall take any estate or property, real or personal, by descent, transmission, gift, devise, limitation, or otherwise in the same manner as if absolutely born at the demise of its parent. If such child is not born alive, the effect shall be the same, to all intents and purposes, as if no such child had ever existed.

Section 505. Posthumous children.

Posthumous children, born alive, shall be considered as though living at the death of their parent.

Section 508. Meaning of child and related terms.

If, for purposes of intestate succession, a relationship of parent and child must be established to determine succession by, through, or from a person:

(1) An adopted person is the child of an adopting parent and not of the natural parent except that adoption of a child by the spouse of a natural parent has no effect on the relationship between the child and that natural parent.

(2) In cases not covered by subdivision (1) of this section, a person born out of wedlock is a child of the mother. That person is also a child of the father, if:

a. The natural parents participated in a marriage ceremony before or after the birth of the child, even though the attempted marriage is void; or

b. The paternity is established by an adjudication before the death of the father or is established thereafter by preponderance of the evidence; except that the paternity established under this paragraph is ineffective to qualify the father or his kindred to inherit from or through the child unless the father has openly treated the child as his and has not refused to support the child.[38]

DISTRICT OF COLUMBIA: DESCENT AND DISTRIBUTION; ADOPTION

Section 19-314. Share of posthumous children.

A right in the inheritance to real or personal property does not accrue to or vest in a person other than the children of the intestate and their descendants, unless the person is in being and capable in law to take as heir or distributee at the time of the intestate's death; but a child or descendant of the intestate born after the death of the intestate has the same right of inheritance as if born before his death.

Section 19-316. Share of children born out of wedlock; their heirs; mother; father.

Children born out of wedlock and the heirs of children born out of wedlock are capable of taking real and personal estate by inheritance from their mother or from their father if parenthood has been established, or from each other, or from heirs of each other, as the case may be, in like manner as if born in lawful wedlock, and the mother and such father, and their respective heirs, are capable of inheriting from such children.

Section 16-312. Legal effects of adoption.

(a) A final decree of adoption establishes the relationship of natural parent and natural child between adoptor (adopter) and adoptee for all purposes including mutual rights of inheritance and succession as if adoptee were born to adoptor (adopter). The adoptee takes from, through, and as a representative of his adoptive parent or parents in the same manner as a child by birth, and upon the death of an adoptee intestate, his property shall pass and be distributed in the same manner as if the adoptee had been born to the adopting parent or parents in lawful wedlock. All rights and duties including those of inheritance and succession between the adoptee, his natural parents, their issue, collateral relatives, and so forth, are cut off, except that when one of the natural parents is the spouse of the adoptor (adopter), the rights and relations as between adoptee, that natural parent, and his parents and collateral relatives, including mutual rights of inheritance and succession, are in no way altered.

(b) While it is in force, an interlocutory decree of adoption has the same legal effect as a final decree of adoption. Upon the revocation of an interlocutory decree of adoption, the status of the adoptee, the natural parents of the adoptee, and the petitioners are as though the interlocutory decree were null and void ab initio.

(c) The family name of the adoptee shall be changed to that of the adopter unless the decree otherwise provides, and the given name of the adoptee may be fixed or changed at the same time.

Section 16-313. Child as including adopted person.

In the district, "child" or its equivalent in a deed, grant, will, or other written instrument includes an adopted person, unless the contrary plainly appears by the terms thereof, whether the instrument was executed before or after the entry of the interlocutory decree of adoption, if any, or before or after the final decree of adoption became effective.[39]

FLORIDA: ESTATES AND TRUSTS

732.108. Adopted persons and persons born out of wedlock.

(1) For the purposes of intestate succession by or from an adopted person, the adopted person is a lineal descendant of the adopting parent and is one of the natural kindred of all members of the adopting parent's family, and he is not a lineal descendant of his natural parents, nor is he one of the kindred of any member of his natural parent's family or any prior adoptive parent's family, except that:

(a) Adoption of a child by the spouse of a natural parent has no effect on the relationship between the child and the natural parent or the natural parent's family.

(b) Adoption of a child by a natural parent's spouse who married the natural parent after the death of the other natural parent has no effect on the relationship between the child and the family of the deceased natural parent.

(2) For the purpose of intestate succession in cases not covered by subsection (1), a person born out of wedlock is a lineal descendant of his mother and is one of the natural kindred of all members of the mother's family. The person is also a lineal descendant of his father and is one of the natural kindred of all members of the father's family, if:

(a) The natural parents participated in a marriage ceremony before or after the birth of the person born out of wedlock, even though the attempted marriage is void.

(b) The paternity of the father is established by an adjudication before or after the death of the father.

(c) The paternity of the father is acknowledged in writing by the father.

732.106. Afterborn heirs.

Heirs of the decedent conceived before his death, but born thereafter, inherit intestate property as if they had been born in the decedent's lifetime.

732.302. Pretermitted children.

When a testator omits to provide in his will for any of his children born or adopted after making the will and the child has not received a part of the testator's property equivalent to a child's part by way of advancement, the child shall receive a share of the estate equal in value to that he would have received if the testator had died intestate, unless:

(1) It appears from the will that the omission was intentional; or

(2) The testator had one or more children when the will was executed and devised substantially all his estate to the other parent of the pretermitted child.

The share of the estate that is assigned to the pretermitted child shall be obtained in accordance with Section 733.805.[40]

GEORGIA: WILLS, TRUSTS, AND ESTATES

53-4-4. Inheritance by illegitimates and their offspring.

(a) Illegitimate children have no inheritable blood except that given to them by express law.

(b) An illegitimate child may inherit in the same manner as if legitimate from and through his mother, from and through the other children of the mother, and from and through any other maternal kin, whether collateral or lineal.

(c) An illegitimate child may not inherit from or through his father or any paternal kin by reason of the paternal kinship unless, during the lifetime of the father and after the conception of the child, a court of competent jurisdiction has entered an order declaring the child to be legitimate, under the authority of Code Section 19-7-22 or such other authority as may be provided by law, or has otherwise entered a court order establishing the father of the illegitimate child. If such an order has been entered, an illegitimate child may inherit in the same manner as if legitimate from and through his father, from and through the other children of the father, and from and through any other paternal kin, whether collateral or lineal.

(d) In distributions under this code section, the children of a deceased illegitimate child shall represent the deceased parent.[41]

HAWAII: DESCEDENTS' ESTATES; ADOPTION

Section 532-6. To illegitimate child.

Every illegitimate child shall be considered as an heir to his mother and shall inherit her estate, in whole or in part, as the case may be, in like manner as if he had been born in lawful wedlock.

Section 532-7. From illegitimate persons.

If any illegitimate person dies intestate, without leaving lawful issue, or a widow, his estate shall descend to his mother; but if he leaves a widow, she shall take one-half, and his mother the other half, and if his mother is not living, but his widow is, then the widow shall take one-half, and the remaining half shall go to his brothers and sisters in equal parts, the children of any deceased brother or sister taking by right of representation. In default of surviving brothers or sisters, or their issue, such one-half shall go to the brothers and sisters of his mother in equal shares, the issue of any such brother or sister who is deceased taking by right of representation. In default of any relatives as are in this section mentioned, the half, and the whole in the event that he leaves no widow, shall go to his next of kin. No action shall be commenced or prosecuted on behalf of the state to recover or hold any property which but for this section might have been held to have escheated to the state.

Section 532-9. Posthumous children.

Posthumous children shall, in all cases, inherit the same as if they had been born during their father's lifetime.

Section 578–16. Effect of adoption.

A legally adopted individual shall be considered to be a natural child of the whole blood of the adopting parent or parents as provided in the Uniform Probate Code, relating to the descent of property, and the former legal parent or parents of an adopted individual and any other formal legal relatives or next of kin shall not be considered to be related to the individual as provided in the Uniform Probate Code; and for all other purposes an adopted individual and his adopting parent or parents shall sustain towards each other the legal relationship of parents and child and shall have all the rights and be subject to all the duties of that relationship, the same as if the individual were the natural child of the adopting parent or parents, and all such duties and rights as between the individual and his former legal parent or parents shall cease from the time of the adoption; provided, that if the individual is adopted by a person married to a legal parent of the individual, the full reciprocal rights and duties which theretofore existed between the legal parent and the individual, and the rights of inheritance as between the individual and the legal parent and the legal relatives of the parent, as provided in Chapter 560, shall continue, notwithstanding the adoption, subject only to the rights acquired by and the duties imposed upon the adoptive parents by reason of the adoption. An individual legally adopted under the laws of any state or territory of the United States or under the laws of any nation shall be accorded the same rights and benefits in all respects as an individual adopted under this chapter.[42]

IDAHO: INTESTATE SUCCESSIONS—WILLS

15-2-109. Meaning of child and related terms.

If, for the purposes of intestate succession, a relationship of parents and child must be established to determine succession by, through, or from a person:

(a) An adopted person is a child of an adopting parent and not of the natural parents except that adoption of a child by the spouse of a natural parent has no effect on the relationship between the child and the natural parent, and adoption by the spouse of a natural parent has no effect on the relationship between the child and a deceased, undivorced natural parent.

(b) In cases not covered by subsection (a) of this section, a person born out of wedlock is a child of the mother. That person is also a child of the father, if:

(1) The natural parents participated in a marriage ceremony before or after the birth of the child, even though the attempted marriage is void; or

(2) The paternity is established by an adjudication before the death of the

father or is established thereafter by clear and convincing proof, except that the paternity established under this subparagraph (2) is ineffective to qualify the father or his kindred to inherit from or through the child unless the father has openly treated the child as his and has not refused to support the child.

15-2-302. Pretermitted children.

(a) If a testator fails to provide in his will for any of his children born or adopted after the execution of his will, the omitted child receives a share in the estate equal in value to that which he would have received if the testator had died intestate unless:

(1) it appears from the will that the omission was intentional;

(2) when the will was executed the testator had one (1) or more children and devised substantially all his estate to the other parent of the omitted child; or

(3) the testator provided for the child by transfer outside the will and the intent that the transfer be in lieu of a testamentary provision is shown by statements of the testator or from the amount of the transfer or other evidence.

(b) If at the time of execution of the will the testator fails to provide in his will for a living child solely because he believes the child to be dead, the child receives a share in the estate equal in value to that which he would have received if the testator had died intestate.

(c) In satisfying a share provided by this section, the devises made by the will abate as provided in section 15-3-902 of this code.[43]

ILLINOIS: DESCENT AND DISTRIBUTION

Section 2-2. Illegitimates.

The intestate real and personal estate of a resident decedent who was illegitimate at the time of death and the intestate real estate in this state of a nonresident decedent who was illegitimate at the time of death, after all just claims against his estate are fully paid, descends and shall be distributed as follows:

(a) If there is a surviving spouse and also a descendant of the decedent: 1/3 of the entire estate to the surviving spouse and 2/3 to the decedent's descendants per stirpes.

(b) If there is no surviving spouse but a descendant of the decedent: the entire estate to the decedent's descendants per stirpes.

(c) If there is a surviving spouse but no descendant of the decedent: the entire estate to the surviving spouse.

(d) If there is no surviving spouse or descendant but the mother or a descendant of the mother of the decedent: the entire estate to the mother and her descendants, allowing 1/2 to the mother and 1/2 to her descendants per stirpes.

(e) If there is no surviving spouse, descendant, mother, or descendant of the mother of the decedent, but a maternal grandparent or descendant of a maternal grandparent of the decedent: the entire estate to the decedent's maternal grandparents in equal parts, or to the survivor of them, or if there is none surviving, to their descendants per stirpes.

(f) If there is no surviving spouse, descendant, mother, descendant of the mother, maternal grandparent, or descendant of a maternal grandparent of the decedent: the entire estate to the decedent's maternal great-grandparents in equal parts or to the survivor of them, or if there is none surviving, to their descendants per stirpes.

(g) If there is no surviving spouse, descendant, mother, descendant of the mother, maternal grandparent, descendant of a maternal grandparent, maternal great-grandparent, or descendant of a maternal great-grandparent of the decedent: the entire estate in equal parts to the nearest kindred of the mother of the decedent in equal degree (computing by the rules of the civil law) and without representation.

(h) If there is no surviving spouse or mother of the decedent and no known kindred of the mother of the decedent: the real estate escheats to the county in which it is located, the personal estate physically located within this state and the personal estate physically located or held outside this state which is the subject of ancillary administration within this state escheats to the county of which the decedent was a resident or, if the decedent was not a resident of this state, to the county in which it is located; all other personal property of the decedent of every class and character, wherever situated, or the proceeds thereof, shall escheat to this state and be delivered to the Director of Financial Institutions of this state pursuant to the Uniform Disposition of Unclaimed Property Act.

An illegitimate child is heir of his mother and of any maternal ancestor and of any person from whom his mother might have inherited, if living; and the lawful issue of an illegitimate person shall represent such person and take by descent any estate which the parent would have taken, if living. A child who was illegitimate whose parents intermarry and who is acknowledged by the father as the father's child is legitimate.

Section 2–4. Adopted child and adopting parent.

(a) An adopted child is a descendant of the adopting parent for purpose of inheritance from the adopting parent and from the lineal and collateral kindred of the adopting parent.

(b) An adopting parent and the lineal and collateral kindred of the adopting parent shall inherit property from an adopted child to the exclusion of the natural parent and the lineal and collateral kindred of the natural parent in the same manner as though the adopted child were a natural child of the adopting parent, except that the natural parent and the lineal or collateral kindred of the natural parent shall take from the child and the child's kindred the property that the child has taken from or through the natural parent or the lineal or collateral kindred of the natural parent by gift, by will or under intestate laws.

(c) For purposes of inheritance from the child and his kindred (1) the person who at the time of the adoption is the spouse of an adopting parent is an adopting parent and (2) a child is adopted when the child has been or is declared by any court to have been adopted or has been or is declared or assumed to be the adopted child of the testator or grantor in any instrument bequeathing or giving property to the child.

(d) If an adopted child is related by blood to the adopting parent, the adopted child and his descendants shall take property from the estate of the adopting parent only as an adopted child or descendants of an adopted child and not as relatives by blood.

(e) For the purpose of determining the property rights of any person under any instrument executed on or after September 1, 1955, an adopted child is a natural child unless the contrary intent plainly appears by the terms of the instrument. This subsection does not apply in determining the taker of the property under any instrument executed before September 1, 1955.

Section 4–10. Effect of child born after will.

Unless provision is made in the will for a child of the testator born after the will is executed or unless it appears by the will that it was the intention of the testator to disinherit the child, the child is entitled to receive the portion of the estate to which he would be entitled if the testator died intestate, and all legacies shall abate proportionately therefor.[44]

INDIANA: PROBATE—INTESTATE SUCCESSION; DISTRIBUTION AND DISCHARGE

29-1-2-6. Afterborn children; inheritance.

Descendants of the intestate, begotten before his death but born thereafter, shall inherit as if they had been born in the lifetime of the intestate and had survived him. With this exception, the descent and distribution of intestate estates shall be determined by the relationships existing at the time of the death of the intestate.

29-1-2-7. Illegitimate children; inheritance.

(a) For the purpose of inheritance to, through, and from an illegitimate child, such child shall be treated the same as if he were the legitimate child of his mother, so that he and his issue shall inherit from his mother and from his maternal kindred, both descendants and collaterals, in all degrees, and they may inherit from him. Such child shall also be treated the same as if he were a legitimate child of his mother for the purpose of determining homestead rights and the making of family allowances.

(b) For the purpose of inheritance to, through, and from an illegitimate child, such child shall be treated the same as if he were the legitimate child of his father if, but only if, (1) the paternity of such child has been established by law, during the father's lifetime; or (2) if the putative father marries the mother of the child and acknowledges the child to be his own.

The testimony of the mother may be received in evidence to establish such paternity and acknowledgment, but no judgment shall be made upon the evidence of the mother alone. The evidence of the mother must be supported by corroborative evidence or circumstances.

When such paternity is established as provided herein, such child shall be treated the same as if he were the legitimate child of his father, so that he and his issue shall inherit from his father and from his paternal kindred, both descendants and collateral, in all degrees, and they may inherit from him. Such child shall also be treated the same as if he were a legitimate child of his father for the purposes of determining homestead rights and the making of family allowance.

29-1-2-8. Adopted children; inheritance.

For all purposes of intestate succession, including succession by, through, or from a person, both lineal and collateral, an adopted child shall be treated as a natural child of his adopting parents; and he shall cease to be treated as a child of his natural parents and of any previous adopting parents: Provided, That if a natural parent of a legitimate or illegitimate child shall have married the adopting parent, the adopted child shall inherit from his natural parent as though he had not been adopted and from his adoptive parent as though he were the natural child; and Provided further, That if a person who is related to a child within the sixth degree adopts such child, such child shall upon the occasion of each death in his family have the right of inheritance through his natural parents or adopting parents, whichever is greater in value in each case.

29-1-17-3. Abatement of distributee shares.

(a) Except as provided in subsection (b) hereof, shares of the distributees shall abate, for the payment of claims, legacies, the widow's or family allowance, the shares of pretermitted heirs, or the share of the surviving spouse who elects to take against the will, without any preference or priority as between real and personal property, in the following order:

(1) Property not disposed of by the will;

(2) Property devised to the residuary devisee;

(3) Property disposed of by the will but not specifically devised and not devised to the residuary devisee;

(4) Property specifically devised.

A general devise charged on any specific property or fund shall, for purposes of abatement, be deemed property specifically devised to the extent of the value of the thing on which it is charged. Upon the failure or insufficiency of the thing on which it is charged, it shall be deemed property not specifically devised to the extent of such failure or insufficiency.

(b) If the provisions of the will or the testamentary plan or the express or implied purpose of the devise would be defeated by the order of abatement stated in subsection (a) hereof, the shares of distributees shall abate in such other manner as may be found necessary to give effect to the intention of the testator.[45]

IOWA: PROBATE CODE AND INTESTATE SUCCESSION

633.220. Afterborn heirs—time of determining relationship.

Descendants and other heirs of an intestate, begotten before his death but born thereafter, shall inherit as if they had been born in the lifetime of the intestate and had survived him. With this exception, the intestate succession shall be determined by the relationships existing at the time of the death of the intestate.

633.221. Illegitimate child—inherit from mother.

Unless he has been adopted, an illegitimate child shall inherit from his natural mother, and she from the child.

633.222. Illegitimate child—inherit from father.

Unless he has been adopted, an illegitimate child shall inherit from his natural father when the paternity is proven during the father's lifetime, or when the child has been recognized by the father as his child; but such recognition must have been general and notorious or else in writing. Under such circumstances, if the recognition has been mutual, and the child has not been adopted, the father may inherit from his illegitimate child.

633.223. Effect of adoption.

A lawfully adopted person and his heirs shall inherit from and through the adoptive parents the same as a natural-born child. The adoptive parents and their heirs shall inherit from and through the adopted person the same as though he were a natural-born child.

633.267. Children born or adopted after execution of will.

When a testator fails to provide in his will for any of his children born to or adopted by him after the making of his last will, such child, whether born before or after the testator's death, shall receive a share in the estate of the testator equal in value to that which he would have received if the testator had died intestate, unless it appears from the will that such omission was intentional.[46]

KANSAS: WILLS; INTESTATE SUCCESSION

59-2103. Effect of adoption; name; rights of child, parents, grandparents.

(a) Any child adopted as herein provided shall assume the surname of the person or persons by whom the child is adopted except that the court in its discretion may permit a different surname when requested by the person or persons adopting the child. When requested by the person or persons petitioning to adopt a child, the court, in its discretion, may change the given name or names of the child.

(b) When adopted, a child shall be entitled to the same personal and property rights as a natural child of the adoptive parent. The adoptive parent shall be entitled to exercise all the rights of a natural parent and be subject to all the liabilities of that relationship. Upon adoption all the rights of natural parents to the adopted child, including their right to inherit from the child, shall cease, except the rights of a natural parent who is the spouse of the adopting parent.

(c) If a parent of a child is deceased and the surviving parent's spouse adopts the child, the parents of the deceased parent may be granted reasonable visitation rights to the child in accordance with K.S.A. 38-129 and amendments.

59-501. Definitions.

As used in this article, the word ''children'' means natural children, including a posthumous child, and children adopted as provided by law, and includes illegitimate children when applied to mother and child and also when applied to father and child where the father has notoriously or in writing recognized his paternity of the child, or his paternity thereof has been determined in his lifetime in any action or proceeding involving that question in a court of competent jurisdiction. The word ''issue'' includes adopted children of deceased children or issue.[47]

KENTUCKY: DESCENT AND DISTRIBUTION; ADOPTION

391.070. Posthumous child—Inheritance by.

A child born of a widow, within ten (10) months after the death of the intestate, shall inherit from him in the same manner as if he were being at the time of the intestate's death.

391.090. Bastards—Inheritance from and by—Effect of marriage of parents.

(1) The estate of a bastard shall descend and be distributed in the same manner as that of a person born in lawful wedlock, except that the inheritance shall go to the mother and her kindred and not to the father and his kindred.

(2) A bastard shall inherit from his mother and his mother's kindred.

(3) If a man who has had a child by a woman afterward marries her, the child or its descendants, if recognized by him before or after marriage, shall be deemed legitimate.

199.520. Judgment—Prerequisites—Order—Name and legal status of child.

(1) After hearing the case the court shall enter a judgment of adoption, if it finds that the facts stated in the petition were established; that all legal requirements including jurisdiction, relating to the adoption, have been complied with; that the petitioners are of good moral character, of reputable standing in the community, and of ability to properly maintain and educate the child, and that the best interest of the child will be promoted by the adoption and that the child is suitable for adoption. In the judgment the name of the child shall be changed to conform with the prayer of the petition. The judgment and all orders required to be entered and recorded in the order book, including the caption, shall contain

only the names of the petitioners and the proposed adopted name of the child, without any reference whatsoever to its former name or the names of its birth parents.

(2) Upon entry of the judgment of adoption, from and after the date of the filing of the petition, the child shall be deemed the child of petitioners and shall be considered for purposes of inheritance and succession and for all other legal consideration the natural, legitimate child of the parents adopting it the same as if born of their bodies. Except where a natural parent is the spouse of an adoptive parent an adopted child from the time of adoption shall have no legal relationship to its birth parents in respect to either personal or property rights.

(3) The clerk of the court shall notify the department of any action of the court with respect to entering a judgment granting an adoption, the amendment of an adoption, or the denial or dismissal of a petition for adoption.[48]

LOUISIANA: ADOPTION; IRREGULAR SUCCESSION

Art. 214. Reciprocal rights and duties of adopter and adopted.

The adopted and his lawful issue and the adopter shall have the same rights and shall be subject to the same duties and legal incidents towards each other as if the adopted were the legitimate child of the adopter. The adopted and his lawful issue have the same rights as legal and forced heirs to the succession of the adopter as his legitimate children. Also, except as provided in Article 214.7, the adopter has the same rights to the succession of the adopted and his lawful issue as if the adopted were his legitimate child.

Art. 917. Irregular heirs.

When the deceased has left neither lawful descendants, nor lawful ascendants, nor collateral relations, the law calls to his inheritance either the surviving husband or wife, or his or her natural children, or the state, in the manner and order hereafter directed.

Art. 918. Acknowledged natural children of mother.

Natural children are called to the legal succession of their natural mother, when they have been duly acknowledged by her, if she has left no lawful children or descendants, to the exclusion of her father and mother and other ascendants or collaterals of lawful kindred.

In case the natural mother has lawful children or descendants, the rights of the natural children are reduced to a moderate alimony, which is determined by the rules established in the title: Of Father and Child.

Art. 919. Acknowledged natural children of father.

Natural children are called to the inheritance of their natural father, who has duly acknowledged them, when he has left no descendants or ascendants, or collateral relations, or surviving wife, and to the exclusion only of the state.

In all other cases, they can only bring an action against their natural father or his heirs for alimony, the amount of which shall be determined, as is directed in the title: Of Father and Child.

Art. 920. Other illegitimate children.

Bastard, adulterous, or incestuous children shall not enjoy the right of inheriting the estates of their natural father or mother, in any of the cases above mentioned, the law allowing them nothing more than a mere alimony.[49]

MAINE: INTESTATE SUCCESSION AND WILLS

Section 2-109. Meaning of child and related terms.

If, for purposes of intestate succession, a relationship of parent and child must be established to determine succession by, through, or from a person:

(1) An adopted person is the child of an adopting parent and not of the natural parents except that an adopted child will also inherit from the natural parents and their respective kin if the adoption decree so provides, and except that adoption of a child by the spouse of a natural parent has no effect on the relationship between the child and either natural parent;

(2) In cases not covered by paragraph (1), a person born out of wedlock is a child of the mother; that person is also a child of the father if:

(i) The natural parents participated in a marriage ceremony before or after the birth of the child, even though the attempted marriage is void; or

(ii) The father adopts the child into his family; or

(iii) The father acknowledges in writing before a justice of the peace or notary public that he is the father of the child, or the paternity is established by an adjudication before the death of the father or is established thereafter by clear and convincing proof, but the paternity established under this subparagraph is ineffective to qualify the father or his kindred to inherit from or through the child unless the father has openly treated the child as his and has not refused to support the child.

Section 2-302. Pretermitted children.

(a) If a testator fails to provide in his will for any of his children born or adopted after the execution of his will, the omitted child receives a share in the estate equal in value to that which he would have received if the testator had died intestate unless:

(1) It appears from the will that the omission was intentional;

(2) When the will was executed, the testator had one or more children and devised substantially all his estate to the other parent of the omitted child; or

(3) The testator provided for the child by transfer outside the will and the intent that the transfer be in lieu of a testamentary provision is shown by statements of the testator or from the amount of the transfer or other evidence.

(b) If at the time of the execution of the will the testator fails to provide in his will for a living child solely because he believes the child to be dead, the child receives a share in the estate equal in value to that which he would have received if the testator had died intestate.

(c) In satisfying a share provided by this section, the devises made by the will abate as provided in Section 3-902.

Adopted children.

An adopted child shall be "to all intents and purposes the child of his adoptors, the same as if born of them in lawful wedlock"; such child is a lineal descendant of its adopting parents and as such may take a legacy by will given to one of its adopting parents and thus prevent the legacy from lapsing, when the legatee dies before the testator. *Warren v. Prescott* (1892) 84 Me. 483, 24 A. 948, 30 Am.St.Rep. 370, 17 L.R.A. 435.[50]

MARYLAND: ESTATES AND TRUSTS

Section 3-107. After-born child.

A child of the decedent who is conceived before the death of the decedent, but born afterwards, shall inherit as if he had been born in the lifetime of the decedent. No other after-born relation may be considered as entitled to distribution in his own right.

Section 3-108. Inheritance from illegitimate person.

Property of an illegitimate person passes in accordance with the usual rules of intestate succession, except that the father or his relations can inherit only if the person is treated as the child of the father pursuant to Section 1-208.

Section 3-301. When entitled to share.

(a) Birth after execution of will. A will may not be revoked by the subsequent birth, adoption, or legitimation of a child by the testator except under the circumstances referred to in Section 4-105(c).

(b) Legacy to a child. A child described in subsection (a) or issue, if any, of such child who does not survive the testator is entitled to a share in the estate to be determined and paid in accordance with Section 3-302 and Section 3-303, if:

(1) The will contains a legacy for a child of the testator but makes no provision for a person who becomes a child of the testator subsequent to the execution of the will;

(2) The child was born, adopted, or legitimated after the execution of the will;

(3) The child, or his issue, survive the testator; and

(4) The will does not expressly state that the child, or issue, should be omitted.

Section 3-302. Amount of share.

A child permitted to share in the estate of a decedent pursuant to Section 3-301 shall receive from the personal representative an amount equal to the lesser of

(1) The distribution which the child would have taken in the event of intestacy; or

(2) The value of all legacies to children of the testator and issue of deceased children divided by time total number of children of the testator who survive him and deceased children leaving issue who take under this subtitle, including the pretermitted child. The issue of a pretermitted child who did not survive the testator may take the amount by representation.

Section 3-303. Payment.

Property distributed pursuant to Section 3-302 shall be paid by the personal representative from the legacies of children of the testator and issue of deceased children who take by representation. Each person shall contribute in the proportion which his legacy bears to all legacies of children of the testator and issue of deceased children taking by representation. Instead of contributing an interest in specific property to the pretermitted child, a legatee may pay the pretermitted child or his issue, in cash or other property acceptable to the pretermitted child or his issue, an amount equal to the fair market value of the interest in specific property as of the date of death of the testator.

Section 1-207. Adopted child.

(a) General rule.—An adopted child shall be treated as a natural child of his adopting parent or parents. On adoption, a child no longer shall be considered a child of either natural parent, except that upon adoption by the spouse of a natural parent, the child shall still be considered the child of that natural parent.

(b) More than one adoption. A child who has been adopted more than once shall be considered to be a child of the parent or parents who have adopted him most recently and shall cease to be considered a child of his previous parents.

Section 1-208. Illegitimate child.

(a) Child of his mother. A child born to parents who have not participated in a marriage ceremony with each other shall be considered to be the child of his mother.

(b) Child of his father. A child born to parents who have not participated in a marriage ceremony with each other shall be considered to be the child of his father only if the father

(1) Has been judicially determined to be the father in an action brought under the statutes relating to paternity proceedings; or

(2) Has acknowledged himself, in writing, to be the father; or

(3) Has openly and notoriously recognized the child to be his child; or

(4) Has subsequently married the mother and has acknowledged himself, orally or in writing, to be the father.

Section 3-107. After-born child.

A child of the decedent who is conceived before the death of the decedent, but born afterwards, shall inherit as if he had been born in the lifetime of the decedent. No other after-born relation may be considered as entitled to distribution in his own right.[51]

MASSACHUSETTS: DESCENT AND DISTRIBUTION; ADOPTION OF CHILDREN

Section 5. Rights of illegitimate child.

An illegitimate child shall be heir of his mother and of any maternal ancestor, and the lawful issue of an illegitimate person shall represent such person and take by descent any estate which such person would have taken if living.

Section 8. Inheritance or succession by right of representation; posthumous children.

Inheritance or succession by right of representation is the taking by the descendants of a deceased heir of the same share or right in the estate of another person as their parent would have taken if living. Posthumous children shall be considered as living at the death of their parent.

Section 7. Succession to property; rights of adopted child.

A person adopted in accordance with this chapter shall take the same share of the property which the adopting parent could dispose of by will as he would have taken if born to such parent in lawful wedlock, and he shall stand in regard to the legal descendants, but to no other of the kindred of such adopting parent, in the same position as if so born to him. If the person adopted dies intestate, his property acquired by himself or by gift of inheritance from his adopting parent or from the kindred of such parent shall be distributed according to chapters one hundred and ninety and one hundred and ninety-six among the persons who would have been his kindred if he had been born to his adopting parent in lawful wedlock; and property received by gift or inheritance from his natural parents or kindred shall be distributed in the same manner as if no act of adoption had taken place. The apportionment and distribution shall be ascertained by the court. A person shall not by adoption lose his right to inherit from his natural parents or kindred. The court may decree that the rights of succession to property under this section shall vest in the person as of the date of the filing of the petition for adoption.[52]

MICHIGAN: ADMINISTRATION AND PROBATE

700.108. Representation, division of estate; posthumous children.

When representation is called for by Section 106(a), (c), or (d), the estate shall be divided into as many equal shares as there are surviving heirs in the nearest degree of kinship and deceased persons in the same degree who left issue who survived decedent, each surviving heir in the nearest degree receiving 1 share and the share of each deceased person in the same degree being divided among his issue in the same manner. Posthumous children are considered as living at the death of their parent.

Adopted persons.

C.L.1897, Section 8780, subsec. 5 (see, now, Section 710.60), providing that an adopted child was to become heir at law of person adopting it, did not make adopted child an heir of kindred of person who adopted it, by right of representation. *Van Derlyn v. Mack* (1904) 100 N.W. 278, 137 Mich. 146, 66 L.R.A. 437.

700.110. Parental rights terminated; adopted persons.

(1) The permanent termination of parental rights to and concerning a minor child by order of a court of competent jurisdiction, by a release for purposes of adoption by the parent, but not a guardian, to a licensed child placement agency or before a probate or juvenile court, or, excepting termination by emancipation or death by any other process recognized by the law governing the parent-child status at the time of termination, ends kinship between the parent whose rights are so terminated and the child for all purposes of intestate succession.

(2) The entry by a court of competent jurisdiction of an interlocutory decree of adoption which is not thereafter vacated or reversed makes the adopted kin of the adopting parents for all purposes of intestate succession.

(3) If a person was adopted or in the future is adopted, the adopted person is an heir of the adopting parents and an heir of the lineal and collateral kindred of the adopting parents and the adopted person shall no longer be an heir of his natural parent or an heir of the lineal and collateral kindred of his natural parents, except that a right, title, or interest vested before this act shall not be divested by this section.

700.111. Legitimacy and illegitimates.

(1) For all purposes of intestate succession, a child is the heir of each of his or her natural parents notwithstanding the relationship between the parents except as otherwise provided by Section 110.

(2) If a child is born or conceived during a marriage, both spouses are presumed to be the natural parents of the child for all purposes of intestate succession. A child conceived following artificial insemination of a married woman with the consent of her husband shall be considered as their child for all purposes of intestate succession. Consent of the husband is presumed unless the contrary is shown by clear and convincing evidence. If a man and a woman participated in a marriage ceremony in apparent compliance with the law before the birth of a child, even though the attempted marriage is void, the child is considered to be their child for all purposes of intestate succession.

(3) Only the person presumed to be the natural parent of a child under subsection (2) may disprove any presumption that may be relevant to the relationship, and this exclusive right to do so terminates upon the death of the presumed parent.

(4) If a child is born out of wedlock or if a child is born or conceived during a marriage but not the issue of that marriage, a man is considered to be the natural father of that child for all purposes of intestate succession if any of the following occurs:

(a) The man joins with the mother of the child and acknowledges that child as his child in a writing executed and acknowledged by them in the same manner provided by law for the execution and acknowledgment of deeds of real estate and recorded at any time during the child's lifetime in the office of the judge of probate in the county in which the man or mother of the child reside at the time of execution and acknowledgment. It shall not be necessary for the mother of the child to join in the acknowledgment if she is disqualified to act by reason of mental incapacity, death, or any other reason satisfactory to the probate judge of the country in which the acknowledgment may be recorded.

(b) The man joins with the mother in a written request for a correction of certificate of birth pertaining to the child which results in issuance of a substituted certificate recording the birth of the child.

(c) The man and the child have borne a mutually acknowledged relationship of parent and child which began before the child became age 18 and continued until terminated by the death of either.

(5) Property of a child born out of wedlock or a child born or conceived during a marriage but not the issue of that marriage passes in accordance with the law of intestate succession except that the father and his kindred shall not be considered as relatives of the child unless the child might have inherited from the father as provided in this section.

(6) If a person is considered or presumed by a provision of this section to be the natural parent of a child born out of wedlock or a child born or conceived during a marriage but not the issue of that marriage, that child shall bear the same relationship to that person as a child born or conceived during a marriage for all other purposes and shall have the identical status, rights, and duties of a child born in lawful wedlock effective from birth.

700.127. Pretermitted heir.

(1) If a child is born or adopted after the making of his parent's will and a provision for the child is not made in the will, that child shall have the same share in the estate of the testator as if the parent died intestate. The child's share shall be assigned to the child as provided by law in case of intestate estates, unless it is apparent from the will that it was the testator's intention not to make a provision for the child.

(2) If a testator fails to provide in his will for any of his children, or for the issue of any deceased child, and it appears that the omission was not intentional

but was made by mistake or accident, the child, or the issue of the child, shall have the same share in the estate of the testator as if he had died intestate. The share shall be assigned as provided in the preceding subsection.

(3) If a share of the estate of a testator is assigned to a child born after the making of a will, or to a child, or the issue of a child omitted in the will, pursuant to subsection (1) or (2), the share shall first be taken from the estate not disposed of by the will, if any. If the portion of the estate passing intestate, if any, is not sufficient, so much as is necessary shall be taken from all the devisees in proportion to the value of the estate which they would have otherwise received respectively under the will, unless the obvious intention of the testator, in relation to some specific devise or other provision in the will, would thereby be defeated, in which event, the specific devise or provision may be exempted from the apportionment, and a different apportionment may be adopted in the discretion of the court.[53]

MINNESOTA: WILLS AND INTESTATE SUCCESSION

Adopted Children.

Adopted child has same property rights as natural child. *Bakke v. Bakke,* 1928, 175 Minn. 193, 220 N.W. 601.

525.171. Posthumous child.

A posthumous child shall be considered as living at the death of its parent.

525.172. Illegitimate as heir.

An illegitimate child shall inherit from his mother the same as if born in lawful wedlock and also from the person who in writing and before a competent attesting witness shall have declared himself to be his father, provided such writing or an authenticated copy thereof shall be produced in the proceeding in which it is asserted or from the person who has been determined to be the father of such child in a paternity proceeding before a court of competent jurisdiction; but such child shall inherit from the kindred of the father by right of representation.[54]

MISSISSIPPI: DESCENT AND DISTRIBUTION; ADOPTION, LEGITIMATION, ETC.

Section 91-1-15. Descent among illegitimates.

(1) The following terms shall have the meaning ascribed to them herein:

(a) "Remedy" means the right of an illegitimate to commence and maintain a judicial proceeding to enforce a claim to inherit property from the estate of the natural mother or father of such illegitimate, said claim having been heretofore prohibited by law, or prohibited by statutes requiring marriage between the natural parents, or restrained, or enjoined by the order of process of any court in this state.

(b) ''Claim'' means the right to assert a demand on behalf of an illegitimate to inherit property, either personal or real, from the estate of the natural mother or father of such illegitimate.

(c) ''Illegitimate'' means a person who at the time of his birth was born to natural parents not married to each other and said person was not legitimized by subsequent marriage to said parents or legitimized through a proper judicial proceeding.

(d) ''Natural parents'' means the biological mother or father of the illegitimate.

(2) An illegitimate shall inherit from and through the illegitimate's mother and her kindred, and the mother of an illegitimate and her kindred shall inherit from and through the illegitimate according to the statutes of descent and distribution. However, if an illegitimate shall die unmarried and without issue, and shall also predecease the natural father, the natural mother or her kindred shall not inherit any part of the natural father's estate from or through the illegitimate. In the event of the death of an illegitimate, unmarried and without issue, any part of the illegitimate's estate inherited from the natural father shall be inherited according to the statutes of descent and distribution.

(3) An illegitimate shall inherit from and through the illegitimate's natural father and his kindred, and the natural father of an illegitimate and his kindred shall inherit from and through the illegitimate according to the statutes of descent and distribution if:

(a) The natural parents participated in a marriage ceremony before the birth of the child, even though the marriage was subsequently declared null and void or dissolved by a court; or

(b) There has been an adjudication of paternity or legitimacy before the death of the intestate; or

(c) There has been an adjudication of paternity after the death of the intestate, based upon clear and convincing evidence, in an heirship proceeding under Sections 91-1-27 and 91-1-29. However, no such claim of inheritance shall be recognized unless the action seeking an adjudication of paternity is filed within one (1) year after the death of the intestate or within ninety (90) days after the first publication of notice to creditors to present their claims, whichever is less; and such time period shall run notwithstanding the minority of a child. No claim of inheritance based on an adjudication of paternity, after death of the intestate, by a court outside the state of Mississippi shall be recognized unless:

(i) Such court was in the state of residence of the intestate at the time of the intestate's death;

(ii) The action adjudicating paternity was filed within ninety (90) days after the death of the intestate;

(iii) All known heirs were made parties to the action; and

(iv) Paternity or legitimacy was established by clear and convincing evidence.

Section 91-5-5. Children born after making of the will.

If a testator or testatrix, having a child or children born at the time of making and publishing his or her last will and testament, shall, at his or her death, leave a child or children born after the making and publishing of such last will and testament, the child or children so after-born, if unprovided for by settlement and neither provided for nor disinherited, but only pretermitted, by the last will and testament, shall succeed to the same portion of the father's or mother's estate as such child or children would have been entitled to if the father or mother had died intestate, towards raising which portion the devisees and legatees shall contribute.

Section 93-17-13. Final decree and effect thereof.

A final decree of adoption shall not be entered before the expiration of six (6) months from the entry of the interlocutory decree except (a) when a child is a stepchild of a petitioner or is related by blood to the petitioner within the third degree according to the rules of the civil law or in any case in which the chancellor in the exercise of his discretion shall determine from all the proceedings and evidence in said cause that the six-month waiting period is not necessary or required for the benefit of the court, the petitioners, or the child to be adopted and shall so adjudicate in the decree entered in said cause, in either of which cases the final decree may be entered immediately without any delay and without an interlocutory decree; or (b) when the child has resided in the home of any petitioner prior to the granting of the interlocutory decree, in which case the court may, in its discretion, shorten the waiting period by the length of time the child has thus resided.

The final decree shall adjudicate, in addition to such other provisions as may be found by the court to be proper for the protection of the interests of the child; and its effect, unless otherwise specifically provided, shall be that (a) the child shall inherit from and through the adopting parents and shall likewise inherit from the other children of the adopting parents to the same extent and under the same conditions as provided for the inheritance between brothers and sisters of the full blood by the laws of descent and distribution of the state of Mississippi, and that the adopting parents and their other children shall inherit from the child, just as if such child had been born to the adopting parents in lawful wedlock; (b) the child and the adopting parents and adoptive kindred are vested with all of the rights, powers, duties, and obligations, respectively, as if such child had been born to the adopting parents in lawful wedlock, including all rights existing by virtue of Section11-7-13, Mississippi Code of 1972; provided, however, that inheritance by or from the adopted child shall be governed by subsection (a) above; (c) that the name of the child shall be changed if desired; and (d) that the natural parents and natural kindred of the child shall not inherit by or through the child except as to a natural parent who is the spouse of the adopting parent, and all parental rights of the natural parent, or parents, shall be terminated, except as to a natural parent who is the spouse of the adopting parent. Nothing in this chapter shall restrict the right of any person to dispose of property under a last will and testament.[55]

MISSOURI: DESCENT AND DISTRIBUTION; ADOPTION AND FOSTER CARE

474.060. Illegitimate children inherit from mother, etc.

Illegitimate children are capable of inheriting and transmitting inheritance on the part of their mother, and a mother may inherit from her illegitimate children, in like manner, as if they had been lawfully begotten of her.

474.050. Posthumous children to inherit.

All posthumous children, or descendants, of the intestate shall inherit in like manner, as if born in the lifetime of the intestate; but no right of inheritance accrues to any person other than the children or descendants of the intestate, unless they are born and capable in law to take as heirs at the time of the intestate's death.

453.090. Consequences of adoption.

1. When a child is adopted in accordance with the provisions of this chapter, all legal relationships and all rights and duties between such child and his natural parents (other than a natural parent who joins in the petition for adoption as provided in section 453.010) shall cease and determine. Said child shall thereafter be deemed and held to be for every purpose the child of his parent or parents by adoption, as fully as though born to him or them in lawful wedlock.

2. Said child shall be capable of inheriting from, and as the child of, said parent or parents by adoption as fully as though born to him or them in lawful wedlock and, if a minor, shall be entitled to proper support, nurture, and care from said parent or parents by adoption.

3. Said parent or parents by adoption shall be capable of inheriting from and as the parent or parents of said adopted child as fully as though said child had been born to him or them in lawful wedlock and, if said child is a minor, shall be entitled to the services, wages, control, and custody of said adopted child.

4. Said adopted child shall be capable of inheriting from and taking through his parent or parents by adoption property limited expressly to heirs of the body of such parent or parents by adoption.

5. The word "child" as used in this section, shall, unless the context hereof otherwise requires, be construed to mean either a person under or over the age of twenty-one years.[56]

MONTANA: INTESTATE SUCCESSION AND WILLS

72-2-205. Requirement that heir survive decedent by one hundred twenty hours.

Any person who fails to survive the decedent by 120 hours is deemed to have predeceased the decedent for purposes of homestead allowance, exempt property, and intestate succession, and the decedent's heirs are determined accordingly. If the time of death of the decedent or of the person who would otherwise be an heir or the times of death of both cannot be determined and it cannot be established that the person who would otherwise be an heir has survived the decedent by 120 hours, it is deemed that the person failed to survive for the required period. This section is not to be applied where its application would result in a taking of intestate estate by the state under 72-2-207.

72-2-212. Afterborn heirs.

Relatives of the decedent conceived before his death but born thereafter inherit as if they had been born in the lifetime of the decedent.

72-2-213. Establishment of parent-child relationship.

If, for the purposes of intestate succession, a relationship of parent and child must be established to determine succession by, through, or from a person:

(1) An adopted person is the child of an adopting parent and not of the natural parents, except that adoption of a child by the spouse of a natural parent has no effect on the relationship between the child and either natural parent.

72-2-602. Pretermitted child.

(1) If a testator fails to provide in his will for any of his children born or adopted after the execution of his will, the omitted child receives a share in the estate equal in value to that which he would have received if the testator had died intestate unless:

(a) it appears from the will that the omission was intentional;

(b) when the will was executed the testator had one or more children and devised substantially all his estate to the other parent of the omitted child; or

(c) the testator provided for the child by transfer outside the will and the intent that the transfer be in lieu of a testamentary provision is shown by statements of the testator or from the amount of the transfer or other evidence.

(2) If at the time of the execution of the will the testator fails to provide in his will for a living child solely because he believes the child to be dead, the child receives a share in the estate equal in value to that which he would have received if the testator had died intestate.

(3) In satisfying a share provided by this section, the devises made by the will abate as provided in 72-3-901.[57]

NEBRASKA: INTESTATE SUCCESSION AND WILLS

30-2308. Afterborn heirs.

Relatives of the decedent conceived before his death but born thereafter inherit as if they had been born in the lifetime of the decedent.

30-2309. Meaning of child and related terms.

If, for purposes of intestate succession, a relationship of parent and child must be established to determine succession by, through, or from a person,

(1) an adopted person is the child of an adopting parent and not of the natural parents except that adoption of a child by the spouse of a natural parent has no effect on the relationship between the child and that natural parent.

(2) in cases not covered by (1), a person born out of wedlock is a child of the mother. That person is also a child of the father, if:

(i) the natural parents participated in a marriage ceremony before or after the birth of the child, even though the attempted marriage is void; or

(ii) the paternity is established by an adjudication before the death of the father or is established thereafter by strict, clear, and convincing proof. The open cohabitation of the mother and alleged father during the period of conception shall be admissible as evidence of paternity. The paternity established under this subparagraph (ii) is ineffective to qualify the father or his kindred to inherit from or through the child unless the father has openly treated the child as his and has not refused to support the child.

30-2321. Pretermitted children.

(a) If a testator fails to provide in his will for any of his children born or adopted after the execution of his will, the omitted child receives a share in the estate equal in value to that which he would have received if the testator had died intestate unless:

(1) it appears from the will that the omission was intentional;

(2) when the will was executed the testator had one or more children and devised substantially all his estate to the other parent of the omitted child; or

(3) the testator provided for the child by transfer outside the will in an amount equal to or greater than such child's share had the testator died intestate.

(b) If at the time of the execution of the will the testator fails to provide in his will for a living child solely because he believes the child to be dead, the child receives a share in the estate equal in value to that which he would have received if the testator had died intestate.

(c) In satisfying a share provided by this section, the devises made by the will abate as provided in section 30-24,100.[58]

NEVADA: ADOPTION; WILLS

127.160. Rights and duties of adopted child and adoptive parents.

Upon the entry of an order of adoption, the child shall become the legal child of the persons adopting him, and they shall become his legal parents with all the rights and duties between them of natural parents and legitimate child. By virtue of such adoption he shall inherit from his adoptive parents and their relatives the same as though he were the legitimate child of such parents, and in case of his death intestate the adoptive parents and their relatives shall inherit his estate as if they had been his natural parents and relatives in fact. After a decree of adoption is entered, the natural parents of an adopted child shall be relieved of all parental responsibilities for such child, and they shall not exercise or have any rights over such adopted child or his property. The child shall not owe his natural parents or their relatives any legal duty nor shall he inherit from his natural parents or kindred. Notwithstanding any other provisions to the contrary in this section, the adoption of a child by his stepparent shall not in any way change the status of the relationship between the child and his natural parent who is the spouse of the petitioning stepparent.

133.160. Rights of children born after making of parent's will.

When any child shall have been born after the making of its parent's will, and no provision shall have been made for him or her therein, such child shall have the same share in the estate of the testator as if the testator had died intestate, unless it shall be apparent from the will that it was the intention of the testator that no provision should be made for the child.[59]

NEW HAMPSHIRE: WILLS

551:10. Child Not Named, etc.

Every child born after the demise of the testator, and every child or issue of a child of the deceased not named or referred to in his will, and who is not a devisee or legatee, shall be entitled to the same portion of the estate, real and personal, as he would be if the deceased were intestate.

Adopted child.

An adopted child, although given the status of a natural child for the purpose of inheritance and other consequences of the relationship created by the adoption, is not ''issue'' for the purpose of determining the right of a surviving spouse in the estate of the deceased spouse under a statute granting certain rights in the absence of issue. *Morse v. Osborne* (1910) 75 NH 487, 77 A 403, 30 LRA NS 914.

Illegitimate child.

That a child is illegitimate does not make him any the less an heir of his mother in the descending line, within the meaning of this section. *Goodwin v. Colby* (1887) 64 NH 401, 13 A 866.[60]

NEW JERSEY: INTESTATE SUCCESSION

3B:5-8. Afterborn heirs.

Relatives of the decedent conceived before his death but born thereafter inherit as if they had been born in the lifetime of the decedent.

3B:5-9. Adopted child.

If, for the purposes of intestate succession, a relationship of parent and child

must be established to determine succession by, through, or from a person, the relationships and rights of a minor adopted child shall be those as provided in Section 14 of P.L. 1977, c. 367 (C.9:3-50), and the relationships and rights of an adopted adult shall be as provided in N.J.S.
2A:22-3.

3B:5-10. Child born out of wedlock.

If, for the purposes of intestate succession, a relationship of parent and child must be established to determine succession by, through, or from a person, a child born out of wedlock is a child of the mother. That child is also a child of the father, if:

a. The natural parents, before or after the birth of the child, participated in a ceremonial marriage or shall have consummated a common-law marriage where the marriage is recognized as valid in the manner authorized by the law of the place where the marriage took place, even though the attempted marriage is void; or

b. The paternity is established by an adjudication before the death of the father or is established thereafter by clear and convincing proof, except that the paternity established under this subsection is ineffective to qualify the father or his kindred to inherit from or through the child unless the father has openly treated the child as his and has not refused to support the child.[61]

NEW MEXICO: INTESTATE SUCCESSION AND WILLS

45-2-107. Kindred of half blood.

Relatives of the half blood inherit the same share they would inherit if they were of the whole blood.

45-2-108. Afterborn children.

Children of the decedent conceived before his death but born thereafter inherit as if they had been born in the lifetime of the decedent.

45-2-109. Meaning of child and related terms.

If, for purposes of intestate succession, a relationship of parent and child must be established to determine succession by, through, or from a person:

A. An adopted person is the child of an adopting parent and not of the natural parents, and in the event of the death of the adopted child, his estate shall pass as provided by law for natural-born children of the same family, all to the exclusion of the natural parents of such child; provided, however, the adoption of a child by the spouse of a natural parent has no effect on the relationship between the child and that natural parent; and

B. in cases not covered by subsection A of this section, a person born out of wedlock is a child of the mother. That person is also a child of the father, if:

(1) the natural parents participated in a marriage ceremony before or after the birth of child, even though the attempted marriage is void;

(2) the reputed father has recognized the child in writing by an instrument signed by him, which shows upon its face that it was so signed with the intent of recognizing the child as an heir. In event of loss or destruction of such an instrument, declarations of deceased persons shall be admissible to prove such loss or destruction, as well as the existence and contents thereof, whether or not lost or destroyed, and the genuineness of such an instrument. Such declarations shall be corroborated by proof of general and notorious recognition of such child by the father; or

(3) the paternity is established by an adjudication before the death of the father or is established thereafter by a preponderance of the evidence. However, the paternity established under this paragraph is ineffective to qualify the father or his kindred to inherit from or through the child unless the father has openly treated the child as his and has not refused to support the child.

45-2-301. Omitted spouse.

A. If a testator fails to provide by will for the surviving spouse who married the testator after the execution of the will, the omitted spouse shall receive the same share of the estate he would have received if decedent left no will unless it appears from the will that the omission was intentional, or the testator provided for the spouse by transfer outside the will and the intent that the transfer be in lieu of a testamentary provision is shown by statements of the testator or from the amount of the transfer or other evidence.

B. In satisfying a share provided by this section, the devises made by the will abate as provided in Section 45-3-902 NMSA 1978.

45-2-302. Pretermitted children.

A. If a testator fails to name or provide in his will for any of his children born or adopted before or after the execution of his will, the omitted child or his issue receives a share in the estate equal in value to that which he would have received if the testator had died intestate unless:

(1) it appears from the will that the omission was intentional;

(2) when the will was executed, the testator had one or more children and devised substantially all his estate to the other parent of the omitted child; or

(3) the testator provided for the child by transfer outside the will and the intent that the transfer be in lieu of a testamentary provision is shown by statements of the testator or from the amount of the transfer or other evidence.

B. If at the time of execution of the will the testator fails to provide in his will for a living child solely because he believes the child to be dead, the child receives a share in the estate equal in value to that which he would have received if the testator had died intestate.

C. In satisfying a share provided by this section, the devises made by the will abate as provided in Section 45-3-902 NMSA 1978.[62]

NEW YORK; DESCENT AND DISTRIBUTION

Section 4-1.2. Inheritance by or from born-out-of-wedlock persons.

(a) For the purposes of this article:

(1) A child born out of wedlock is the legitimate child of his mother so that he and his issue inherit from his mother and from his maternal kindred.

(2) A child born out of wedlock is the legitimate child of his father so that he and his issue inherit from his father and his paternal kindred if:

(A) a court of competent jurisdiction has, during the lifetime of the father, made an order of filiation declaring paternity or;

(B) the father of the child has signed an instrument acknowledging paternity, provided that

(i) such instrument is acknowledged or executed or proved in the form required to entitle a deed to be recorded in the presence of one or more witnesses and acknowledged by such witness or witnesses, in either case, before a notary public or other officer authorized to take proof of deeds and

(ii) such instrument is filed within sixty days from the making thereof with the putative father registry established by the state department of social services pursuant to section three hundred seventy-two-c of the social services law, as added by chapter six hundred sixty-five of the laws of nineteen hundred seventy-six and

(iii) the department of social services shall, within seven days of the filing of the instrument, send written notice by registered mail to the mother and other legal guardian of such child, notifying them that an acknowledgment of paternity instrument acknowledged or executed by such father has been duly filed or;

(C) paternity has been established by clear and convincing evidence and the father of the child has openly and notoriously acknowledged the child as his own.

(3) The existence of an agreement obligating the father to support the child born out of wedlock does not qualify such child or his issue to inherit from the father in the absence of an order of filiation made or acknowledgment of paternity as prescribed by subparagraph (2).

(4) A motion for relief from an order of filiation may be made only by the father and a motion for relief from an acknowledgment of paternity may be made by the father, mother, or other legal guardian of such child, or the child, provided however, such motion must be made within one year from the entry of such order or from the date of written notice as provided for in subparagraph (2).

(b) If a child born out of wedlock dies, his surviving spouse, issue, mother, maternal kindred, father, and paternal kindred inherit and are entitled to letters of administration as if the decedent were legitimate, provided that the father and paternal kindred may inherit or obtain such letters only if the paternity of the child born out of wedlock has been established pursuant to provisions of subparagraph (A) of paragraph (2) of subdivision (a) or the father has signed an instrument acknowledging paternity and filed the same in accordance with the provisions of subparagraph (B) of paragraph (2) of subdivision (a) or paternity has been established by clear and convincing evidence and the father of the child has openly and notoriously acknowledged the child as his own.

Section 5-3.2 Revocatory effect of birth of child after execution of will.
(a) Whenever a testator, during his lifetime or after his death, has a child born after the execution of a last will and dies leaving the after-born child unprovided for by any settlement, and neither provided for nor in any way mentioned in the will, every such child shall succeed to a portion of the testator's estate as herein provided:

(1) If the testator has one or more children living when he executes his will, and:

(A) No provision is made therein for any such child, an after-born child is not entitled to share in the testator's estate.

(B) Provision is made therein for one or more of such children, an after-born child is entitled to share in the testator's estate, as follows:

(i) The portion of the testator's estate in which the after-born child may share is limited to the disposition made to children under the will.

(ii) The after-born child shall receive such share of the testator's estate, as limited in subparagraph (i), as he would have received had the testator included all after-born children with the children upon whom benefits were conferred under the will and given an equal share of the estate to each such child.

(iii) To the extent that it is feasible, the interest of the after-born child in the testator's estate shall be of the same character, whether an equitable or legal life estate or in fee, as the interest which the testator conferred upon his children under the will.

(2) If the testator has no child living when he executes his last will, the after-born child succeeds to the portion of such testator's estate as would have passed to such child had the testator died intestate.

(b) The after-born child may recover the share of the testator's estate to which he is entitled, either from the other children under subparagraph (a) (1) (B) or the testamentary beneficiaries under subparagraph (a) (2), ratably, out of the portions of such estate passing to such persons under the will. In abating the interests of such beneficiaries, the character of the testamentary plan adopted by the testator shall be preserved to the maximum extent possible.

Section 6-5.7 Posthumous children.

(a) Where a future estate is limited to children, distributees, heirs, or issue, posthumous children are entitled to take in the same manner as if living at the death of their ancestors.

(b) A future estate conditioned upon the death of a person without children, distributees, heirs, or issue is defeated by the birth of a child conceived before but born alive after the death of such person.[63]

NORTH CAROLINA: INTESTATE SUCCESSION; WILLS

Section 29-17. Succession by, through, and from adopted children.

(a) A child, adopted in accordance with Chapter 48 of the General Statutes or in accordance with the applicable law of any other jurisdiction, and the heirs of such child are entitled by succession to any property by, through, and from his adoptive parents and their heirs the same as if he were the natural legitimate child of the adoptive parents.

(b) An adopted child is not entitled by succession to any property, by, through, or from his natural parents or their heirs, except as provided in subsection (e) of this section.

(c) The adoptive parents and the heirs of the adoptive parents are entitled by succession to any property, by, through, and from an adopted child the same as if the adopted child were the natural legitimate child of the adoptive parents.

(d) The natural parents and the heirs of the natural parents are not entitled by succession to any property, by, through, or from an adopted child, except as provided in subsection (e) of this section.

(e) If a natural parent has previously married, is married to, or shall marry an adoptive parent, the adopted child is considered the child of such natural parent for all purposes of intestate succession.

Section 29-19. Succession by, through, and from illegitimate children.

(a) For purposes of intestate succession, an illegitimate child shall be treated as if he were the legitimate child of his mother, so that he and his lineal descendants are entitled to take by, through, and from his mother and his other maternal kindred, both descendants and collaterals, and they are entitled to take from him.

(b) For purposes of intestate succession, an illegitimate child shall be entitled to take by, through, and from:

(1) Any person who has been judicially determined to be the father of such child pursuant to the provisions of G.S. 49-14 through 49-16;

(2) Any person who has acknowledged himself during his lifetime to be the father of such child in a written instrument executed or acknowledged before a certifying officer named in G.S. 52-6(c) and filed during his own lifetime in the office of the clerk of superior court of the county where either he or the child resides.

Notwithstanding the above provisions, no person shall be entitled to take hereunder unless he has given written notice of the basis of his claim to the personal representative of the putative father within six months after the date of the first publication or posting of the general notice to creditors.

(c) Any person described under subdivision (b) (1) or (2) above and his lineal and collateral kin shall be entitled to inherit by, through, and from the illegitimate child.

(d) Any person who acknowledges himself to be the father of an illegitimate child in his duly probated last will shall be deemed to have intended that such child be treated as expressly provided in such will or, in the absence of any express provision, the same as a legitimate child.

Section 28A-22-2. Shares of after-born and after-adopted children.

The share of an after-born or after-adopted child, as provided by G.S. 29-9 and 31-5.5, shall be allotted to him out of any undevised real or personal property, or out of both, if there is enough such undevised property for that purpose. If there is no undevised real or personal property, or if there is not enough, then the whole of the child's share, or the deficiency, shall be made up from the devised real or personal property or from both. The portion contributed by a devisee shall bear the same ratio to his devise as the after-born or after-adopted child's share bears to the net estate.[64]

NORTH DAKOTA: INTESTATE SUCCESSION

30.1-04-08 (2-108). Afterborn heirs.

Relatives of the decedent conceived before his death but born thereafter inherit as if they had been born in the lifetime of the decedent.[65]

OHIO: DESCENT AND DISTRIBUTION

Section 2105.17 Children born out of wedlock.

Children born out of wedlock shall be capable of inheriting or transmitting inheritance from and to their mother, and from and to those from whom she may inherit, or to whom she may transmit inheritance, as if born in lawful wedlock.[66]

OKLAHOMA: WILLS AND SUCCESSION

Section 215. Inheritance by and from illegitimate child.

For inheritance purposes, a child born out of wedlock stands in the same relation to his mother and her kindred, and she and her kindred to the child, as if that child had been born in wedlock. For like purposes, every such child stands in identical relation to his father and his kindred and the latter and his kindred to the child, whenever: (a) the father, in writing, signed in the presence of a competent witness, acknowledges himself to be the father of the child, (b) the father and mother intermarried subsequent to the child's birth, and the father, after such marriage, acknowledged the child as his own or adopted him into his family, (c) the father publicly acknowledged such child as his own, receiving it as such, with the consent of his wife, if he is married, into his family and otherwise treating it as if it were a child born in wedlock, or (d) the father was judicially determined to be such in a paternity proceeding before a court of competent jurisdiction.

For all purposes, the issue of all marriages null in law, or dissolved by divorce, are deemed to have been born in wedlock.

Section 216. Inheritance from illegitimate child.

If an illegitimate child, who has not been acknowledged or adopted by his father, dies intestate, without lawful issue, his estate goes to his mother or, in case of her decease, to her heirs at law.

Section 217. Degrees of kindred.

The degree of kindred is established by the number of generations, and each generation is called a degree.

Section 218. Lineal and collateral.

The series of degrees from the line; the series of degrees between persons who descend one from the other is called direct or lineal consanguinity; and the series of degrees between persons who do not descend from one another, but spring from a common ancestor, is called the collateral line or collateral consanguinity.

Section 219. Ascending and descending lines.

The direct line is divided into a direct line descending and the direct line ascending. The first is that which connects the ancestor with those who descend from him. The second is that which connects a person with those from whom he descends.

Section 220. Degrees in direct line.

In the direct line there are as many degrees as there are generations. Thus the son is, with regard to the father, in the first degree; the grandson in the second; and vice versa with regard to the father and grandfather toward the sons and grandsons.

Section 221. Collateral degrees; how reckoned.

In the collateral line the degrees are counted by generations, from one of the relations up to the common ancestor, and from the common ancestor to the other relations. In such computation the decedent is excluded, the relative included, and the ancestor counted but once. Thus brothers are related in the second degree, uncle and nephew in the third degree, cousins germane in the fourth degree, and so on.

Section 222. Kindred of the half-blood.

Kindred of the half-blood inherit equally with those of the whole blood in the same degree, unless the inheritance come to the intestate by descent, devise, or gift of some one of his ancestors, in which case all those who are not of the blood of such ancestors must be excluded from such inheritance.

Section 228. Representation defined—Posthumous children.

Inheritance or succession by right of representation takes place when the descendants of any deceased heir take the same share or right in the estate of another person that their parents would have taken if living. Posthumous children are considered as living at the death of their parents.[67]

OREGON: INTESTATE SUCCESSION AND WILLS

112.075. Time of determining relationships; afterborn heirs.

The relationships existing at the time of the death of the decedent govern the passing of his net intestate estate, but persons conceived before his death and born alive thereafter inherit as though they were alive at the time of his death.

112.095. Persons of the half-blood.

Persons of the half-blood inherit the same share that they would inherit if they were of the whole blood.

112.105. Succession where parents not married.

(1) For all purposes of intestate succession, full effect shall be given to all relationships as described in ORS 109.060, except as otherwise provided by law in case of adoption.

(2) For all purposes of intestate succession and for those purposes only, before the relationship of father and child and other relationships dependent upon the establishment of paternity shall be given effect under subsection (1) of this section:

(a) The paternity of the child shall have been established under ORS 109.070 during the lifetime of the child or;

(b) The father shall have acknowledged himself to be the father in writing signed by him during the lifetime of the child.

112.175 Adopted persons.

(1) An adopted person, his issue, and kindred shall take by intestate succession from his adoptive parents, their issue, and kindred, and his adoptive parents, their issue, and kindred shall take by intestate succession from the adopted person, his issue, and kindred, as though the adopted person were the natural child of his adoptive parents.

(2) An adopted person shall cease to be treated as the child of his natural parents for all purposes of intestate succession by the adopted person, his issue, and kindred and his natural parents, their issue, and kindred, except:

(a) If a natural parent of a person marries or remarries and the person is adopted by his stepparent, the adopted person shall continue also to be treated, for all purposes of intestate succession, as the child of the natural parent who is the spouse of the adoptive parent.

(b) If a natural parent of a person dies, the other natural parent remarries and the person is adopted by his stepparent, the adopted person shall continue also to be treated, for all purposes of intestate succession by any person through the deceased natural parent, as the child of the deceased natural parent.

(3) ORS Chapters 111, 112, 113, 114, 115, 116, and 117 apply to adopted persons who were adopted in this state or elsewhere.

112.185. Effect of more than one adoption.

For all purposes of intestate succession, a person who has been adopted more than once shall be treated as the child of the parents who have most recently adopted him and, except as otherwise provided in this section, shall cease to be treated as the child of his previous adoptive parents. He shall continue also to be treated as the child of his natural parent or previously adoptive parent only to the extent provided in ORS 112.175(2), and for the purpose of applying that subsection with reference to a previous adoptive parent, ''natural parent'' in that subsection means the previous adoptive parent.

112.405. Children born or adopted after execution of will; pretermitted children.

(1) As used in this section, ''pretermitted child'' means a child of a testator who is born or adopted after the execution of the will of the testator, who is neither provided for in the will nor in any way mentioned in the will and who survives the testator.

(2) If a testator has one or more children living when he executes his will and no provision is made in the will for any such living child, a pretermitted child shall not take a share of the estate of the testator disposed of by the will.

(3) If a testator has one or more children living when he executes his will and provision is made in the will for one or more of such living children, a pretermitted child is entitled to share in the estate of the testator disposed of by the will as follows:

(a) The pretermitted child may share only in the portion of the estate devised to the living children by the will.

(b) The share of each pretermitted child shall be the total value of the portion of the estate devised to the living children by the will divided by the number of pretermitted children plus the number of living children for whom provision, other than nominal provision, is made in the will.

(c) To the extent feasible, the interest of a pretermitted child in the estate shall be of the same character, whether equitable or legal, as the interest the testator gave to the living children by the will.

(4) If a testator has no child living when he executes his will, a pretermitted child shall take a share of the estate as though the testator had died intestate.

(5) A pretermitted child may recover the share of the estate to which he is entitled, as provided in this section, either from the other children under subsection (3) of this section or from the testamentary beneficiaries under subsection (4) of this section, ratably, out of the portions of the estate passing to those persons under the will. In abating the interests of those beneficiaries, the character

of the testamentary plan adopted by the testator shall be preserved so far as possible.[68]

PENNSYLVANIA: INTESTATE SUCCESSION

Section 2107. Persons born out of wedlock.

(a) Child of mother. For purposes of descent by, from, and through a person born out of wedlock, he shall be considered the child of his mother but not of his father.

(b) Marriage of parents. When the parents of a person born out of wedlock shall have married each other, he shall be legitimated for purposes of descent by, from, and through him as if he had been born during the wedlock of his parents.

Section 2108. Adopted person.

For purposes of descent by, from, and through an adopted person he shall be considered the issue of his adopting parent or parents and not the issue of his natural parents: Provided, That if a natural parent shall have married the adopting parent, the adopted person for purposes of descent by, from and through him shall also be considered the issue of such.[69]

RHODE ISLAND: RULES OF DESCENT

33-1-8. Children born out of wedlock.

A child born out of wedlock shall be capable of inheriting or transmitting inheritance on the part of his mother in like manner as if born in lawful wedlock. Any such child whose parents shall lawfully intermarry and shall acknowledge him as their child shall be deemed legitimate.

33-6-23. Pretermitted issue.

When a testator omits to provide in his will for any child of his born after the execution of his will, either during his lifetime or after his death, or for any issue of a deceased child of his dying after the execution of his will, or for any issue born after the execution of his will of a deceased child of his dying before such execution, such child or issue shall take the same share of the testator's estate as such child or issue would have been entitled to if the testator had died intestate, unless it appears that the omission was intentional and not occasioned by accident or mistake. The term ''will,'' as used in this section, shall be deemed to include the testator's will and all codicils thereto effective at the testator's death; and the term ''the execution of his will'' shall be deemed, in a case in which there is a codicil or codicils, to refer to the execution of the latest codicil effective at the testator's death.[70]

SOUTH CAROLINA: DECEDENTS' ESTATES GENERALLY; ADOPTION

Section 21-1-30. Posthumous child shall take under will or settlement.

A posthumous child shall take under any will or settlement as though born in the lifetime of the father and shall not be liable to be defeated on the ground that the remainder was contingent and did not vest at the instant that the prior estate terminated and that there was no trustee to preserve the contingent remainder.

Section 21-3-30. Inheritance by or from illegitimates.

Any illegitimate child or children whose mother shall die intestate possessed of any real or personal property shall be, so far as such property is concerned, an heir or heirs at law as to such property, notwithstanding any law or usage to the contrary. Whenever any illegitimate child shall die in this state leaving property, real or personal, the mother of such child shall have the same right to inherit from such child as she would have if such child had been legitimate. Illegitimate children of the same mother shall have the same right to inherit from each other that they would have had had they been legitimate and all children of the same mother, whether legitimate or illegitimate, shall likewise inherit from each other as to any property, real or personal.

In the event of the death of any illegitimate intestate, leaving no one to take under the statute law of this state regulating the descent of property of intestates as it would exist had this section not been enacted, the property of such illegitimate shall descend to and be distributed among the next of kin of such illegitimate on the mother's side as if such illegitimate had been born in lawful wedlock. And in the event that the next of kin of such illegitimate child on the mother's side dies intestate and without leaving anyone to take his property under the statute law of this state regulating the descent of property of intestates as it would exist had this section not been enacted, then before such property escheats to the state it shall descend to the child or children of the mother through whom the kinship exists, both legitimate and illegitimate.

Section 15-45-130. Effect of final decree.

(a) After the final decree of adoption is entered, the relation of parent and child and all the rights, duties, and other legal consequences of the natural relation of child and parent shall thereafter exist between such adopted child and the person adopting such child and the kindred of the adoptive parents. From the date the final decree of adoption is entered, the adopted child shall be considered a natural child of the adopting parents for all inheritance purposes, both by and from such child, to the exclusion of the natural or blood parents or kin of such child. These rules of inheritance shall also apply to all the parties where one of the natural parents is united in bonds of matrimony to the other adopting parent.

(b) After a final decree of adoption is entered, the natural parents of the adopted child, unless they are the adoptive parents, shall be relieved of all parental responsibilities for the child and have no rights over such adopted child.[71]

SOUTH DAKOTA: DESCENT AND DISTRIBUTION

2-104. Requirement that heir survive decedent for 120 hours.

Any person who fails to survive the decedent by 120 hours is deemed to have predeceased the decedent for purposes of homestead allowance, exempt property, and intestate succession, and the decedent's heirs are determined accordingly. If the time of death of the decedent or of the person who would otherwise be an heir, or the times of death of both, cannot be determined, and it cannot be established that the person who would otherwise be an heir has survived the decedent by one hundred twenty hours, it is deemed that the person failed to survive for the required period. This section is not to be applied where its application would result in a taking of intestate estate by the state under Section 2-105.

2-108. Afterborn heirs.

Relatives of the decedent conceived before his death but born thereafter inherit as if they had been born in the lifetime of the decedent.

2-109. Meaning of child and related terms.

If, for purposes of intestate succession, a relationship of parent and child must be established to determine succession by, through, or from a person

(1) An adopted person is the child of an adopting parent and not of the natural parents except that adoption of a child by the spouse of a natural parent has no effect on the relationship between the child and that natural parent.

(2) In cases not covered by (1), a person born out of wedlock is a child of the mother. That person is also a child of the father, if

(i) the natural parents participated in a marriage ceremony before or after the birth of the child, even though the attempted marriage is void; or

(ii) the paternity is established by an adjudication before the death of the father or is established thereafter by clear and convincing proof, except that the paternity established under this subparagraph (ii) is ineffective to qualify the father of his kindred to inherit from or through the child unless the father has openly treated the child as his and has not refused to support the child.

2-302. Pretermitted children.

(a) If a testator fails to provide in his will for any of his children born or adopted after the execution of his will, the omitted child receives a share in the estate equal in value to that which he would have received if the testator had died intestate unless:

(1) it appears from the will that the omission was intentional;

(2) when the will was executed the testator had one or more children and devised substantially all his estate to the other parent of the omitted child; or

(3) the testator provided for the child by transfer outside the will, and the

intent that the transfer be in lieu of a testamentary provision is shown by statements of the testator or from the amount of the transfer or other evidence.

(b) If at the time of the execution of the will the testator fails to provide in his will for a living child solely because he believes the child to be dead, the child receives a share in the estate equal in value to that which he would have received if the testator had died intestate.

(c) In satisfying a share provided by this section, the devises made by the will abate.

2-611. Construction of generic terms to accord with relationships as defined for intestate succession.

Half bloods, adopted persons, and persons born out of wedlock are included in class gift terminology and terms of relationship in accordance with rules for determining relationships for purposes of intestate succession, but a person born out of wedlock is not treated as the child of the father unless the person is openly and notoriously so treated by the father.[72]

TENNESSEE: DESCENT AND DISTRIBUTION

31-114. Illegitimate children inherit with legitimate.

Where any woman shall die intestate, having a child or children born out of wedlock, whether she also leaves a child or children born in wedlock, or otherwise, such child or children born out of wedlock shall take equally with the other child or children in the property, both real and personal, of his or their mother, and, should either of such children die intestate, without child, his brothers and sisters shall, in like manner, take his portion.

31-115. Posthumous child inheriting.

A posthumous child of a testator, born within ten (10) months after his death, not provided for in his will, shall take such share of the estate as would have fallen to such child in case of intestacy, to be contributed by the beneficiaries in the proportion of their shares of the whole estate.

31-116. Adopted child inheriting from adoptive parents.

Any adopted child shall be equally capable with any child born to the intestate of inheriting under the provisions of Section 31-110, and for that purpose wherever child or children may appear in Section 31-110, such reference shall include adopted child or adopted children. Adoptive parents and their lineal and collateral kindred shall be capable of inheriting from the adopted child real and personal property acquired by him after the adoption, as described in Section 36-126.[73]

TEXAS: DESCENT AND DISTRIBUTION

Section 40. Inheritance by and from an adopted child.

For purposes of inheritance under the laws of descent and distribution, an adopted child shall be regarded as the child of the parent or parents by adoption, such adopted child and its descendants inheriting from and through the parent or parents by adoption and their kin the same as if such child were the natural legitimate child of such parent or parents by adoption, and such parent or parents by adoption and their kin inheriting from and through such adopted child the same as if such child were the natural legitimate child of such parent or parents by adoption. The natural parent or parents of such child and their kin shall not inherit from or through said child, but said child shall inherit from and through its natural parent or parents. Nothing herein shall prevent any parent by adoption from disposing of his property by will according to law. The presence of this section specifically relating to the rights of adopted children shall in no way diminish the rights of such children, under the laws of descent and distribution or otherwise, which they acquire by virtue of their inclusion in the definition of "child" which is contained in this code.

Illegitimate children:

An illegitimate child does not inherit from its father by descent and distribution. *Guidry v. Denkins* (Civ.App.1970) 460 S.W. 2d 943.

Daughters of decedent could not inherit from decedent where he had never married their mother. *Wells v. Hames* (Civ.App.1971) 464 S.W. 2d 393, ref. n. r. e.

Section 67. After-born or after-adopted children.

(a) Where a child was living when will was executed. If a testator having a child or children born or adopted at the time of making his last will and testament shall, at his death, leave a child or children born or adopted after the making of such last will and testament, the child or children so after-born or after-adopted and pretermitted shall, unless provided for by settlement, succeed to the same portion of the testator's estate as they would have been entitled to if the testator had died intestate; toward raising which portion the devisees and legatees shall contribute proportionately out of the parts devised and bequeathed to them by such last will and testament; provided, however, that where the surviving husband or wife is the father or mother of all of testator's children, exclusive of adopted children, and said surviving husband or wife is the principal beneficiary in said testator's last will and testament, to the entire exclusion, by silence or otherwise, of all of said testator's children, then and in that event the foregoing provisions of this section shall not apply or be considered in the construction of said last will and testament.

(b) Where no child was living when will was executed. Every last will and testament made when the testator had no child living, wherein any child he might have is not provided for or mentioned, if at the time of his death he shall leave a child, either born to him or adopted by him, or shall leave his wife enceinte of a child which shall be born, shall have no effect during the life of such after-born or after-adopted child and shall be void, unless such child dies within one year after the death of the testator; provided, however, that where a surviving husband or wife is the father or mother of all of the testator's children, exclusive of adopted children, and said surviving husband or wife is the principal beneficiary in said testator's last will and testament, to the entire exclusion, by silence or otherwise, of all of said testator's children, then and in that event the foregoing provisions of this section shall not apply or be considered in the construction of said last will and testament.

(c) Definition of "Children." As used in this section and in the preceding section, the term "children" includes descendants of whatever degree they may be, it being understood that they are counted only for the child they represent.[74]

UTAH: INTESTATE SUCCESSION AND WILLS

75-2-108. Afterborn heirs.

Relatives of the decedent conceived before his death but born thereafter inherit as if they had been born in the lifetime of the decedent.

75-2-109. Meaning of child and related terms.

(1) If, for purposes of intestate succession, a relationship of parent and child must be established to determine a succession by, through, or from a person:

(a) An adopted person is the child of an adopting parent and not of the natural or previously adopting parents except that adoption of a child by the spouse of a natural or previously adopting parent has no effect on the relationship between the child and that natural or previously adopting parent.

(b) In cases not covered by subsection (1) (a), a person born out of wedlock is a child of the mother. That person is also a child of the father, if:

(i) The natural parents participated in a marriage ceremony before or after the birth of the child, even though the attempted marriage is void; or

(ii) The paternity is established by an adjudication before the death of the father or is established thereafter by clear and convincing proof, except that the paternity established under this section (1) (b) (ii) is ineffective to qualify the father or his kindred to inherit from or through the child unless the father has openly treated the child as his and has not refused to support the child.[75]

VERMONT: DECEDENTS' ESTATES

Section 553. Illegitimate children; inheritance by and from.

(a) An illegitimate child shall inherit from or through his mother as if born in lawful wedlock. The estate of an illegitimate person dying intestate and leaving no issue nor husband nor wife shall descend to the mother and, if the mother is dead, through the line of the mother as if the person so dying were born in lawful wedlock.

(b) An illegitimate child shall inherit from or through his father as if born in lawful wedlock, under any of the following conditions:

(1) The father has been declared the putative father of the child under Section 339 of Title 15.

(2) The father has openly and notoriously claimed the child to be his own.

Section 557. Omitted or after-born child, from what part of estate share taken.

When a share of a testator's estate is assigned to a child born after the making of a will, or to a child or the issue of a child omitted in the will, such share shall be taken first from the estate not disposed of by the will, if there is any. If that is not sufficient, so much as is necessary shall be taken from the devisees or legatees in proportion to the value of the estate they respectively receive under the will. If the obvious intention of the testator, as to some specific devise or legacy or other provision in the will, would thereby be defeated, such specific devise, legacy, or provision may be exempted from such apportionment and a different apportionment adopted in the discretion of the court.[76]

VIRGINIA: DESCENT AND DISTRIBUTION

Section 64.1-5.1 Meaning of child and related terms.

If, for purposes of Title 64.1, a relationship of parent and child must be established to determine succession by, through, or from a person:

1. An adopted person is the child of the adopting parent and not of the biological parents, except that adoption of a child by the spouse of a biological parent has no effect on the relationship between the child and either biological parent;

2. In cases not covered by paragraph 1 hereof, a person born out of wedlock is a child of the mother. That person is also a child of the father, if:

(a) The biological parents participated in a marriage ceremony before or after the birth of the child, even though the attempted marriage was prohibited by law, deemed null or void, or dissolved by a court; or

(b) The paternity is established by clear and convincing evidence as set forth in Section 64.1-5.2; provided, however, that the paternity establishment pursuant to this subparagraph (b) shall be ineffective to qualify the father or his kindred to inherit from or through the child unless the father has openly treated the child as his and has not refused to support the child.

3. No claim of succession based upon the relationship between a child born out of wedlock and a parent of such child shall be recognized in the settlement of any decedent's estate unless an affidavit by such child or by someone acting for such child alleging such parenthood has been filed within one year of the date of the death of such parent in the clerk's office of the circuit court of the jurisdiction wherein the property affected by such claim is located and an action seeking adjudication of parenthood is filed in an appropriate circuit court within said time; provided, however, such one-year period shall run notwithstanding the minority of such child. The limitation period of the preceding sentence shall not apply in those cases where the relationship between the child born out of wedlock and the parent in question is (i) established by a birth record prepared

upon information given by or at the request of such parent; or (ii) by admission by such parent of parenthood before any court or in writing under oath; or (iii) by a previously concluded proceeding pursuant to the provisions of Section 20-61.1.

Section 64.1-5.2. Evidence of paternity.

For the purposes of Title 64.1, evidence that a man is the father of a child born out of wedlock shall be clear and convincing and shall be limited to the following:

1. That he cohabited openly with the mother during all of the ten months immediately prior to the time the child was born;
2. That he gave consent to a physician or other person, not including the mother, charged with the responsibility of securing information for the preparation of a birth record that his name be used as the father of the child upon the birth records of the child;
3. That he allowed by a general course of conduct the common use of his surname by the child;
4. That he claimed the child as his child on any statement, tax return, or other document filed and signed by him with any local, state, or federal government or any agency thereof;
5. That he admitted before any court having jurisdiction to try and dispose of the same that he is the father of the child; or
6. That he voluntarily admitted paternity in writing, under oath.

If a proceeding has been initiated and concluded pursuant to Section 20.61.1 of the code and the court enters a judgment against a man for the support, maintenance, and education of a child as if the child were born in lawful wedlock to the man, that judgment shall be sufficient evidence of paternity for the purposes of this section.

Section 64.1-70. Provision for pretermitted children when no child living when will made.

If any person dies leaving a child, or his wife with child, which shall be born alive, and leaving a will made when such person had no child living, wherein any child he might have is not provided for or mentioned, such child, or any descendant of his, shall succeed to such portion of the testator's estate as he would have been entitled to if the testator had died intestate; towards raising which portion the devisees and legatees shall, out of what is devised and bequeathed to them, contribute ratably, either in kind or in money, as a court of equity, in the particular case, may deem most proper. But if any such child, or descendant, die under the age of eighteen years, unmarried, and without issue, his portion of the estate or so much thereof as may remain unexpended in his support and education shall revert to the person or persons to whom it was given by the will.

Section 64.1-7.1. Children conceived by artificial insemination presumed legitimate.

Any child born to a married woman, which was conceived by means of artificial insemination performed by a licensed physician at the request of and with the consent in writing of such woman and her husband, shall be presumed, for all purposes, the legitimate natural child of such woman and such husband the same as a natural child not conceived by means of artificial insemination.

Section 64.1-8.1. Afterborn heirs.

Relatives of the decedent conceived before his death but born thereafter shall inherit as if they had been born during the lifetime of the decedent.[77]

VIRGIN ISLANDS

Section 84: Descent and distribution of estate of decedent.

The real property of a deceased person, male or female, not devised, shall descend, and the surplus of his or her personal property, after payment of debts and legacies, and if not bequeathed, shall be distributed to the surviving spouse, children, or next of kin or other persons, in manner following:

12. Descendants and other distributees of the deceased, begotten before his death, but born thereafter, shall take in the same manner as if they had been born in the lifetime of the deceased and had survived him

13. An illegitimate child shall be considered to have the same status, for the purpose of the descent and distribution of the property of his or her ancestors, as if he or she were born in lawful wedlock provided that in cases where the ancestor in question is a father, he admitted of record paternity of such child by signing the official birth certificate; or he was adjudged the father of such child by a court of competent jurisdiction; or by written acknowledgment he recognized such child as his.

14. The right of an adopted child to take a share of the estate and the right of succession to the estate of an adopted child shall continue as provided in Title 16.[78]

WASHINGTON: PROBATE LAW AND PROCEDURE

11.04.081. Inheritance by and from illegitimate child.

For the purpose of inheritance to, through, and from an illegitimate child, such child shall be treated the same as if he were the legitimate child of his mother, so that he and his issue shall inherit from his mother and from his maternal kindred, in all degrees, and they may inherit from him. Such child shall also be treated the same as if he were a legitimate child of his mother for the purpose of determining homestead rights, the distribution of exempt property and the making of family allowances. When the parents of an illegitimate child shall marry subsequent to his birth, or the father shall acknowledge said child in writing, such child shall be deemed to have been made the legitimate child of both of the parents for purposes of intestate succession.

11.04.085. Inheritance by adopted child.

A lawfully adopted child shall not be considered an "heir" of his natural parents for purposes of this title.

11.12.090. Intestacy as to pretermitted children.

If any person make his last will and die leaving a child or children or desendants of such child or children not named or provided for in such will, although born after the making of such will or the death of the testator, every such testator, as to such child or children not named or provided for, shall be deemed to die intestate, and such child or children or their descendants shall be entitled to such proportion of the estate of the testator, real and personal, as if he had died intestate, and the same shall be assigned to them, and all the other heirs, devisees, and legatees shall refund their proportional part.[79]

WEST VIRGINIA: DESCENT AND DISTRIBUTION

Section 42-1-5. From whom bastards inherit.

Bastards shall be capable of inheriting and transmitting inheritance on the part of their mother, as if lawfully begotten.

Section 42-1-8. Posthumous children to take.

Any child in the womb of its mother at, and which may be born after, the death of the intestate, shall be capable of taking by inheritance in the same manner as if such child were in being at the time of such death.

Section 48-4-5. Effect of order as to relations of parents and child and as to rights of inheritance, intestacy, of adopted child.

Upon the entry of such order of adoption, the natural parent or parents, any parent or parents by any previous legal adoption, and the lineal or collateral kindred of any such parent or parents, except any such parent who is the husband or wife of the petitioner for adoption, shall be divested of all legal rights, including the right of inheritance from or through the adopted child under the statutes of descent and distribution of this state, and shall be divested of all obligations in respect to the said adopted child, and the said adopted child shall be free from all legal obligations, including obedience and maintenance, in respect to any such parent or parents. From and after the entry of such order of adoption, the adopted child shall be, to all intents and for all purposes, the legitimate issue of the person or persons so adopting him or her and shall be entitled to all the rights and privileges and subject to all the obligations of a natural child of such adopting parent or parents.

For the purpose of descent and distribution, from and after the entry of such order of adoption, a legally adopted child shall inherit from and through the parent or parents of such child by adoption and from or through the lineal or collateral kindred of such adopting parent or parents in the same manner and to the same extent as though said adopted child were a natural child of such adopting parent or parents, but such child shall not inherit from his or her natural parent or parents nor their lineal or collateral kindred except that a child legally adopted by a husband or wife of the natural parent shall inherit from the natural parent of such child as well as from the adopting parent. If a legally adopted child shall die intestate, all property, including real and personal, of such adopted child shall pass, according to the statutes of descent and distribution of this state, to those persons who would have taken had the decedent been the natural child of the adopting parent or parents.[80]

WISCONSIN: INTESTATE SUCCESSION AND WILLS

851.51. Status of adopted persons for purposes of inheritance, wills, and class gifts.

(1) Inheritance rights between adopted person and adoptive relatives. A legally adopted person is treated as a natural child of his adoptive parents for purposes of intestate succession by, through, and from the adopted person and for purposes of any statute conferring rights upon children, issue, or relatives in connection with the law of intestate succession or wills.

(2) Inheritance rights between adopted person and natural relatives. A legally adopted person ceases to be treated as a child of his natural parents for the same purposes, except:

(a) If a natural parent marries or remarries and the child is adopted by the stepparent, the child is treated as the child of his natural parent for all purposes;

(b) If a natural parent of a legitimate marital child dies and the other natural parent remarries and the child is adopted by the stepparent, the child is treated as the child of the deceased natural parent for purposes of inheritance through that parent and for purposes of any statute conferring rights upon children, issue, or relatives of that parent under the law of intestate succession or wills.

(3) Construction of class gift as including adopted persons. A gift of property by will, deed, or other instrument to a class of persons described as issue, lawful issue, children, grandchildren, descendants, heirs, heirs of the body, next of kin, distributees, or the like includes a person adopted by a person whose natural child would be a member of the class or issue of the adopted person, if (a) the instrument does not expressly exclude adopted persons, (b) the conditions for membership in the class are otherwise satisfied, and (c) the adopted person was a minor at the time of adoption or was adopted after having been raised as a member of the household by the adoptive parent from the child's 15th birth-

day or before. Unless the instrument expressly provides otherwise, such a gift excludes a natural child and his issue otherwise within the class if the child has been adopted and would cease to be a child of his natural parents under sub. (2) for purposes of inheritance from the testator. This subsection applies to all wills, deeds, trusts, or other instruments executed on or after April 1, 1971.

852.05. Status of illegitimate person for purposes of intestate succession

(1) An illegitimate child or his issue is entitled to take in the same manner as a legitimate child by intestate succession from and through (a) his mother and (b) his father if the father has either been adjudicated to be such under ss. 52.21 to 52.45, or has admitted in open court that he is the father, or has acknowledged himself to be the father in writing signed by him.

(2) Property of an illegitimate person passes in accordance with s. 852.01 except that the father or his kindred can inherit only if the father has been adjudicated to be such under ss. 52.21 to 52.45.

(3) This section does not apply to a child legitimated by the subsequent marriage of his parents under s. 245.25, and status of an illegitimate child who is legally adopted is governed by s. 851.51.

853.25. Unintentional failure to provide for issue of testator.

(1) Children born or adopted after making of the will. If a testator fails to provide in his will for any child born or adopted after the making of the will, that child is entitled to receive a share in the estate of the testator equal in value to the share which the child would have received if the testator had died intestate, unless: (a) the testator left all or substantially all of his estate to the mother of the child, or (b) the testator eliminated all of his children known to him to be living at the time of the execution of the will from any share under the will, or (c) the testator provided for the subsequently born or adopted child by transfers outside the will and the intent that the transfers be in lieu of a testamentary gift is either shown by statements of the testator or inferred from the amount of the transfers and other circumstances, or (d) in any other case it appears from the will or evidence outside the will that the omission was intentional. If a child entitled to a share under this section dies before the testator, and the child leaves issue who survive the testator, the issue who represent the child are entitled to his share.

(2) Living issue omitted by mistake. If clear and convincing evidence proves that by mistake or accident the testator failed to provide in his will for a child living at the time of making of the will, or for the issue of any then deceased child, the child or issue is entitled to receive a share in the estate of the testator equal in value to the share which he or they would have received if the testator had died intestate. But failure to mention a child or issue in the will is not in itself evidence of mistake or accident.[81]

WYOMING: WILLS AND DECEDENTS' ESTATES

Section 2-4-103. Posthumous persons.

Persons conceived before the decedent's death but born thereafter inherit as if they had been born in the lifetime of the decedent.

Section 2-4-107. Determination of relationship of parent and child.

(a) If for purposes of intestate succession, a relationship of parent and child shall be established to determine succession by, through, or from a person:

(i) An adopted person is the child of an adopting parent and of the natural parents for inheritance purposes only. The adoption of a child by the spouse of a natural parent has no effect on the relationship between the child and that natural parent;

(ii) An adopted person shall inherit from all other relatives of an adoptive parent as though he was the natural child of the adoptive parent and the relatives shall inherit from the adoptive person's estate as if they were his relatives;

(iii) In cases not covered by paragraph (i) of this subsection, a person born out of wedlock is a child of the mother. That person is also a child of the father, if the relationship of parent and child has been established under the Uniform Parentage Act, W.S. 14-2-101 through 14-2-120.[82]

6 The Law of Intestacy

In the normal course of administration of a decedent's estate, in particular when an individual dies intestate, various questions arise as to the rights a beneficiary may have with regard to his or her distributive share. These rights vary substantially from state to state. In addition, the estate taxation by the respective state on property of a decedent often depends upon the nature of the asset and the assets res. This chapter briefly summarizes the types of state death taxes that presently exist and their impact on the decedent's estate. Included is a table of appropriate statutory citations for each state. Also, a digest of state intestacy laws is provided, which often includes ancillary information on the right of a surviving spouse (right of elections) as against the estate. In terms of practicality, a general practitioner should be able to comprehend and acknowledge the differences in the intestacy statutes between his home state and that of a sister state with easy access. Often times, retrieving this information is time consuming. Therefore, the primary purpose of this chapter is to provide you with a quick reference to respective state statutes that will expedite the management process for your office. The actual statutory material should, of course, be consulted for use in any proceedings. A summary of executor's rights and duties is also furnished along with a commentary.

STATE DEATH TAXATION

In the United States, every sovereign state including the District of Columbia has exercised its power by statute to impose death taxes upon real property located within its jurisdiction with the exception of Nevada. The fact that a decedent may not have resided there is immaterial. The state statutes are not consistent, however, with regard to the taxability of estates when property ownership may have been jointly owned. The individual state statutes must be researched to determine what value will be placed on a decedent's property to determine ultimately the taxability status.

There is a major difference between an inheritance tax levied by an individual state and the federal estate tax. The *federal estate tax* is levied upon the transfer of the estate in its entirety, whereas the *state (inheritance) tax* is imposed on the succession to the individual shares left to individual beneficiaries.

Many state inheritance laws divide the heirs into beneficiary classes. Those heirs who bear the closest family ties to a decedent usually receive larger exemptions and, therefore, pay lower taxes (in those states that have these types of inheritance tax statutes). Generally, a decedent's state of domicile will levy an inheritance tax on all real estate located in the state jurisdiction. In many states, life insurance proceeds paid to named beneficiaries are exempt from inheritance tax; however, intangible personal property may not be exempt.

Some states impose a death tax on the right of a person to transfer his or her property at death. Therefore, this tax is like the federal estate tax, because it is based upon the value of the net taxable estate.

Credit estate taxes are distinctly different from a regular state estate type of death tax. Although a credit estate tax will usually be imposed in addition to a regular inheritance or estate tax, a state may impose all or any combination of the types of death taxes.

Counsel for an estate owner should determine if a client is a resident of a state that has a state estate tax. The state's statutes will dictate whether, or which, property is subject to a death tax. The state and federal taxing power will not be the same. For example, states are without power, to impose a death tax on a resident's real property, located outside of their jurisdictions, according to traditional conflict-of-law rules. However, the federal government has no such limitation, and it is able to tax a United States resident citizen's real property even if it is located in a foreign country.

Generally, state estate tax laws are patterned after federal law but with some variations. One significant variation is that most states provide some exemption for life insurance paid to certain beneficiaries, even if at the time of death the decedent had incidents of ownership in said policy. Furthermore, when real property is held jointly with right of survivorship between the spouses, some states will provide some type of favorable treatment.

States have the power to impose a death tax but may choose not to by statute. However, almost all of the states have chosen to institute a death tax. A few states have adopted only the credit estate tax, not enacting either an inheritance or estate tax. In these states no state death tax is payable in the estate of a decedent unless there is a taxable estate for federal purposes that is in excess of the statutory threshold (the minimum amount for which a federal estate tax credit is available). In such an instance the amount of the state tax would equal the amount of the credit obtained. There are only a few states that have *only* a credit estate tax, just as there are only a few that have declined to levy the tax.

A few states have, in addition to the basic death tax and the credit estate tax, enacted a special death tax. Almost all of the states that have this tax have simply imposed a surtax on the amount of their basic tax or on the total of their basic

Uniform Simultaneous Death Act: Table of Jurisdictions Wherein Act Has Been Adopted

Jurisdiction	Statutory Citation
Alabama	Code of Ala., Tit. 16, Secs. 34 to 41.
Arizona	A.R.S. Secs. 14–2804 to 14–2810.
Arkansas	Ark. Stats. Secs. 61–124 to 61–130.
California	West's Ann. Prob. Cod, Secs. 296 to 296.8.
Colorado	C.R.S. '73, 15–11–613.
Connecticut	C.G.S.A. Sec. 45–287.
Delaware	12 Del.C. Secs. 701 to 707.
District of Columbia	D.C.C.E. Secs. 19–501 to 19–506.
Florida	West's F.S.A. Sec. 732.601.
Georgia	Code, Secs. 113–2901 to 113–2907.
Hawaii	HRS Secs. 534–1 to 534–5.
Idaho	I.C. Sec. 15–2–613.
Illinois	S.H.A. ch. 3, Secs. 41a to 41g.
Indiana	I.C.1971, 29–2–14–1 to 29–1–14–8.
Iowa	I.C.A. Secs. 633.523 to 633.528.
Kansas	K.S.A. 58–701 to 58–707.
Kentucky	KRS 397.010 to 397.080.
Maine	18 M.R.S. Secs. 1101 to 1108.
Maryland	Code, Courts and Judicial Proceedings, Secs. 10–801 to 10–807.
Massachusetts	M.G.L.A. c. 190A Secs. 1 to 8.
Michigan	M.C.L.A. Secs. 720.101 to 720.108.
Minnesota	M.S.A. Sec. 525.90.
Mississippi	Code 1972, Secs. 91–3–1 to 91–3–15.
Missouri	V.A.M.S. Secs. 471.010 to 471.080.
Montana	R.C.M.1947, Secs. 91–423 to 91–430.
Nebraska	R.R.S.1943, Secs. 30–121 to 30–126.
Nevada	N.R.S. 135.010 to 135.090.
New Hampshire	RSA 563:1 to 563:9.
New Jersey	N.J.S.A. 3A:5–1 to 3A:5–8.
New Mexico	1953 Comp. Secs. 29–1–24 to 29–1–31.
New York	EPTL 2–1.6.
North Carolina	G.S. Secs. 28A–24–1 to 28A–24–7.
North Dakota	NDCC 31–12–01 to 31–12–06.
Oklahoma	58 Okl.St.Ann. Secs. 1001 to 1008.
Oregon	ORS 112.575 to 112.645.
Panama Canal Zone	7 C.Z.C. Secs. 651 to 659.
Pennsylvania	20 Pa.C.S.A. Secs. 8501 to 8505.
Rhode Island	Gen.Laws 1956, Secs. 33–2–1 to 33–2–9.
South Carolina	Code 1962, Secs. 19–301 to 19–308.
South Dakota	SDCL 29–8–1 to 29–8–8.
Tennessee	T.C.A. Secs. 31–501 to 31–508.

Uniform Simultaneous Death Act: Table of Jurisdictions Wherein Act Has Been Adopted (*continued*)

Jurisdiction	Statutory Citation
Texas	V.A.T.S. Probate Code, Sec. 47.
Utah	U.C.A.1953, 74–5–1 to 74–5–8.
Vermont	14 V.S.A. Secs. 621 to 627.
Virgin Islands	15 V.I.C. Sec. 88.
Virginia	Code 1950, Secs. 64.1–97 to 64.1–104.
Washington	RCWA 11.05.010 to 11.05.910.
West Virginia	Code, 42–5–1 to 45–5–10.
Wisconsin	W.S.A. 851.55.
Wyoming	W.S.1957, Secs. 34–100 to 34–106.

and credit estate tax. The other less-used method is to impose a special tax on contingent interests. For example:

Under Colorado Inheritance Tax Law, a surtax of 10 percent is levied on the total amount payable. Moneys collected from the surtax are added to the state fund for the Colorado old-age pension.

Under Connecticut Inheritance Tax Law, a surtax of 30 percent of the total amount payable is levied. The moneys collected from the surtax are not designated for any specific purpose.

Under Massachusetts Inheritance Tax Law, a surtax of 14 percent of the total amount payable is levied. This surtax is used to guarantee a minimum distribution amount to cities and towns.

Under Wisconsin Inheritance Tax Law, a surtax of 30 percent on the total amount due under the inheritance tax and the credit estate tax is levied. The moneys raised from this surtax are added to a state fund used for relief purposes as well as the construction and improvement of state institutions and other state property. This surtax is only on property within the state and is not extended to a Wisconsin decedent's property outside of the state.

In Rhode Island, a special tax is imposed if any part of the decedent's property is devised, bequeathed, or conveyed in a manner that postpones the beneficial enjoyment or possession of it. This tax is equal to 2 percent of such property's value and is for the advantage of delaying the final tax calculation on the remaining interest until after the happening of the contingency.

REAL ESTATE AND TANGIBLE PERSONAL PROPERTY

Most states impose their inheritance and estate taxes upon a non-resident's real estate and tangible personal property located within their borders at his or her death. Accordingly, if a decedent leaves either tangible or personal property located in any other state besides his or her domicile at death, this other state will impose a death tax upon the property. The domicile state is forbidden by the 14th Amendment to the U.S. Constitution to tax such property, and thus the latter state should not include it when calculating the total estate that is subject to a tax. When calculating the total amount of all taxes, the death taxes of the state of domicile must be added to the taxes imposed by outside states upon the real estate and tangible personal property found within its borders.

INTANGIBLES: STOCKS, BONDS, AND OTHER INTANGIBLE PROPERTY

Foreign states sometimes tax intangibles (stocks, bonds, and so on) as property in the decedent's estate. This intangible property may, under certain circumstances, be taxed by other states besides the domicile state.

SOME STATES DO NOT TAX INTANGIBLES OF NON-RESIDENTS

Several states choose not to exercise their power to tax the intangibles of a non-resident, limiting the inheritance and estate taxes to a non-resident's real estate and tangible personal property located in the state. For example, the New York State Constitution provides that moneys, credit, securities, and other intangible property within the state, which is not used for any business therein, for taxation purposes will be considered to be located in the owner's domicile. A property that is held in trust will not be considered to be located in the state even though the trustee is in the state. Accordingly, upon a non-resident's death, New York will ordinarily tax only his or her real estate and tangible personal property that is found in the state.

RECIPROCAL EXEMPTION OF NON-RESIDENT'S ESTATES

In addition to the aforementioned taxing schemes, some state laws contain reciprocal exemption provisions. These reciprocal exemption laws provide that a non-resident's intangible property will not be taxed when the state of residence provides either or similar provisions or does not tax the transfer of a non-resident's intangible property. Each case should be checked carefully, because there are many variations in state laws.

SUMMARY

In general, unless there are special circumstances, a non-resident's intangibles will be subject to a tax only by the state of residence. Examples of special situations that would lead to taxing in this case would be uncertainty as to domicile, the existence of a trust, or the employment of the intangibles in a business outside the owner's, home state.

THE EXECUTOR

This summary includes principal duties of the executor that are basic to the office or that arise in most jurisdictions and estates. Depending upon the local law and practice of a particular jurisdiction, this summary may have to be modified and in special cases added to. Determining if this summary needs to be altered is an important prerequisite to its proper use.

The first duties of an executor may be called preprobate responsibilities, which form a foundation for the duties to follow. The fact and time of the death must be established. The will and witnesses have to be located, and if the will is not found, the fact of intestacy must be determined. If the will is located, it must be examined to see if there were any special instructions or provisions by the testator. The executor must then qualify to act as a fiduciary. If the executor does not qualify, he or she must renounce. Steps should be taken to protect the estate pending probate while also determining whether the need for temporary administration is necessary. It is also customary for the executor to make or assist the family in funeral arrangements and provide interim assistance to the family.

Subsequently, the executor must offer the will for probate, or if no will exists, someone must apply for administration. If required, the executor must arrange for bond. The final initial steps are to obtain a facsimile copy of the will and letters testamentary, which make possible the collection of the decedent's assets.

In order for the decedent's assets to be properly collected they must first be identified and protected. Because assets could be kept in a variety of places, it is best first to examine the decedent's records, income tax returns, checkbooks, bank and broker's statements, and so on to locate the assets. The executor should open a bank account for the estate and into it deposit a compilation of all of the decedent's bank accounts plus any cash in the decedent's possession at time of death. Furthermore, the decedent's safe deposit box must be opened, and the cash contents, if any, should also be deposited in the estate account. Also, if necessary, a new safe deposit box should be rented to store other valuables. The home and office of the decedent also should be searched, so that valuable records can be taken into custody. Appraisals of real property and personalty should be obtained as required, since it may be necessary to seal the home or office to protect their contents. If required, the executor must file an inventory. The executor should also cancel open orders for purchase or sale of securities, terminate margin accounts with brokers, and obtain any securities the brokers or custodians may possess. Claims for insurance and veteran's and social security benefits should also be made with all moneys made payable to the estate. It may also be necessary to examine employment contracts, employee benefit plans, and so on to see if any additional amounts will be paid to the estate. If the decedent owned a business, it is the executor's duty to protect it, the records, and the inventory thereof.

After all assets are identified and protected, a review of financial records and business affairs must be made. The executor must note if there are any executed contracts for the purchase or sale of property. The policies of casualty insurance on real and personal property should be reviewed to check the adequacy of coverage and endorsement of policies to the estate. If the decedent held a title to real property, the executor must ascertain whether same was held solely, jointly, or by the entirety. If there is a lease of home, apartment, or office, a termination or sublease should be considered. The executor must tend to any partnership agreements, buy-sell agreements, and other business arrangements, including current debts and obligations. The interest of a decedent as a fiduciary or beneficiary of an estate or trust should also be noted. The executor must determine whether business and personal employees should be discharged and then arrange for the appropriate withholding and social security taxes and filing. The income tax returns for the five years preceding a decedent's death must be studied and data collected for the preparation of the decedent's final income tax return. Any gifts made during the decedent's lifetime must be examined to see if there is any return due or if the gift must be reportable for estate tax purposes. The executor must also determine the date of the gift, the person who received the gift, the nature of the gift, and the state of health of the decedent when the gift was made.

The executor will also have to attend to those duties that relate to administration in general, which involves a collection of all income, accounts, fees, and other receivables. An estimate of cash requirements will have to be made that includes expenses, taxes, debts, and cash legacies. Furthermore, if the decedent owned United States Treasury bonds, a determination should be made as to eligibility and application on federal estate tax returns. United States savings bonds should be redeemed within a limited time after death, if they have reached maturity. Also, any corporate stock should be disposed of. The liquidation of these assets should be done if and as necessary to provide cash requirements for preservation of values and eventual distribution. The funds should be made productive pending expenditure or distribution. The securities should be registered in the name of a nominee, if it is permitted. There must be an examination and allowance for rejection of claims. The executor is responsible for continuing, defending, or terminating pending litigation by or against the decedent and appropriately managing or supervising real property. There should also be discovery proceedings to find or recover the decedent's property in possession of others.

The executor must also pay due attention to non-probate assets, obtaining information as to the nature and amounts subject to death taxation. Those non-probate assets passing pursuant to a residuary clause must also be determined. The executor should also see to the facilitating of the collection of insurance, social security benefits, joint bank accounts, and so on by the taker or beneficiary.

Finally, the tax returns and payments must be drafted. The decedent's final return must be filed, as well as the return for the preceding tax year (if it has not already been filed). A joint return with the decedent's spouse should also be considered by reviewing open years as to possible deficiency assessments and fraud penalties. The audit of returns must also be prepared and a request for a prompt audit should be considered. The fiscal year of the estate must be determined, by considering interests of and effects on beneficiaries, for income tax purposes. The executor will have to determine whether to include an accrued increment on United States savings bonds and whether to take certain expenses as income tax or estate tax deductions. The executor must be certain to file returns for the estate.

When dealing with the decedent's gift taxes, the executor has to determine whether taxable gifts were made in the quarter of the decedent's death or the preceding quarter. In the appropriate case, the executor may have to obtain the consent of the spouse to treat certain gifts as joint gifts. The executor should also determine whether any taxable gifts were made in prior years for which returns were not filed. Once again, all of the necessary returns have to be filed.

Finally, the executor must arrange for the payment of the death taxes on the decedent's estate. For each life insurance policy, a Form 712 (in the United States) must be obtained. To enable collection or transfer of securities or other assets, the executor must obtain the required releases or consents. The Federal Estate Tax Return must then be filed as must the State Inheritance or Estate Tax Return, or the Executor must institute proceedings for the fixation of the tax. The executor should be sure to establish credits where appropriate against federal tax for state death taxes paid. If taxes are to be apportioned, the executor should estimate the apportionable shares and withhold from the legatees and collect from other takers.

The next step is to determine the order of priority of the expenses, debts, and claims, as well as the property applicable to their payment. The estate's solvency or insolvency must be ascertained. The executor should then see to the timely payment of the allowed claims and avoidance of interest.

The rights of the spouse and children must be recognized. This involves ascertainment and segregation of "exempt" property and allowances. The rights of pretermitted children must also be established. Then the executor should see to the statutory election by the surviving spouse, if appropriate.

The satisfaction of legacies should be accomplished while paying attention to the order of priority, the time for satisfaction (as affected by the factors), and the satisfaction of cash legacy in property. Partial distributions may be made if justified. Further consideration should be given to the income tax effects of distributions to residuary beneficiaries. The executor must also leave reserves for any expenses, contingencies, tax deficiencies, and so on that may arise and distribute the residue in cash or in kind. The executor should establish a trust pursuant to the will, if appropriate. In addition, if appropriate, the proper intestacy statutes should be consulted and researched in depth.

The executor is also responsible for all accounts and accountings. He or she is to keep full and accurate records and make them available to the beneficiaries and the court. Additionally, where necessary or proper, the executor is to give intermediate accountings. When a final accounting is anticipated, it should be settled by judicial proceeding or by voluntary agreement of all beneficiaries (receipt and release). Subsequently, the executor is to see to the payment of administrative expenses, fees, and compensation. It is also the executor's duty to comply with the final decree. The executor may then obtain his or her discharge from further accountability and from office.

It may be necessary to make provisions for a successor and substituted executors or administrators. The qualification of the successor or substitute is to be done as in the case of the original executor, and the powers and duties of the replacement will generally be the same as for the original executor. Subsequent to substitution, a settlement of the account of the predecessor must be accomplished. Furthermore, it is the successor's duty to take all necessary steps that were not taken or completed by the predecessor. The successor will also be able to exercise the same discretionary powers the predecessor had, unless those powers were personal to the predecessor.

INTESTACY LAWS AND THE SURVIVING SPOUSE RIGHT OF ELECTION

The following statutes indicate the rules of descent and distribution and the disposition of assets of those persons who die without a valid will. Although it is a fact that approximately two out of every five persons with estates to administer die without a will, the statutes relating to intestacy are designed for general application and rarely coincide with a decedent's individual wishes. Procrastination and antipathy to thoughts of death are the primary reasons intestacy results. The state statutes are clearly impersonal and inflexible. The limited share passing to a decedent's spouse under a state statute can also result in unwarranted hardship to the widow or widower. In addition, most state statutes treat a decedent's children equally despite unequal needs. There may be estate losses due to forced liquidation, as well as restrictions regarding investments and increased administration expenses and estate taxes.

If a decedent dies testate, his or her surviving spouse may be entitled to elect to take against the decedent's will. Many states permit the surviving spouse to assert rights against the will. In general, when the survivor elects against the will, he or she will receive the intestate share, which is in effect the share he or she would have received had the decedent died without a will.

Each state statute must be clearly researched to determine the rights of the interested parties concerned. In addition, the state statutes must be investigated to determine the minimum-age requirements for drafting a will, number of witnesses required, status of holographic and nuncupative wills, charitable gift limitations, and the application of the rule against perpetuities.

The statutes that follow address several of the issues and problems that arise from statutory descent and distribution, as well as the right of election predicament that may be asserted by a decedent's surviving spouse.

ALABAMA

Section 43–8–40. Intestate estate generally.

Any part of the estate of a decedent not effectively disposed of by his will passes to his heirs as prescribed in the following sections of this chapter.

Section 43–4–41. Share of the spouse.

The intestate share of the surviving spouse is as follows:

(1) If there is no surviving issue or parent of the decedent, the entire intestate estate;

(2) If there is no surviving issue but the decedent is survived by a parent or parents, the first $100,000.00 in value, plus one-half of the balance of the intestate estate;

(3) If there are surviving issue all of whom are issue of the surviving spouse also, the first $50,000.00 in value, plus one-half of the balance of the intestate estate;

(4) If there are surviving issue one or more of whom are not issue of the surviving spouse, one-half of the intestate estate;

(5) If the estate is located in two or more states, the share shall not exceed in the aggregate the allowable amounts under this chapter.

Section 43–8–42. Share of heirs other than surviving spouse.

The part of the intestate estate not passing to the surviving spouse under Section 43–8–41, or the entire intestate estate if there is no surviving spouse, passes as follows:

(1) To the issue of the decedent; if they are all of the same degree of kinship to the decedent they take equally, but if of unequal degree, then those of more remote degree take by representation;

(2) If there is no surviving issue, to his parent or parents equally;

(3) If there is no surviving issue or parent, to the issue of the parents or either of them by representation;

(4) If there is no surviving issue, parent, or issue of a parent, but the decedent is survived by one or more grandparents or issue of grandparents, half of the estate passes to the paternal grandparents if both survive, or to the surviving paternal grandparent, or to the issue of the paternal grandparents if both are deceased, the issue taking equally if they are all of the same degree of kinship to the decedent, but if of unequal degree, those of more remote degree take by representation; and the other half passes to the maternal relatives in the same manner; but if there be no surviving grandparent or issue of grandparent on either the paternal or the maternal side, the entire estate passes to the relatives on the other side in the same manner as the other half.

Section 43–8–44. When estate passes to state.

If there is no taker under the provisions of this article, the intestate estate passes to the state of Alabama.[83]

ALASKA

Section 13.11.005. Intestate estate.

Any part of the estate of a decedent not effectively disposed of by his will passes to his heirs as prescribed in the following sections of this code.

Section 13.11.010. Share of the Spouse.

The intestate share of the surviving spouse is:

(1) if there is no surviving issue or parent of the decedent, the entire intestate estate;

(2) if there is no surviving issue but the decedent is survived by a parent or parents, the first $50,000.00 plus one-half of the balance of the intestate estate;

(3) if there are surviving issue all of whom are issue of the surviving spouse also, the first $50,000.00, plus one-half of the balance of the intestate estate;

(4) if there are surviving issue one or more of whom are not issue of the survivng spouse, one-half of the intestate estate.

Section 13.11.015. Share of heirs other than surviving spouse.

The part of the intestate estate not passing to the surviving spouse under Section 10 of this chapter, or the entire intestate estate if there is no surviving spouse, passes as follows:

(1) to the issue of the decedent; if they are all of the same degree of kinship to the decedent they take equally, but if of unequal degree, then those of more remote degree take by representation;

(2) if there is no surviving issue, to his parent or parents equally;

(3) if there is no surviving issue or parent, to the brothers and sisters and the issue of each deceased brother or sister by representation; if there is no surviving brother or sister, the issue of brothers and sisters take equally if they are all of the same degree of kinship to the decedent, but if of unequal degree, then those of more remote degree take by representation;

(4) if there is no surviving issue, parent, or issue of a parent, but the decedent is survived by one or more grandparents or issue of grandparents, half of the estate passes to the paternal grandparents if both survive or to the issue of the paternal grandparents if both are deceased, the issue taking equally if they are all of the same degree of kinship to the decedent, but if of unequal degree, those of more remote degree take by representation; but if there be no surviving grandparent or issue of grandparent on either the paternal or the maternal side, the entire estate passes to the relatives on the other side in the same manner as the half.

Section 13.11.025. No taker.

If there is no taker under the provisions of this chapter, the intestate estate passes to the state.[84]

ARIZONA

Section 14–2101. Intestate estate.

Any part of the estate of a decedent not effectively disposed of by his will passes to his heirs as prescribed in the following sections of this title.

Section 14–2102. Intestate share of surviving spouse.

The following part of the intestate estate, as to both separate property and the one-half of community property which belongs to the decedent, passes to the surviving spouse:

1. If there is no surviving issue, or if there are surviving issue all of whom are issue of the surviving spouse also, the entire intestate estate.

2. If there are surviving issue one or more of whom are not issue of the surviving spouse, one-half of the intestate separate property and no interest in the one-half of the community property which belonged to the decedent.

Section 14–2103. Share of heirs other than surviving issue.

A. The part of the intestate estate not passing to the surviving spouse under Section 14–102, or the entire intestate estate if there is no surviving spouse, passes as follows:

1. The the issue of the decedent.

2. If there is no surviving issue, to the decedent's parent or parents equally.

3. If there is no surviving issue or parent, to the issue of the decedent's parents or issue of either of the parents.

4. If there is no surviving issue, parent, or issue of a parent, but the decedent is survived by one or more grandparents or issue of grandparents, half of the estate passes to the paternal grandparent or grandparents equally or to their issue if both grandparents are deceased; the other half passes to maternal grandparents or their issue in the same manner. If there is no surviving grandparent or issue on either the paternal or maternal side, the entire estate passes to the relatives on the other side in the same manner as the half.

B. Whenever the heirs are issue of the decedent, or of his parents, or of his grandparents, the issue take equally if they are all of the same degree of kinship to the decedent; but if they are of unequal degree, then those of more remote degree take by representation as provided in Section 14–2106.

Section 14–2105. No taker.

If there is no taker under the provisions of this chapter, the intestate estate passes to the state.[85]

ARKANSAS

61–132. Dying intestate—Intestate defined.

"Dying intestate" means dying without a valid Last Will and Testament. A person so dying is referred to in this act [Sections 61–131 to 61–155] as an "Intestate"; and it is recognized that a person may die wholly or partially intestate.

61–149. Tables of descents.

The heritable estate (as defined in Section 7 [Section 61–137] of this act) of an Intestate shall upon his death pass as follows:

(a) First, to the children of the Intestate and the descendants of each child of the Intestate who may have predeceased him or her, which children and descendants will take per capita or per stirpes according to Sections 4 [Section 61–134] and 5 [Section 61–135] of this act.

(b) Second, if the Intestate is survived by no descendant, to the Intestate's surviving spouse unless the Intestate and such surviving spouse had been continuously married less than three [3] years next preceding the death of the Intestate, in which event the surviving spouse will take merely 50% of the Intestate's heritable estate.

(c) Third, if the Intestate is survived by no descendant or spouse, to the Intestate's surviving parents, sharing equally, or to the sole surviving parent if only one [1] of them shall be living.

(d) Fourth, if the Intestate is survived by no descendant but is survived by a spouse to whom Intestate has been continuously married less than three [3] years next preceding the death of the Intestate, the entire portion of his or her heritable estate which does not pass to the surviving spouse under subparagraph (b) above shall pass to the Intestate's surviving parents, sharing equally, or to the sole surviving parent if only one [1] of them shall be living.

(e) Fifth, if the Intestate be survived by no descendant or parent, then all of his or her heritable estate which under subparagraphs (c) and (d) would have vested in Intestate's surviving parent or parents will pass to Intestate's brothers and sisters and the descendants of any brothers and sisters of Intestate who may have predeceased him or her, such brothers, sisters, and descendants taking per capita or per stirpes according to Sections 4 [Section 61–134] and 5 [Section 61–135] of this act.

(f) Sixth, if the Intestate be survived by no descendant, then in respect to such portion of his or her heritable estate as does not pass under the foregoing subparagraphs (b) to (e) inclusive, the inheriting class will be the surviving grandparents, uncles, and aunts of the Intestate. In this situation each surviving grandparent shall take the same share as each surviving uncle and aunt, and no distinction shall be made between the paternal and maternal sides. In other words, a maternal grandparent, uncle, or aunt shall take the same share as a paternal grandparent, uncle, or aunt and vice versa. If any uncle or aunt of the Intestate shall predecease him, the decendants of such deceased uncle or aunt will take, per capita or per stirpes according to Sections 4 [Section 61–134] and 5 [Section 61–135] hereof, the share the decedent would have taken if he or she had survived the Intestate.

(g) Seventh, if the Intestate be survived by no descendant, then in respect to such portion of his or her estate as does not pass under the foregoing subparagraph (b) to (f) inclusive, the inheriting class will be the surviving great-grandparents and great-uncles and great-aunts of the Intestate. In this situation each surviving great-grandparent shall take the same share as each surviving great-uncle and great-aunt, and no distinction shall be made between the paternal and maternal sides. In other words, a maternal great-grandparent, great-uncle, or great-aunt shall take the same share as a paternal great-grandparent, great-uncle, or great-aunt and vice versa. If any great-uncle or great-aunt shall predecease the Intestate, the descendants of the decedent will take, per capita or per stirpes according to Sections 4 [Section 61–134] and 5 [Section 61–135] hereof, the share the decedent would have taken if he or she had survived the Intestate.

(h) Eighth, if heirs capable of inheriting the entire heritable estate cannot be found within the inheriting classes prescribed in subparagraphs (a), (b), (c), (d), (e), (f), and (g) of this section, the real and personal property of the Intestate, or the portion thereof not passing under said subparagraphs, shall pass according to Section 20 [Section 61–150] (devolution where all or some portion of heritable estate does not pass under Section 19 [this section] of this act).

61–150. Devolution where all or some portion of heritable estate does not pass under Section 61–149—Escheat.

If an heir to the heritable estate, or some portion thereof, cannot be found under Section 19 [Section 61–149], then such portion of the heritable estate as does not pass under Section 19 [Section 61–149] will pass as follows:

First, to the surviving spouse of the Intestate even though they had been married less than three [3] years.

Second, if there be no such surviving spouse, to the heirs, determined as of the date of the Intestate's death in accordance with Section 19 [Section 61–149] of this act, of the Intestate's deceased spouse (meaning the spouse to whom the Intestate was last married if there had been more than one marriage); provided that, in case a marriage was terminated by divorce, rather than by death, the heirs of the divorced spouse shall not inherit.

Third, if there be no person capable of inheriting under First or Second, the estate shall escheat to the state.[86]

CALIFORNIA

CHAPTER 1. COMMUNITY PROPERTY

Section 201. Title of surviving spouse; portion subject to testamentary disposition or succession.

Upon the death of either husband or wife, one-half of the community property belongs to the surviving spouse; the other half is subject to the testamentary disposition of the decedent, and in the absence thereof goes to the surviving spouse, subject to the provisions of Sections 202 and 203 of this code.

Section 201.5. Personal property; portion belonging to surviving spouse; distribution of other portion.

Upon the death of either husband or wife one-half of all personal property, wherever situated, heretofore or hereafter acquired after marriage by either husband or wife, or both, while domiciled elsewhere, which would not have been the separate property of either if acquired while domiciled in this state, shall belong to the surviving spouse; the other one-half is subject to the testamentary disposition of the decedent and in the absence thereof goes to the surviving spouse, subject to the debts of the decedent and to administration and disposal under the provisions of Division 3 of this code.

Section 202. Death of husband, property subject to debts and administration, disposal; death of wife, husband's powers, and duties relating to property.

Community property passing from the control of the husband, either by reason of his death or by virtue of testamentary disposition by the wife, is subject to his debts and to administration and disposal under the provisions of Division 3 of this code; but in the event of such testamentary disposition by the wife, the husband, pending administration, shall retain the same power to sell, manage, and deal with the community personal property as he had in her lifetime; and his possession and control of the community property shall not be transferred to the personal representative of the wife except to the extent necessary to carry her will into effect.

Section 203. Surviving spouse's power over property; notice of claim by another under decedent's will; status of property.

After 40 days from the death of a spouse, the surviving spouse or the personal representative, guardian of the estate, or conservator of the property of surviving spouse shall have full power to sell, lease, mortgage, or otherwise deal with and dispose of the community or quasi-community real property, unless a notice is recorded in the county in which the property is situated to the effect that an interest in the property is claimed by another under the will of the deceased spouse. The notice must also (1) describe the property in which an interest is claimed, and (2) set forth the name or names of the owner or owners of the record title to the property. There shall be endorsed on the notice instructions that it shall be indexed by the recorder in the name or names of the owner or owners of the record title to the property, as grantor or grantors, and in the name of the person claiming an interest in the property, as grantee. The right, title, and interest of any grantee, purchaser, encumbrancer, or lessee shall be as free of rights of divisees or creditors of the deceased spouse to the same extent as if the property had been owned as the separate property of the surviving spouse.

CHAPTER 2. SEPARATE PROPERTY

Section 221. Distribution to surviving spouse and issue.

If the decedent leaves a surviving spouse and only one child or the lawful issue of a deceased child, the estate goes one-half to the surviving spouse and one-half to the child or issue. If the decedent leaves a surviving spouse and more than one child living or one child living and the lawful issue of one or more deceased children, the estate goes one-third to the surviving spouse and the remainder in equal shares to his children and to the lawful issue of any deceased child, by right of representation; but if there is no child of decedent living at his death, the remainder goes to all of his lineal decendants; and if all of the decendants are in the same degree of kindred to the decedent they share equally, otherwise they take by right of representation.

Section 222. Distribution to issue where no surviving spouse.

If the decendent leaves no surviving spouse but leaves issue, the whole estate goes to such issue; and if all of the decendants are in the same degree of kindred to the decedent they share equally, otherwise they take by right of representation.

Section 223. Distribution to surviving spouse and immediate family where no issue.

If the decedent leaves a surviving spouse and no issue, the estate goes one-half to the surviving spouse and one-half to the decedent's parents in equal shares, or if either is dead to the survivor, or if both are dead to their issue and the issue of either of them, by right of representation.

Section 224. Distribution to surviving spouse where neither issue nor immediate family.

If the decedent leaves a surviving spouse and neither issue, parent, brother, sister, nor descendant of a deceased brother or sister, the whole estate goes to the surviving spouse.

Section 225. Distribution to immediate family where neither issue nor spouse.

If the decedent leaves neither issue nor spouse, the estate goes to his parents in equal shares, or if either is dead to the survivor, or if both are dead, in equal shares to his brothers and sisters and to the descendants of deceased brothers and sisters by right of representation.

Section 226. Distribution to next of kin where no spouse, issue, or immediate family.

If the decedent leaves neither issue, spouse, parent, brother, sister, nor descendant of a deceased brother or sister, the estate goes to the next of kin in equal degree, excepting that, when there are two or more collateral kindred in equal degree, but claiming through different ancestors, those who claim through the nearest ancestor must be preferred to those claiming through an ancestor more remote.

Section 228. Distribution of community and other property acquired from predeceased spouse where no surviving spouse or issue.

If the decedent leaves neither spouse nor issue, and the estate or any portion thereof was community property of the decedent and a previously deceased spouse, and belonged or went to the decedent by virtue of its community character on the death of such spouse, or came to the decedent from said spouse by gift, descent, devise, or bequest, or became vested in the decedent on the death of such spouse by right of survivorship in a homestead, or in a joint tenancy between such spouse and the decedent, or was set aside as a probate homestead, such property goes in equal shares to the children of the deceased spouse and their descendants by right of representation, and if none, then one-half of such community property goes to the parents of the decedent in equal shares, or if either is dead, to the survivor, or if both are dead, in equal shares to the brothers and sisters of the decedent and their descendants by right of representation, and the other half goes to the parents of the deceased spouse in equal shares, or if either is dead, to the survivor, or if both are dead, in equal shares to the brothers and sisters of said deceased spouse and to their descendants by right of representation.

Section 229. Distribution of former separate property of previously deceased spouse where no surviving spouse or issue.

If the decedent leaves neither spouse nor issue, and the estate or any portion thereof was separate property of a previously deceased spouse and came to the decedent from such spouse by gift, descent, devise, or bequest, or became vested in the decedent on the death of such spouse by right of survivorship in a homestead or in a joint tenancy between such spouse and the decedent, such property goes in equal shares to the children of the deceased spouse and to their descendants by right of representation, and if none, then to the parents of the deceased spouse in equal shares, or if either is dead, to the survivor, or if both are dead, in equal shares to the brothers and sisters of the deceased spouse and to their descendants by right of representation.

Section 230. Distribution to next of kin of property acquired from previously deceased spouse.

If there is no one to succeed to any portion of the property in any of the contingencies provided for in the last two sections, according to the provisions of these sections, such portion goes to the next of kin of the decedent in the manner hereinabove provided for succession by next of kin.

Section 231. Escheat.

If the decedent leaves no one to take his estate or any portion thereof under the laws of this state, the same escheats to the state as of the date of the death of the decedent. Property passing to the state under this section, whether held by the state or its officers, is subject to the same charges and trusts to which it would have been subject if it had passed by succession and is also subject to the provisions of Title 10 of Part 3 of the Code of Civil Procedure relating to escheated estates.[87]

COLORADO

Section 15–11–101. Intestate estate.

Any part of the estate of a decedent not effectively disposed of by his will or otherwise passes to his heirs as prescribed in the following sections of this code.

Section 15–11–102. Share of the spouse.

(1) the intestate share of the surviving spouse is:

(a) If there is no surviving issue of the decedent, the entire intestate estate;

(b) If there are surviving issue all of whom are issue of the surviving spouse also, the first twenty-five thousand dollars, plus one-half of the balance of the intestate estate;

(c) If there are surviving issue of one or more of whom are not issue of the surviving spouse, one-half of the intestate estate.

Section 15–11–103. Share of heirs other than surviving spouse.

(1) The part of the intestate estate not passing to the surviving spouse under Section 15–11–102 or the entire estate if there is no surviving spouse, passes as follows:

(a) to the issue of the decedent; if they are all of the same degree of kinship to the decedent, they take equally, but if of unequal degree, then those of more remote degree take by representation;

(b) If there is no surviving issue, to his parent or parents equally;

(c) If there is no surviving issue or parent, to the issue of the parents or either of them; if they are all of the same degree of kinship to the decedent, they take equally but if of unequal degree, then those of more remote degree take by representation;

(d) If there is no surviving issue, parent, or issue of a parent, but the decedent is survived by one or more grandparents or issue of grandparents, half of the estate passes to the paternal grandparents if both survive, or to the surviving paternal grandparent, or to the issue of the paternal grandparents, if both are deceased, the issue taking equally if they are all of the same degree of kinship to the decedent, but if of unequal degree, those of more remote degree take by representation; and the other half passes to the maternal relatives in the same manner; but if there be no surviving grandparent or issue of grandparent on either the paternal or the maternal side, the entire estate passes to the relatives on the other side in the same manner as the half; and

(e) If none of the relatives above enumerated be living, then to the nearest lineal ancestors and their descendants, the descendants collectively taking the share of their immediate ancestors in equal parts.[88]

CONNECTICUT

Section 45–273. Distribution of intestate estates.

(a) After payment of expenses and charges, an intestate estate shall be distributed by the administrator or other fiduciary charged witih the administration of the estate; provided the court of probate may, in its discretion, on its own motion or upon application by an interested person, appoint three disinterested persons to make the distribution.

(b) If all the persons interested in the estate legally capable of acting and all fiduciaries for any other persons interested in the estate make and file in the court a division of the estate, made, executed, and acknowledged like deeds of land, such division, being recorded in the records of the court, shall be a valid distribution of the estate. Any such fiduciary may petition the court of probate which appointed him for permission to enter into such a division, and such permission may be granted or, for cause shown, denied by the court, after a hearing on such petition held on such notice as the court may order.

(c) If any intestate estate consists wholly of real property, the court of probate shall issue a certificate of descent to the heirs at law, as provided in Section 45–286, without formal distribution or without a mutual distribution as provided for in this section, unless there is filed in the court of probate, within one month after the acceptance of the administration account, the ascertainment of the distributees and the order of distribution, a mutual distribution executed by all of such heirs at law or a return of distribution by this section.

Section 45–273a. Succession upon death of spouse; election against will; intestate succession.

(a) On the death of a husband or wife, the survivor shall be entitled to the use for life of one-third in value of all the property, real and personal, legally or equitably owned by the other at the time of his or her death, after the payment of all debts and charges against the estate. Such third shall be set out by the fiduciary charged with the administration of the estate or, in the discretion of the probate court on its own motion or upon application by any interested person, by distributors appointed by the court of probate in any property, real or personal or both, according to the judgment of such fiduciary or distributors. The right to such third shall not be defeated by any disposition of the property by will to other parties. If the husband has by will devised or bequeathed a portion of his property to his surviving wife, or if the wife by will has devised or bequeathed a portion of her property to her surviving husband, such provision shall be taken to be in lieu of the share herein-above provided for, unless the contrary is expressly stated in the will or clearly appears therein; but, in any such case, the surviving spouse, with the approval, after public notice and hearing, of the court of probate by which such conservator or guardian was appointed, shall have his or her election whether to accept the provisions of such will or take such life use of one-third. Such election shall be made in writing signed by the party entitled to make the election and lodged with the court of probate before which the estate is in settlement, within two months after the expiration of time limited for the exhibition of claims against the estate. If such election is not so made, such person shall be taken to have accepted the provisions of the will and shall be barred of such statutory share. In any case where the husband or wife by will does not make any provision for the surviving wife or husband, the surviving spouse, or the conservator or guardian of the estate of the surviving spouse, with the approval, after public notice and hearing, of the court of probate by which such conservator or guardian was appointed, shall, within two months after the expiration of the time limited for the exhibition of claims against such estate, file a notice, in writing, of his or her intention to take a life use of one-third of the estate under the provisions of this section with the court of probate before which the estate is in settlement, and if such notice is not so filed, such person shall be barred of such statutory share. A surviving spouse shall also, when in the option of the court of probate it is necessary, be allowed a reasonable sum from the estate for his or her support and for the support of his or her family during the settlement of the estate; but, in that case, such person shall not take his or her statutory share until the expiration of the time for which such allowance is made. The provisions of this section with regard to the statutory share of the surviving husband or wife in the property of the other shall not apply to any case in which, by written contract made before or after marriage, either party has received from the other what was intended as a provision in lieu of such statutory share; nor shall either party be entitled to such statutory share who, without sufficient cause, abandoned the other and continued such abandonment to the time of the other's death.

(b) If there is no will, or if any part of the property, real and personal, legally or equitably owned by the deceased at the time of his or her death, is not effectively disposed of by the will or codicil of the deceased, the portion of the intestate estate of the deceased which the surviving husband or wife of the deceased shall take is: [1] if there is no surviving issue or parent of the deceased, the entire intestate estate absolutely; [2] if there is no surviving issue of the deceased but the deceased is survived by a parent or parents, the first fifty thousand dollars plus three-quarters of the balance of the intestate estate absolutely; [3] if there are surviving issue of the deceased all of whom are also issue of the surviving spouse, the first fifty thousand dollars plus one-half of the balance of the intestate estate absolutely; or [4] if there are surviving issue of the deceased one or more of whom are not issue of the surviving spouse, one-half of the intestate estate absolutely.

(c) The provisions of this section shall apply to estates of all persons dying on or after January 1, 1974.

(d) For the purposes of this section issue shall include children born out of wedlock and the issue of such children who qualify for inheritance under the provisions of Section 45–274.

Section 45–276. Distribution when there are no children or representatives of them.

(a) [1] If there are no children or any legal representative of them, then, after the portion of the husband or wife, if any, is distributed or set out, the residue of the estate shall be distributed equally to the parent or parents of the intestate. [2] If there is no parent, then the residue of the estate shall be distributed equally to the brothers and sisters of the whole blood and those who legally represent them. [3] If there is no such kindred, then the residue of the estate shall be distributed equally to the brothers and sisters of the half blood and those who legally represent them. [4] If there is no parent or brothers and sisters of the whole or half blood and those who legally represent them, then the residue of the estate shall be distributed equally to the next of kin in equal degree, kindred of the whole blood to take in preference of the half blood in equal degree, and no representatives to be admitted among collaterals after the representatives of brothers and sisters.

(b) When any will executed prior to January 1, 1902, fails for any reason to dispose of the whole or any part of the estate of the testator, and such estate becomes intestate, the same shall be distributed in accordance with the statutes of distribution in force at the time such will was executed.

(c) Real property subject to the life use of husband or wife, remaining undivided at the expiration of such life use, shall be distributed in the same manner by the same or other distributors, or the same may be distributed during the continuance of such life interest and subject thereto.

(d) In ascertaining the next of kin in all cases, the rule of the civil law shall be used.[89]

DELAWARE

Section 501. Intestate estate.

Any part of the real or personal estate of a decedent not effectively disposed of by will passes to the decedent's heirs as prescribed in the following sections of this chapter.

Section 502. Share of spouse.

The intestate share of the surviving spouse is:

(1) If there is no surviving issue or parents of the decedent, the entire intestate estate;

(2) If there is no surviving issue but the decedent is survived by a parent or parents, the first $50,000 of the intestate personal estate, plus one-half of the balance of the intestate personal estate, plus a life estate in the intestate real estate;

(3) If there are surviving issue all of whom are issue of the surviving spouse

also, the first $50,000 of the intestate personal estate, plus one-half of the balance of the intestate personal estate, plus a life estate in the intestate real estate;

(4) If there are surviving issue, one or more of whom are not issue of the surviving spouse, one-half of the intestate personal estate, plus a life estate in the intestate real estate.

Section 503. Share of heirs other than surviving spouse.

The part of the intestate estate not passing to the surviving spouse under Section 502 of this title, or the entire intestate estate if there is no surviving spouse, passes as follows:

(1) To the issue of the decedent, per stirpes;

(2) If there is no surviving issue, to the decedent's parent or parents equally;

(3) If there is no surviving issue or parent, to the brothers and sisters and the issue of each deceased brother or sister, per stirpes;

(4) If there is no surviving issue, parent, or issue of a parent, then to the next of kin of the decedent and to the issue of a deceased next of kin, per stirpes;

(5) Any property passing under this section to 2 or more persons passes to such persons as tenants in common.[90]

DISTRICT OF COLUMBIA

Section 19–301. Course of descents generally.

The real estate in the District of Columbia, of a deceased person, male or female, if not devised, shall descend in fee simple, and the surplus of the personal estate of a deceased resident of the District, if not bequeathed, shall be distributed to the surviving spouse, children, and other persons in the manner provided by this chapter. The heirs specified by this subsection [section] take the real estate as tenants in common in the same proportions as they take the surplus personal estate as provided by this chapter.

Section 19–302. When surviving spouse entitled to whole.

When the intestate leaves a surviving spouse and no child, parent, grandchild, brother, or sister, or the child of a brother or sister of the intestate, the surviving spouse is entitled to the whole.

Section 19–303. When surviving spouse entitled to one-third.

When the intestate leaves a surviving spouse and a child or a descendant of a child, the surviving spouse is entitled to one-third.

Section 19–304. When surviving spouse entitled to one-half.

When the intestate leaves a surviving spouse and no child or descendant of the intestate, but a father or mother, or brother or sister, or child of a brother or sister, the surviving spouse is entitled to one-half.

Section 19–305. Distribution of surplus after payment to surviving spouse.

The surplus, above the share of the surviving spouse, or the whole surplus, when there is no surviving spouse, descends and is distributed as provided by this chapter and by Section 19–701.

Section 19–306. Children to share equally.

When the intestate leaves children and no other descendants, the surplus is divided equally among them.

Section 19–307. Grandchildren's share.

(a) Subject to subsection (b) of this section, and to Section 19–319, when the intestate leaves a child and a child of a deceased child, the child of the deceased child takes such share as his deceased parent would, if living, be entitled to, and every other descendant in existence at the death of the intestate stands in the place of his deceased ancestor.

(b) Those in equal degree claiming in the place of an ancestor take equal shares.

Section 19–308. Share of father and mother.

When the intestate leaves no child, or descendant, the whole is divided equally between the father and mother of their survivor.

Section 19–309. Share of brother or sister or their descendants.

When the intestate leaves a brother or sister, or child or descendant of a brother or sister, and no child, descendant, or father or mother, the brother, sister, or child or descendant of a brother or sister is entitled to the whole.

Section 19–310. Brothers and sisters to share equally.

Each brother and sister of the intestate is entitled to an equal share, and the children or descendants of a brother or sister of the intestate stand in the place of their deceased parents respectively.

Section 19–311. Share of collateral relations.

After children, descendants, parents, brothers, and sisters of the deceased and their descendants, all collateral relations in equal degree share, and representation among the collaterals is not allowed.

Section 19–312. Share of grandfather and grandmother.

The grandparents, or such of them as survive, share alike where there are no collaterals.

Section 19–313. Death of distributee before distribution.

When a person entitled to distribution dies before the distribution is made, his share goes to his estate or legal representatives.[91]

FLORIDA

Section 732.101. Intestate estate.

(1) Any part of the estate of a decedent not effectively disposed of by will

passes to the decedent's heirs as prescribed in the following sections of this code.

(2) The decedent's death is the event that vests the heirs' right to intestate property.

Section 732.102. Share of spouse.

(1) The intestate share of the surviving spouse is:

[a] If there is no surviving lineal descendant of the decedent, the entire intestate estate.

[b] If there are surviving lineal descendants of the decedent, all of whom are lineal descendants of the surviving spouse also, the first $20,000 of the intestate estate, plus one-half of the balance of the intestate estate. Property allocated hereunder to the surviving spouse to satisfy the $20,000 shall be valued at the fair market value on the date of the decedent's death.

[c] If there are surviving lineal descendants, one or more of whom are not lineal descendants of the surviving spouse, one-half of the intestate estate.

(2) The court shall allot the property to which the spouse is entitled, treating all beneficiaries equitably.

Section 732.103. Share of other heirs.

The part of the intestate estate not passing to the surviving spouse under Section 732.102, or the entire intestate estate if there is no surviving spouse, descends as follows:

(1) To the lineal descendants of the decedent.

(2) If there is no lineal descendant, to the decedent's father and mother equally, or to the survivor of them.

(3) If there is none of the foregoing, to the decedent's brothers and sisters and the descendants of deceased brothers and sisters.

(4) If there is none of the foregoing, the estate shall be divided, one-half of which shall go to the decedent's paternal and the other half to the (decedent's) maternal kindred in the following order:

[a] To the grandfather and grandmother equally, or to the survivor of them.

[b] If there is no grandfather or grandmother, to uncles and aunts and descendants of deceased uncles and aunts of the decedent.

[c] If there is no paternal kindred or if there is no maternal kindred, the estate shall go to such of the kindred as shall survive in the order aforesaid.

(5) If there is no kindred of either part, the whole (of) such property shall go to the kindred of the last deceased spouse of the decedent as if the deceased spouse had survived the decedent and then died intestate entitled to the estate.[92]

GEORGIA

53–4–2. Rules of inheritance generally.

The following rules shall determine who are the heirs at law of a deceased person:

(1) Upon the death of the husband without lineal descendants, the wife is his sole heir and upon the payment of his debts, if any, may take possession of his estate without administration;

(2) If, upon the death of the husband, there are children or representatives of deceased children, the wife shall have a child's part, unless the shares exceed five in number, in which case the wife shall have one-fifth part of the estate;

(3) Whenever the husband or wife of a deceased person is under the age of 18 years and entitled to a share in the estate of the deceased husband or wife, he or she shall be entitled to take and hold such share without the intervention of a guardian or other trustee;

(4) Children shall stand in the first degree from the intestate and inherit equally all property of every description, accounting for advancements as provided in Article 3 of this chapter. Posthumous children shall stand upon the same footing with children in being upon all questions of inheritance. The lineal descendants of children shall stand in the place of their deceased parents, but in all cases inheritance from a lineal ancestor the distribution is per stirpes and not per capita;

(5) Brothers and sisters of the intestate shall stand in the second degree and shall inherit if there is no surviving spouse, child, or representative of a child. The half blood, both on the paternal and maternal side, shall inherit equally with the whole blood. Brothers and sisters of the whole blood, brothers and sisters of the half blood, and brothers and sisters adopted by a mutual parent of the intestate shall stand in the same degree and inherit equally from each other. The children or grandchildren of deceased brothers and sisters shall represent and stand in the place of their deceased parents, but there shall be no representation further than this among collaterals. If all the brothers and sisters are dead at the time of death of the intestate, then the distribution shall be between nephews and nieces per capita; and if any of the nephews and nieces are dead, leaving children, distribution shall be made as though the nephews and nieces were all alive, the children of the deceased nephew or niece standing in the place of the parent;

(6) The father and mother inherit equally with brothers and sisters and stand in the same degree;

(7) In all degrees more remote than those specified in paragraphs (1) through (6) of this code section, the paternal and maternal next of kin shall stand on equal footing;

(8) The grandfathers and grandmothers of the intestate shall stand next in degree;

(9) Uncles and aunts shall stand next in degree, with the children of any deceased uncle or aunt inheriting in the place of their parent;

(10) First cousins shall stand next in degree; and

(11) The more remote degrees of kinship shall be determined by counting the steps from the claimant to the closest common ancestor and from the ancestor to the intestate. The sum of two chains shall be the degree of kinship.

Section 53–4–3. Inheritance by husband, children, and descendants of intestate.

Upon the death of the wife, the husband is her sole heir and, upon payment of her individual debts, if any, may take possession of her estate without administration unless she died intestate leaving a separate estate without remainder or limitation over, which can and does take effect, and leaves, with the husband, a surviving child or children or descendants of a child or children. In such case, her separate estate shall be equally divided, share and share alike, between the husband and offspring per capita, and the descendants of children shall take per stirpes.

19–8–14. Effect of decree of adoption.

(a) A decree of adoption, whether issued by a court of this state or by a court of any other jurisdiction, shall have the following effect as to matters within the jurisdiction of or before a court in this state:

(1) Except with respect to a spouse of the petitioner and relatives of the spouse, a decree of adoption relieves the natural parent(s) of the adopted individual of all parental rights and responsibilities and terminates all legal relationships between the adopted individual and his relatives, including his natural parent(s), so that the adopted individual thereafter is a stranger to his former relatives for all purposes, including inheritance and the interpretation or construction of documents, statutes, and instruments, whether executed before or after the adopted is decreed, which do not expressly include the individual by name or by some designation not based on a parent and child or blood relationship; and

(2) A decree of adoption creates the relationship of parent and child between the petitioner(s) and the adopted individual, as if the adopted individual were a child of natural bodily issue of the petitioner(s). The adopted individual shall enjoy every right and privilege of a natural child of the petitioner(s), shall be deemed a natural child of the petitioner(s); to inherit under the laws of descent and distribution in the absence of a will, and to take under the provisions of any instrument of testamentary gift, bequest, devise, or legacy, whether executed before or after the adoption is decreed, unless expressly excluded therefrom; shall take by inheritance from relatives of the petitioner(s); and shall also take as a "child" of the petitioner(s) under a class gift made by the will of a third person.

(b) Notwithstanding the provisions of subsection (a) of this code section, if a parent of a child dies without the relationship of parent and child having been previously terminated, the child's right of inheritance from or though the deceased parent shall not be affected by the adoption.[93]

HAWAII: DESCENT OF PROPERTY

Section 532–2. To heirs.

Whenever any person dies intestate, his property, both real and personal, of every kind and description, shall descend to and be divided among his heirs, as in this chapter prescribed; provided that upon his death, testate or intestate, of any occupier or lessee of public land, holding under an existing certification of occupation or an existing nine hundred and ninety-nine-year homestead lease, succession to the decedent's interest in such land shall be determined as provided in Section 171.99(e).

Section 532–4. General rules of descent.

(a) Issue, lineal descendants. The property shall be divided equally among the intestate's children, and the issue of any deceased child by right of representation, and if there is no child of the intestate living at his death, his estate shall descend to all his other lineal descendants; and if all such descendants are in the same degree of kindred to the intestate, they shall share the estate per capita, that is, equally; otherwise they shall inherit per stirpes, that is, by each of the children taking a share, and the grandchildren, the children of a deceased child taking a share, to be afterwards divided among themselves.

(b) Widow; father and mother; brothers and sisters. If the intestate leaves no issue, his estate shall descend one-half to his widow and the other half to his father and mother as tenants in common; and if he leaves no widow, or issue, the whole shall descend to his father and mother or to either of them if only one is alive.

If he leaves no issue, or father, or mother, his estate shall descend one-half to his widow and the other half to his brothers and sisters and to the children of any deceased brother or sister by right of representation. If he leaves no issue, or father, or mother, or widow, his estate shall descend to his brothers and sisters and to the children of any deceased brother or sister by right of representation.

(c) Husband; father and mother; brothers and sisters. If the intestate is a woman and leaves no issue, her estate shall descend one-half to her husband and the other half to her father and mother as tenants in common, and if she leaves no husband, or issue, the whole shall descend to her father and mother or to either of them if only one is alive; if she leaves no issue, or father, or mother, her estate shall descend one-half to her husband and the other half to her brothers and sisters and to the children of any deceased brother or sister by right of representation. If she leaves no issue, or father, or mother, or husband, her estate shall descend to her brothers and sisters and to the children of any deceased brother or sister by right of representation.

(d) Widow or husband. If the intestate leaves no issue or father, mother, brother, sister, or descendants of any deceased brother or sister, the estate shall descend to the intestate's widow, if any; or in the case the intestate is a woman, to her husband, if any.

(e) Otherwise, next of kin. If the intestate leaves none of such relatives surviving, nor widow, nor husband, the estate shall descend in equal shares to the next of kin in equal degree, but no person shall be entitled by right of representation to the shares of the next of kin who have died; provided, that if the estate comes through either parent of the deceased intestate, the brothers and sisters of that parent and their respective heirs shall be preferred to those of the other parent.[94]

IDAHO

PART I: INTESTATE SUCCESSION

15–2–101. Intestate estate.

Any part of the estate of a decedent not effectively disposed of by his will passes to his heirs as prescribed in the following sections of this code.

15–2–102. Share of the spouse.

The intestate share of the surviving spouse is as follows:

(a) As to separate property

(1) if there is no surviving issue or parent of the decedent, the entire intestate estate;

(2) if there is no surviving issue but the decedent is survived by a parent or parents, the first fifty thousand dollars ($50,000), plus one-half [1/2] of the balance of the intestate estate;

(3) if there are surviving issue all of whom are issue of the surviving spouse also, the first fifty thousand dollars ($50,000), plus one-half [1/2] of the balance of the intestate estate;

(4) if there are surviving issue one [1] or more of whom are not issue of the surviving spouse, one-half [1/2] of the intestate estate.

(b) As to community property

(1) the one-half [1/2] of community property which belongs to the decedent passes to the surviving spouse.

15–2–103. Share of heirs other than surviving spouse.

The part of the intestate estate not passing to the surviving spouse under Section 15–2–102 of this part, or the entire intestate estate if there is no surviving spouse, passes as follows:

(a) To the issue of the decedent; if they are all of the same degree of kinship to the decedent they take equally, but if of unequal degree, then those of more remote degree take by representation;

(b) If there is no surviving issue, to his parent or parents, equally;

(c) If there is no surviving issue or parent, to the issue of the parents or either of them by representation;

(d) If there is no surviving issue, parent, or issue of a parent, but the decedent is survived by one (1) or more grandparents or issue of grandparents, half of the estate passes to the paternal grandparents if both survive or to the surviving paternal grandparent, or to the issue of the paternal grandparents if both are deceased, the issue taking equally if they are all of the same degree of kinship to the decedent, but if of unequal degree, those of more remote degree take by representation; and the other half passes to the maternal relatives in the same manner; but if there be no surviving grandparent or issue of grandparents on either the paternal or the maternal side, the entire estate passes to the relatives on the other side in the same manner as the half.

15–2–104. Requirement that heir survive decedent for 120 hours.

Any person who fails to survive the decedent by one hundred twenty [120] hours is deemed to have predeceased the decedent for purposes of homestead allowance, exempt property, and intestate succession, and the decedent's heirs are determined accordingly. If the time of death of the decedent or of the person who would otherwise be an heir, or the times of death of both, cannot be determined, and it cannot be established that the person who would otherwise be an heir has survived the decedent by one hundred twenty [120] hours, it is deemed that the person failed to survive for the required period. This section is not to be applied where its application would result in a taking of intestate by the state under Section 15–2–105 of this part.

15–2–105. No taker.

If there is no taker under the provisions of this chapter, the intestate estate passes to the state of Idaho, subject to administration by the public administrator. After deducting the expenses of administration and causing these to be paid to the county in which such administration occurred, the public administrator shall file the report of abandoned property, required by Section 14–511, Idaho Code, and proceed to dispose of the property in the manner set forth in the "unclaimed property act," provided, however, that if such money is not claimed within eighteen hundred and twenty-seven [1827] days [approximately five (5) years] from the day upon which the property is paid to the state tax commission, it shall escheat to the state and be apportioned to the public school fund without regard to the provisions of said act.[95]

ILLINOIS

Section 2–1. Rules of descent and distribution.

The intestate real and personal estate of a resident decedent and the intestate real estate in this state of a non-resident decedent, after all just claims against his estate are fully paid, descends and shall be distributed as follows:

(a) If there is a surviving spouse and also a descendant of the decedent: 1/2 of the entire estate to the surviving spouse and 1/2 to the decedent's descendants per stirpes.

(b) If there is no surviving spouse but a descendant of the decedent: the entire estate to the decedent's descendants per stirpes.

(c) If there is a surviving spouse but no descendant of the decedent: the entire estate to the surviving spouse.

(d) If there is no surviving spouse or decendant but a parent, brother, sister, or descendant of a brother or sister of the decedent: the entire estate to the parents, brothers, and sisters of the decedent in equal parts, allowing to the surviving parent if one is dead a double portion and to the descendants of a deceased brother or sister per stirpes the portion which the deceased brother or sister would have taken if living.

(e) If there is no surviving spouse, descendant, parent, brother, sister, or descendant of a brother or sister of the decedent but a grandparent or descendant of a grandparent of the decedent: (1) 1/2 of the entire estate to the decedent's maternal grandparents in equal parts or to the survivor of them, or if there is none surviving, to their descendants per stirpes, and (2) 1/2 of the entire estate to the decedent's paternal grandparents in equal parts or to the survivor of them, or if there is none surviving, to their descendants per stirpes. If there is no surviving paternal grandparent or descendant of a paternal grandparent but a maternal grandparent or descendant of a maternal grandparent of the decedent: the entire estate to the decedent's maternal grandparents in equal parts or to the survivor of them, or if there is none surviving, to their descendants per stirpes. If there is no surviving maternal grandparent or descendant of a maternal grandparent, but a paternal grandparent or descendant of a paternal grandparent of the decedent: the entire estate to the decedent's paternal grandparents in equal parts or to the survivor of them, or if there is none surviving, to their descendants per stirpes.

(f) If there is no surviving spouse, descendant, parent, brother, sister, descendant of a brother or sister, or grandparent or descendant of a grandparent of the decedent: (1) 1/2 of the entire estate to the decedent's maternal great-grandparents in equal parts or to the survivor of them, or if there is none surviving, to their descendants per stirpes, and (2) 1/2 of the entire estate to the decedent's paternal great-grandparents in equal parts or to the survivor of them, or if their is none surviving, to their descendants per stirpes. If there is no surviving paternal great-grandparent or descendant of a maternal great-grandparent of the decedent: the entire estate to the decedent's maternal great-grandparents in equal parts or to the survivor of them, or if there is none surviving, to their descendants per stirpes. If there is no surviving maternal great-grandparent or descendant of a maternal great-grandparent, but a paternal great-grandparent or descendant of a paternal great-grandparent of the decedent: the entire estate of the decedent's paternal great-grandparents in equal parts or to the survivor of them, or if there is none surviving, to their descendants per stirpes.[96]

INDIANA

29–1–2–1 [6–201]. General rules of descent.

The net estate of a person dying intestate shall descend and be distributed as follows:

(a) Except as otherwise provided in subsection (b) hereof, the surviving spouse shall receive the following share:

(1) One-third [1/3] of the net estate if the intestate is survived by two [2] or more children, by one or more children and the issue of one or more deceased children, or by the issue of two [2] or more deceased children; or

(2) One-half [1/2] of the net estate if the intestate is survived by one [1] child or by the issue of one [1] deceased child; or

(3) Three-fourths [3/4] of the net estate, if there is no surviving issue but the intestate is survived by one [1] or both of his parents; or

(4) All of the net estate, if there is no surviving issue of parent.

(b) If the surviving spouse be a second or other subsequent spouse who did not at any time have children by the decedent, and the decedent left surviving him a child or children or the descendants of a child or children by a previous spouse, such surviving second or subsequent childless spouse shall take only a life estate in one-third [1/3] of the lands of the deceased spouse, and the fee thereof shall, at the decedent's death, vest at once in such child or children, or the descendants of such as may be dead, subject only to the life estate of surviving spouse. Such second or subsequent childless spouse shall, however, receive the same share of the personal property of the decedent as is provided in subsection (a) hereof with respect to surviving spouses generally.

(c) The share of the net estate not distributable to the surviving spouse, or the entire net estate if there is no surviving spouse, shall descend and be distributed as follows:

(1) To the issue of the intestate, if they are all of the same degree of kinship to the intestate, they shall take equally; or if of unequal degree, then those of more remote degree shall take by representation.

(2) If there is a surviving spouse but no surviving issue of the intestate, then to the surviving parents.

(3) If there is no surviving spouse or issue of the intestate, then to the surviving parents, brothers and sisters, and the issue of deceased brothers and sisters of the intestate. Each living parent of the intestate shall be treated as of the same degree as a brother or sister and shall be entitled to the same share as a brother or sister, provided, however, that the share of each parent shall be not less than one-fourth [1/4] of such net estate. Issue of deceased brothers and sisters shall take by representation.

(4) If there is no surviving parent or brother or sister of the intestate, then to the issue of brothers and sisters. If such distributees are all in the same degree of kinship to the intestate, they shall take equally or, if of unequal degree, then those of more remote degree shall take by representation.

(5) If there is no surviving issue, or parent of the intestate, or issue of a parent, then to the surviving grandparents of the intestate equally.

(6) If there is no surviving issue, or parent, or issue of a parent, or grandparent of the intestate, then the estate of the decedent shall be divided into that number of shares equal to the sum of (a) the number of brothers and sisters of the decedent's parents surviving the decedent plus (b) the number of deceased brothers and sisters of the decedent's parents leaving issue surviving both them

and the decedent, and one [1] of said shares shall pass to each of said brothers and sisters of the decedent's parents, or their respective issue, per stirpes.

(7) Where pursuant to this subsection (c), interests in real estate go to a husband and wife, the aggregate interests so descending shall be owned by them as tenants by the entireties. Interests in personal property so descending shall be owned as tenants in common.

(8) If there is no person mentioned in the preceding seven [7] parts of this subsection, then to the state of Indiana.

29–1–2–2 [6-202]. Inchoate interest of widow.

(a) Any interest acquired by a widow in the decedent's real estate, including contracts for the purchase of real estate, whether by descent or devise, not exceeding one-third [1/3] of said decedent's real estate, shall be received by her, free from all demands of creditors: Provided, however, That where the real estate exceeds in value ten thousand dollars [$10,000], the widow shall have one-fourth [1/4] only, and where the real estate exceeds twenty thousand dollars [$20,000], one-fifth [1/5] only, as against creditors.

(b) If the interest of the widow in the real estate of the decedent be liable to sale to satisfy a lien on such real estate, she shall be entitled to her share of the gross proceeds of the sale after satisfying such lien, insofar as the balance of said proceeds or other assets of the estate are sufficient therefor. The interest of a purchase-money mortgagee, of a mortgage under a mortgage executed prior to the marriage, or of a person holding a mortgage in which said widow has joined shall take precedence over the interest of the widow.

(c) Subsection (a) hereof shall not be construed to prevent the sale of such real estate under the provisions of this [probate] code, and in the event of such sale, the widow shall be entitled to the share provided for in this section out of the proceeds of such sale.

29–1–2–3 [6–203]. Inchoate interest of widow—How barred.

No act or conveyance, performed or executed by the husband without the assent of his wife, evidenced by her acknowledgment thereof in the manner acquired by law; nor any sale, disposition, transfer, or encumbrance of the husband's property, by virtue of any decree, execution, or mortgage to which she shall not be a party (except as provided otherwise by law), shall prejudice or extinguish the right of the wife to her third [1/3] of any real estate owned by him in fee simple during the marriage except to the extent that she may have, pursuant to sections 213 [29–1–2–13] or 306 [29–1–3–6] of this [probate] code, entered into a binding written contract, agreement, or waiver thereof, or preclude her from the recovery thereof, if otherwise entitled thereto.

29–1–2–4 [6–204]. Partial intestacy.

If part but not all of the estate of a decedent is validly disposed of by will, the part not disposed of by will shall be distributed as provided herein for intestate estates.[97]

IOWA

633.210: Rules of descent.

The estate of a person dying intestate shall descend as provided in Sections 633.211 through 633.226.

633.211: Share of surviving spouse if decedent left issue.

If the decedent dies intestate leaving a surviving spouse and leaving issue, the surviving spouse shall receive the following share:

1. One-third in value of all the legal or equitable estates in real property possessed by the decedent at any time during the marriage, which have not been sold on execution or other judicial sale, and to which the surviving spouse has made no relinquishment of his right.

2. All personal property that, at the time of death, was, in the hands of the decedent as the head of a family, exempt from execution.

3. One-third of all other personal property of the decedent which is not necessary for the payment of debts and charges.

4. If the property received by the surviving spouse under subsections one (1), two (2), and three (3) of this section is not equal in value to the sum of fifteen thousand dollars, then so much additional of the remaining real and personal property of the decedent that is subject to payment of debts and charges against the decedent's estate, after payment of such debts and charges, even to the extent of the whole of the net estate, as may be necessary to make the amount of fifteen thousand dollars.

633.212: Share of surviving spouse where decedent left no issue.

If the decedent dies intestate leaving a surviving spouse and leaving no issue, the surviving issue shall receive the following share:

1. One-third in value of all the legal or equitable estates in real property possessed by the decedent at any time during the marriage, which have not been sold on execution or other judicial sale, and to which the surviving spouse has made no relinquishment of his right.

2. All personal property that, at the time of death, was in the hands of the decedent as the head of a family, exempt from execution.

3. One-third of all other personal property of the decedent which is not necessary for the payment of debts and charges.

4. If the property received by the surviving spouse under subsections one (1) and three (3) of this section is not equal in value to the sum of fifteen thousand dollars, then so much additional of the non-exempt real and personal property of the decedent remaining after payment of the debts and charges against the estate, as may be necessary (even to the extent of the entire net estate) to make the amount of fifteen thousand dollars.

5. So much additional of the remaining real and personal property belonging to the decedent as is necessary to make the entire share of the surviving spouse, including the property received under subsections one (1), three (3), and four

(4) of this section, equal in value to the aforesaid sum of fifteen thousand dollars plus one-half of the net value of the estate over and above the sum of fifteen thousand dollars and the value of the exempt personal property.

633.218. Right of spouse to select property.

After such proceedings, and after payment of debts and charges, the surviving spouse shall have the right to select from the property so appraised, at its appraised value thus fixed, property equal in value to the amount to which she is entitled under section 633.211 or 633.212 which selection shall be in writing filed with the clerk of court.

633.219. Share of others than surviving spouse.

The portion of the estate remaining after the payment of the debts and charges, and not distributed to the surviving spouse, as provided in this code, or if there is no surviving spouse, then the remaining estate after payment of the debts and charges, shall descend and be distributed as follows:

1. In equal shares to the decedent's children, unless one or more of them is dead, in which case the issue of such deceased child shall inherit his or her share in accordance with the rules herein prescribed, in the same manner as though said child had outlived his parents.
2. If there is no person to take under subsection one (1) of this section, then to the surviving parents in equal shares; and if either parent is dead, the portion that would have gone to such deceased parent shall go to the survivor.
3. If there is no person to take under subsection one (1) or two (2) of this section, the portion uninherited shall go to such persons as would have been entitled to take if the parents of the decedent had outlived the intestate and had died in possession and ownership of the portion thus falling to their share, and so on, through their ascending ancestors and their heirs.
4. If heirs are not thus found under subsection one (1), two (2), or three (3) of this section, the portion uninherited shall go to the spouse of the intestate; and if the spouse is dead, then to the heirs of the spouse, according to like rules. If such intestate has had more than one spouse who either died or survived in lawful wedlock, it shall be equally divided between the one who is living and the heirs of those who are dead, or between the heirs of all such heirs, taking per stirpes and not per capita.
5. If there is no person who qualifies under either subsection one (1), two (2), three (3), or four (4) of this section, the intestate property shall escheat to the state of Iowa.[98]

KANSAS

59–502. Descent of property of intestate resident.

Subject to any homestead rights, the allowances provided in K.S.A. 59–403, and the payment of reasonable funeral expenses, expenses of last sickness, and costs of administration, taxes, and debts, the property of a resident decedent, who dies intestate, shall at the time of death pass by intestate succession as provided in this article.

59–504. Surviving spouse.

If the decedent leaves a spouse and no children or issue of a previously deceased child, all the decedent's property shall pass to the surviving spouse. If the decedent leaves a spouse and a child, children, or issue of a predeceased child or children, one-half of such property shall pass to the surviving spouse.

59–505. Same; half of realty to surviving spouse.

Also, the surviving spouse shall be entitled to receive one-half of all the real estate of which the decedent at any time during the marriage was seized or possessed and to the disposition whereof the survivor shall not have consented in writing, or by a will, or by an election as provided by law to take under a will, except such real estate as has been sold on execution or judicial sale, or taken by other legal proceeding: Provided, That the surviving spouse shall not be entitled to any interest under the provisions of this section in any real estate of which such decedent in his or her lifetime made a conveyance, when such spouse at the time of the conveyance was not a resident of this state and never had been during the existence of the marriage relation.

59–506. Surviving children or issue.

If the decedent leaves a child, or children, or issue of a previously deceased child or children, and no spouse, all his or her property shall pass to the surviving child, or in equal shares to the surviving children and the living issue, if any, of a previously deceased child, but such issue shall collectively take only the share their parent would have taken had such parent been living. If the decedent leaves such child, children, or issue, and a spouse, one-half of such property shall pass to such child, children, and issue as aforesaid.

59–507. No spouse, child, or issue of the decedent.

If the decedent leaves no surviving spouse, child, or issue but leaves a surviving parent or surviving parents, all of his or her property shall pass to such surviving parent, or in equal shares to such surviving parents, but if the decedent is an adopted child such property shall pass to his or her adoptive parent or parents in like manner including a natural parent who is the spouse of an adoptive parent.

59–508. No spouse, child, issue, or parents.

If the decedent leaves no surviving spouse, child, issue, or parents, the respective shares of his or her property which would have passed to the parents, had both of them been living, shall pass to the heirs of such parents respectively (excluding their respective spouses), the same as it would have passed had such parents owned it in equal shares and died intestate at the time of his or her death; but if either of said parents left no such heirs, then and in that event his or her property shall pass to the living heirs of the other parent.

59–514. Intestate descent; escheat, when.

If an intestate decedent leaves no person entitled to receive property of the decedent as said intestate's heirs under the provisions of K.S.A.

59–503 to 59–513, both sections inclusive, and acts amendatory thereof or supplemental thereto.

Then and in that event said intestate's property shall pass to the living heirs of the intestate's last spouse dying prior to the death of the intestate and if there be no such heir or heirs, then the estate shall escheat to and become the property of the state.[99]

KENTUCKY

391.010. Descent of real estate.

When a person having right or title to any real estate or inheritance dies intestate as to such estate, it shall descend in common to his kindred, male and female, in the following order, except as otherwise provided in this chapter:

(1) To his children and their descendants; if there are none, then

(2) To his father and mother, if both are living, one (1) moiety each; but if the father is dead, the mother, if living, shall take the whole estate; if the mother is dead, the whole estate shall pass to the father; if there is no father or mother, then

(3) To his brothers and sisters and their descendants; if there are none, then

(4) To the husband or wife of the intestate; if there are none surviving, then

(5) One (1) moiety of the estate shall pass to the paternal and the other to the maternal kindred, in the following order:

(a) the grandfather and grandmother equally, if both are living; but if one is dead, the entire moiety shall go to the survivor; if there is no grandfather or grandmother, then

(b) To the uncles and aunts and their descendants; if there are none, then

(c) To the great-grandfathers and great-grandmothers, in the same manner prescribed for grandfather and grandmother by subsection (a); if there are none, then

(d) To the brothers and sisters of the grandfathers and grandmothers and their descendants; and so on in other cases without end, passing to the nearest lineal ancestors and their descendants.

(6) If there is no such kindred to one of the parents as is described in subsection (5), the whole to go to the kindred of the other. If there is neither paternal nor maternal kindred, the whole shall go to the kindred of the husband or wife, as if he or she survived the intestate and died entitled to the estate.

391–020. Descent of real estate acquired from parent.

(1) When a person dies intestate and without issue, owning real estate of inheritance which is the gift of either of his parents, the parent who made the gift, if living, shall inherit the whole of such estate.

(2) If a person under the age of eighteen (18) dies without issue, having the title to real estate derived by gift, devise, or descent from one (1) of his parents, the whole shall descend to that parent and that parent's kindred, and if there is none, then in like manner to the other parent and his kindred. The kindred of one parent shall not be so excluded by the kindred of the other parent, if the latter is more remote than the grandfather, grandmother, uncles and aunts of the intestate, and their descendants.

391.030. Descent of personal property—Exemption for surviving spouse and children—Withdrawal of money from bank by surviving spouse.

(1) Except as otherwise provided in this chapter, where any person dies intestate as to his personal estate, or any part thereof, the surplus, after payment of funeral expenses, charges of administration, and debts, shall pass and be distributed among the same persons, and in the proportions, to whom and in which real estate is directed to descend, except as follows:

(a) The personal estate of an infant shall be distributed as if he had died after full age.

(b) An alien may be distributee as though he were a citizen.

(c) Personal property or money on hand or in bank to the amount of seven thousand five hundred dollars ($7,500) shall be exempt from distribution and sale and shall be set apart by the district court having jurisdiction over the estate on application to the surviving spouse, or, if there is no surviving spouse, to the children surviving.

(2) The surviving spouse of any deceased person may, at any time before the property or money is set apart by the court, procure on petition from the judge of the district court having jurisdiction over administration of his estate an order authorizing him to withdraw from any bank or other depository not exceeding one thousand dollars ($1,000) belonging to the estate of the deceased. Upon presentation of the order, the bank or depository shall permit him to withdraw the sum and shall lodge the order, endorsing thereon the amount withdrawn, with the circuit clerk, and he shall retain it in his files to be considered in connection with further proceedings in the estate, and the withdrawal shall be treated as a charge against the property of the estate exempt from distribution.

(3) In the application for the setting apart of property or money under this section the surviving spouse or, if there is no surviving spouse, the children may make their selection out of the personal property of the estate to the extent that the value of the property selected does not exceed the amount of seven thousand five hundred dollars ($7,500).[100]

LOUISIANA

SECTION 1. GENERAL RULES

Art. 886. Intestate or legal succession.

If there is no testatment or institution of heir, or if the institution is null or without effect, the succession is then open in favor of the legitimate heirs by the mere operation of law.

Art. 887. Classes of legal heirs.

There are three classes of legal heirs, to wit:

The children and other lawful descendants;

The fathers and mothers and other lawful ascendants;

And the collateral kindred.

Art. 888. Inheritance by nearest heir.

The nearest relation in the descending, ascending, or collateral line, conformable to the rules hereafter established, is called to the legal succession.

Art. 890. Direct and collateral consanguinity.

The series of degrees forms the line; the series of degrees between persons who descend from one another is called direct or lineal consanguinity, and the series of degrees between persons who do not descend from one another, but spring from a common ancestor, is called the collateral line or collateral consanguinity.

The direct line is divided into a direct line descending and a direct line ascending. The first is that which connects the ancestor with those who descend from him; the second is that which connects a person with those from whom he descends.

Art. 891. Direct line; degrees of relationship.

In the direct line there are as many degrees as there are generations. Thus the son is with regard to the father, in the first degree, the grandson in the second, and vice versa with regard to the father and grandfather towards the sons and grandsons.

Art. 892. Collateral line; degrees of relationship.

In the collateral line the degrees are counted by the generations from one of the relations up to the common ancestor exclusively and from the common ancestor to the other relations.

Thus brothers are related in the second degree; uncle and nephew in the third degree; cousins german in the fourth; and so on.

SECTION 2. OF REPRESENTATION

Art. 895. Representation in direct descending line.

Representation takes place ad infinitum in the direct descending line.

It is admitted in all cases, whether the children of the deceased concur with the descendants of the predeceased child, or whether all the children having died before him, the descendants of the children be in equal or unequal degrees of relationship to the deceased.

Art. 896. Representation of ascendants not admissible.

Representation does not take place in favor of the ascendants, the nearest relation in any degree always excluding those of a degree superior or more remote.

Art. 897. Representation in collateral line.

In the collateral line, representation is admitted in favor of the children and descendants of the brothers and sisters of the deceased, whether they come to the succession in concurrence with the uncles and aunts, or whether, the brothers and sisters of the deceased having died, the succession devolves on their descendants in equal or unequal degrees.

Art. 898. Basis of partition in cases of representation.

In all cases in which representation is admitted, the partition is made by roots; if one root has produced several branches, the subdivision is also made by roots in each branch, and the members of the branch take between them by heads.

Art. 900. Representation of decedent whose succession was renounced.

One who has renounced the succession of another may still enjoy the right of representation with respect to that other.

Thus it is not necessary that the children who succeed by representation should have been heirs of their father and mother. Although they should have renounced their succession, they are nevertheless competent to represent them in the succession of their grandfather or other ascendants.

Art. 901. Representation of disinherited or unworthy person.

When a person has been disinherited by his father or mother, or excluded from his succession for unworthiness, his children cannot represent him in the succession of their grandfather or other ascendants, if he is alive at the time of the opening of the succession, but they can represent him if he died before.

SECTION 3. OF SUCCESSIONS FALLING TO DESCENDANTS

Art. 902. Inheritance rights of children and grandchildren.

Legitimate children of their descendants inherit from their father and mother, grandfathers, or other ascendants, without distinction of sex or primogeniture, and though they may be born from different marriages.

They inherit in equal portions and by heads, when they are in the same degree, and inherit by their own right; they inherit by roots, when all or part of them inherit by representation.

SECTION 4. OF SUCCESSIONS FALLING TO ASCENDANTS

Art. 903. Inheritance by parents sharing with brothers and sisters.

If any one dies leaving no descendants, but a father and mother and brothers and sisters, or descendants of these last, the succession is divided into two equal portions, one of which goes to the father and mother, who divide it equally between them, the other to the brothers and sisters of the deceased, or their descendants, as is prescribed in the following section.

Art. 904. Inheritance by surviving father or mother sharing with brothers and sisters.

If the father or mother of the person who has died without issue has died before him, the portion which would have been inherited by such deceased parent, according to the terms of the preceding article, will go to the brothers and sisters of the deceased, or to their descendants, in the manner directed by the following section.

Art. 905. Inheritance by ascendants other than parents.

If the deceased has left neither descendants nor brother nor sister, nor descendants from them, nor father nor mother, but only other ascendants, these ascendants inherit the succession to the exclusion of all the collaterals, in conformity with the dispositions of the articles which follow.

Art. 906. Paternal and maternal ascendants in same degree.

If there are ascendants in the paternal and materal lines in the same degree, the estate is divided into two equal shares, one of which goes to the ascendants on the paternal and the other to the ascendants on the maternal side, whether the number of ascendants, on each side, be equal or not. In this case, the ascendants, in each line, inherit by heads.

Art. 908. Ascendant's right to inherit immovables donated to decedent.

Ascendants, to the exclusion of all others, inherit the immovables given by them to their children or their descendants of a more remote degree who died without posterity, when these objects are found in the succession.

If these objects have been alienated, and the price is yet due in whole or in part, the ascendants have the right to receive the price. They also succeed to the right of reversion on the happening of any event which the child or descendant may have inserted, as a condition in his favor, in disposing of those objects.

Art. 909. Ascendant's right to inherit dowry given to decedent.

Ascendants have also the right to take from the succession of their child or descendant who dies without issue the dowry they may have settled in money upon him.

Art. 910. Reversion of property subject to encumbrances and succession debts.

Ascendants inheriting the things mentioned in the preceding articles, which they have given their children or descendants who die without issue, take them subject to all the mortages which the donee may have imposed on them during his life.

Also ascendants exercising the right of reversion are bound to contribute to the payment of the debts of the succession, in proportion to the value of the objects given.

SECTION 5. OF THE SUCCESSION OF COLLATERALS

Art. 911. Inheritance by brothers and sisters sharing with parents.

If a person dies, leaving no descendants, and his father and mother survive, his brothers and sisters, or their descendants, only inherit half of his succession.

If the father or the mother only survive, the brothers and sisters, or their descendants, inherit three-fourths of his succession.

Art. 912. Inheritance by brother and sisters in absence of parents.

If a person dies, leaving no descendants or father or mother, his brothers and sisters, or their descendants, inherit the whole succession to the exclusion of the ascendants and other collaterals.

Art. 913. Brothers and sisters; whole blood and half blood.

The partition of the half, the three-fourths, or the whole of a succession falling to brothers and sisters, as mentioned in two preceding articles, is made in equal portions, if they are all of the same marriage; if they are of different marriages, the succession is equally divided between the paternal and maternal lines of the deceased; the german brothers and sisters take a part in the two lines, the paternal and maternal brothers and sisters take a part in the two lines, the paternal and maternal brothers and sisters, each in their respective lines only; if there are brothers and sisters on one side only, they inherit the whole succession to the exclusion of all other relations of the other line.

In all these cases, the brothers and sisters of the deceased, or their descendants, inherit in their own right or by representation, as is regulated in the section which treats of representation.

Art. 915. Community property; inheritance rights of descendants, surviving spouse, and parents.

When either husband or wife shall die, leaving neither a father nor mother nor descendants, and without having disposed by last will and testament of his or her share of the community property, such undisposed of share shall be inherited by the surviving spouse in full ownership. In the event the deceased leave descendants, his or her share in the community estate shall be inherited by such descendants in the manner provided by law. Should the deceased leave no descendants, but a father and mother, or either, then the share of the deceased in the community estate shall be divided in two equal portions, one of which shall go to the father and mother of the survivor of them, and the other portion shall go to the surviving spouse, who, together with father and mother inheriting in the absence of descendants, as provided above, shall inherit as a legal heir by operation of law, and with the necessity of compliance with the forms of law provided in this chapter for the placing of irregular heirs in possession of the successions to which they are called.

Art. 916. Community property; surviving spouse's usufruct on decedent's share inherited by common issue.

If the deceased spouse is survived by descendants and shall not have disposed by testament of his share in the community property, the surviving spouse shall have a legal usufruct over so much of that share as may be inherited by the descendants. This usufruct terminates when the surviving spouse contracts another marriage, unless confirmed by testament for life or for a shorter period.

The deceased may by testament grant a usufruct for life or for a shorter period to the surviving spouse over all or part of his separate property.

A usufruct authorized by this article is to be treated as a legal usufruct and is not an impingement upon legitime.

If the usufruct authorized by this article affects the rights of heirs other than children of the marriage between the deceased and the surviving spouse or affects separate property, security may be requested by the naked owner.[101]

MAINE

Section 2–101. Intestate estate.

Any part of the estate of a decedent not effectively disposed of by his will passes to his heirs as prescribed in the following sections of this code.

Section 2–102. Share of the spouse.

The intestate share of the surviving spouse is:

(1) If there is no surviving issue or parent of the decedent, the entire intestate estate;

(2) If there is no surviving issue but the decedent is survived by a parent or parents, the first $50,000, plus 1/2 of the balance of the intestate estate;

(3) If there are surviving issue all of whom are issue of the surviving spouse also, the first $50,000, plus 1/2 of the balance of the intestate estate;

(4) If there are surviving issue one or more of whom are not issue of the surviving spouse, 1/2 of the intestate estate.

Section 2–103. Share of heirs other than surviving spouse.

The part of the intestate estate not passing to the surviving spouse under Section 2–102, or the entire estate if there is no surviving spouse, passes as follows:

(1) To the issue of the decedent; to be distributed per capita at each generation as defined in Section 2–106;

(2) If there is no surviving issue, to the decedent's parent or parents equally;

(3) If there is no surviving issue or parent, to the issue of the parents or either of them to be distributed per capita at each generation as defined in Section 2–106.

(4) If there is no surviving issue, parent, or issue of a parent, but the decedent is survived by one or more grandparents or issue of grandparents, half of the estate passes to the paternal grandparents if both survive or to the issue of the

paternal grandparents if both are deceased to be distributed per capita at each generation as defined in Section 2–106; and the other half passes to the maternal relatives in the same manner; but if there be no surviving grandparent or issue of grandparents on either the paternal or maternal side, the entire estate passes to the relatives on the other side in the same manner as the half.

(5) If there is no surviving issue, parent or issue of a parent, grandparent or issue of a grandparent, but the decedent is survived by one or more great-grandparents or issue of great-grandparents, half of the estate passes to the paternal great-grandparents who survive, or to the issue of the paternal great-grandparents if all are deceased, to be distributed per capita at each generation as defined in Section 2-106; and the other half passes to the maternal relatives in the same manner; but if there is no surviving great-grandparent or issue of a great-grandparent on either the paternal or maternal side, the entire estate passes to the relatives on the other side in the same manner as the half.

Section 2-106. Per capita at each generation.

If per capita at each generation representation is called for by this code, the estate is divided into as many shares as there are surviving heirs in the nearest degree of kinship which contains any surviving heirs and deceased persons in the same degree who left issue who survived the decedent. Each surviving heir in the nearest of degree which contains any surviving heir is allocated one share, and the remainder of the estate is divided in the same manner as if the heirs already allocated a share and their issue had predeceased the decedent.[102]

MARYLAND

Section 3-101. Order of distribution of net intestate estate.

Any part of the net estate of a decedent not effectively disposed of by his will shall be distributed by the personal representative to the heirs of the decedent in the order prescribed in this subtitle.

Section 3-102. Share of surviving spouse.

(a) General. The share of a surviving spouse shall be as provided in this section.

(b) Surviving minor child. If there is a surviving minor child, the share shall be one half.

(c) No surviving minor child, but surviving issue. If there is no surviving issue or parent, the share shall be the whole estate.

(d) No surviving issue, but surviving parent. If there is no surviving issue but a surviving parent, the share shall be the first $15,000 plus one-half of the residue.

(e) No surviving issue or parent. If there is no surviving issue or parent, the share shall be the whole estate.

(f) Calculation of net estate. For the purposes of this section, the net estate shall be calculated without a deduction for the tax as defined in Section 11-109.

Section 3-103. Division among surviving issue.

The net estate, exclusive of the share of the surviving spouse, or the entire net estate if there is no surviving spouse, shall be divided equally among the surviving issue, by representation as defined in Section 1-210.

Section 3-104. Distribution when there is no surviving issue.

(a) General. If there is no surviving issue the net estate exclusive of the share of the surviving spouse, or the entire net estate if there is no surviving spouse, shall be distributed by the personal representative pursuant to the provisions of this section.

(b) Parents and their issue. It shall be distributed to the surviving parents equally, or if only one parent survives, to the survivor; or if neither parent survives, to the issue of the parents, by representation.

(c) Grandparents and their issue. If there is no surviving parent or issue of a parent, it shall be distributed one-half to the surviving paternal grandparents equally, or if only one paternal grandparent survives, to the survivor, or if neither paternal grandparent survives, to the issue of the paternal grandparents, by representation, and one-half to the surviving maternal grandparents equally, or if only one maternal grandparent survives, to the survivor, or if neither maternal grandparent survives, to the issue of the maternal grandparents, by representation. In the event that neither of one pair of grandparents and none of the issue of either of that pair survives, the one-half share applicable shall be distributed to the other pair of grandparents, the survivor of them or the issue of either of them, in the same manner as prescribed for their half share.

(d) Great-grandparents and their issue. If there is no surviving parent or issue of a parent, or surviving grandparent or issue of a grandparent, it shall be distributed one-quarter to each pair of great-grandparents equally or all to the survivor, or if neither survives, all to the issue of either or of both of that pair of great-grandparents, by representation. In the event that neither member of a pair of great-grandparents nor any issue of either of that pair survives, the quarter share applicable shall be distributed equally among the remaining pairs of great-grandparents or the survivor of a pair or issue of either of a pair of great-grandparents, in the same manner as prescribed for a quarter share.

(e) No surviving blood relative. If there is no surviving blood relative entitled to inherit under this section, it shall be divided into as many equal shares as there are stepchildren of the decedent who survive the decedent and stepchildren of the decedent who did not survive the decedent but of whom issue did survive the decedent. Each stepchild of the decedent who did survive the decedent shall receive one share and the issue of each stepchild of the decedent who did not survive the decedent but of whom issue did survive the decedent shall receive one share apportioned by applying the pattern of representation set forth in Section 1-210. As used in this subsection, "stepchild" shall mean the child of any spouse of the decedent if such spouse was not divorced from the decedent.

Section 3-105. Escheat.

(a) General. If there is no person entitled to take under Sections 3-102 through 3-104, the net estate shall be converted to cash and paid to the board of education in the county in which the letters were granted and shall be applied for the use of the public schools in the county.

(b) Refund. After payment has been made to the board of education, if a claim for refund is filed by a relative within the third degree living at the death of the decedent or by the personal representative of the relative, and the claim is allowed, the claimant shall be entitled to a refund, without interest, of the sum paid.

Section 3-110. Certain heirs not surviving decedent for 30 days.

If a descendant, ancestor, or descendant of an ancestor of the decedent fails to survive the decedent by 30 full days, he shall be considered to have predeceased the decedent for purposes of intestate succession and is not to be entitled to the rights of an heir. If the time of death of the decedent or of the descendant, ancestor, or descendant of an ancestor of the decedent, who would otherwise be an heir, or the times of death of both cannot be determined, so that it cannot be established that he has survived the decedent by 30 full days, that person shall not be considered to have survived for the required period.

Section 3-201. Family allowance.

(a) Amount of allowance. The surviving spouse is entitled to receive an allowance of $2,000 for his personal use, and an additional allowance of $1,000 for the use of each unmarried child of the decedent who has not attained the age of 18 years at the time of the death of the decedent. Upon receipt of an allowance for an unmarried child under 18 years of age of the decedent who is not also a child of the surviving spouse, the surviving spouse shall distribute that allowance as provided in Section 13-501 of this article.

(b) Tax exemption. The allowance, which is available in both testate and intestate estates, is exempt from the Maryland inheritance tax.

Section 3-203. Right to elective share.

(a) General. Instead of property left to him by will, the surviving spouse may elect to take the share which he might take in intestacy under Section 3-102.

(b) Limitation. The surviving spouse who makes this election may not take more than the share described in Section 3-102.

Section 3-204. Right of election personal to surviving spouse.

The right of election to the surviving spouse is personal to him. It is not transferable and cannot be exercised subsequent to his death. If the surviving spouse is under 18 years of age or under disability, the election may be exercised by order of the court having jurisdiction of the person or property of the spouse or person under disability.

Section 3-205. Waiver of rights in decedent's estate.

The right of election of a surviving spouse may be waived before or after marriage by a written contract, agreement, or waiver signed by the party waiving the right of election. Unless it provides to the contrary, a waiver of "all rights" in the property or estate of a present or prospective spouse, or a complete property settlement entered into after or in anticipation of separation or divorce, is a waiver of any right to his family allowance as well as to his elective share by each spouse in the property of the spouse, his right to letters under Section 5-104, and is an irrevocable renunciation of any benefit which would pass to him from the other by intestate succession, by statutory share, or by virtue of the provisions of a will executed before the waiver of property settlement.

Section 3-208. Effect of election upon will.

(a) No benefits under will. Upon the election of the surviving spouse to take his intestate share of the property of the decedent, all property or other benefits which would have passed to the surviving spouse under the will shall be treated as if the surviving spouse had died before the execution of the will. The surviving spouse and a person claiming through him may not receive property under the will.

(b) Contribution to payment of intestate share of surviving spouse. If there is an election to take an intestate share, contribution to the payment of it shall be prorated among all legatees. Instead of contributing an interest in specific property to the intestate share, a legatee may pay the surviving spouse in cash, or other property acceptable to the spouse, an amount equal to the fair market value of the interest in specific property on the date the election to take an intestate share was made by the spouse. Unless specifically provided in the will, a legatee is not entitled to sequestration or compensation from another legatee, or from another part of the estate of the decedent, except that an interest renounced by the surviving spouse and not included in the share of the net estate received by the surviving spouse under this section may be subject to sequestration for the benefit of individuals who are the natural objects of the bounty of the decedent, in order to avoid a substantial distortion of the intended dispositions of the testator.[103]

MASSACHUSETTS

Chapter 190, Section 1: Spouse's share of property not disposed of by will.

A surviving husband or wife shall, after the payment of the debts of the deceased and the charges of his last sickness and funeral and of the settlement of his estate, and subject to chapter one hundred and ninety-six, be entitled to the following share in his real and personal property not disposed of by will:

(1) If the deceased leaves kindred and no issue, and it appears on determination by the probate court, as hereinafter provided, that the whole estate does not exceed twenty-five thousand dollars in value, the surviving husband or wife shall take the whole thereof; otherwise such survivor shall take twenty-five thousand dollars and one half of the remaining personal and one half of the remaining

real property. If the personal property is insufficient to pay said twenty-five thousand dollars, the deficiency shall, upon the petition of any party in interest, be paid from the sale or mortgage, in the manner provided for the payment of debts or legacies, of any interest of the deceased in real property which he could have conveyed at the time of his death; and the surviving husband or wife shall be permitted, subject to the approval of the court, to purchase at any such sale, notwithstanding the fact that he or she is the administrator of the estate of the deceased person. A further sale or mortgage of any real estate of the deceased may later be made to provide for the deficiency still remaining. Whenever it shall appear, upon petition to the probate court of any party in interest, and after such notice as the court shall order, and after a hearing thereon, that the whole amount of the estate of the deceased, as found by the inventory and upon such other evidence as the court shall deem necessary, does not exceed the sum of twenty-five thousand dollars over and above the amount necessary to pay the debts and charges of administration, the court shall itself by decree determine the value of said estate, which decree shall be binding upon all parties. If additional property is later discovered, the right or title to the estate covered by such decree shall not be affected thereby, but the court may take such further orders and decrees as are necessary to effect the distribution herein provided for.

(2) If the deceased leaves issue, the survivor shall take one third of the personal and one third of the real property.

(3) If the deceased leaves no issue and no kindred, the survivor shall take the whole.

Chapter 190, Section 2: Distribution of personal property.

The personal property of a deceased person not lawfully disposed of by will shall, after the payment of his debts and the charges of his last sickness and funeral and of the settlement of the estate, and subject to the preceding section and to chapter one hundred and ninety-six, be distributed among the persons and in the proportions hereinafter prescribed for the descent of real property.

Chapter 190, Section 3: Descent of land, tenements, or hereditaments.

When a person dies seized of land, tenements, or hereditaments, or of any right thereto, or entitled to any interest therein, in fee simple or for the life of another, not having lawfully devised the same, they shall descend, subject to his debts and to the rights of the husband or wife and minor children of the deceased as provided in this and in the two preceding chapters and in chapter one hundred and ninety-six, as follows:

(1) In equal shares to his children and to the issue of any deceased child by right of representation; and if there is no surviving child of the intestate, then to all his other lineal descendants. If all such descendants are in the same degree of kindred to the intestate, they shall share the estate equally; otherwise, they shall take according to the right of representation.

(2) If he leaves no issue, in equal shares to his father and mother.

(3) If he leaves no issue and no mother, to his father.

(4) If he leaves no issue and no father, to his mother.

(5) If he leaves no issue and no father or mother, to his brothers and sisters and to the issue of any deceased brother or sister by right of representation; and, if there is no surviving brother or sister of the intestate, to all the issue of his deceased brothers and sisters. If all such issue are in the same degree of kindred to the intestate, they shall share the estate equally, otherwise, according to the right of representation.

(6) If he leaves no issue, and no father, mother, brother, or sister, and no issue of any deceased brother or sister, then to his next of kin in equal degree; but if there are two or more collateral kindred in equal degree claiming through different ancestors, those claiming through the nearest ancestor shall be preferred to those claiming through an ancestor more remote.

(7) If an intestate leaves no kindred and no widow or husband, his estate shall escheat to the commonwealth.[104]

MICHIGAN

Section 104. Intestate Succession.

Any part of the estate of a decedent not effectively disposed of by his will passes to his heirs or the state as prescribed in Sections 105 to 113.

Section 105. Surviving spouse; intestate share.

The intestate share of the surviving spouse shall be 1 of the following:

(a) If there is not a surviving issue or parent of the decedent, the entire intestate estate.

(b) If there is not a surviving issue but the decedent is survived by at least 1 parent, the first $60,000.00 which shall be reduced in case of partial intestacy by any amount given the spouse by will, plus 1/2 of the balance of the intestate estate.

(c) If there are surviving issue all of whom are issue of the surviving spouse also, the first $60,000.00 plus 1/2 of the balance of the intestate estate.

(d) If there are surviving issue, 1 or more of whom are not the issue of the surviving spouse, 1/2 of the intestate estate.

Section 106. Intestate share of kindred; escheat.

The part of the intestate estate not passing to the surviving spouse under Section 105 or the entire intestate estate if there is not a surviving spouse shall pass as follows:

(a) To the issue of the decedent. If they are all in the same degree of kinship to the decedent, they shall take equally, but if of unequal degree, then those of more remote degrees take by representation.

(b) If there is no surviving issue, to his or her surviving parents equally.

(c) If there is no surviving issue or parent, to the brothers and sisters and children of deceased brothers and sisters of the decedent. If they are all in the same degree of kinship to the decedent, they shall take equally, but if of unequal degree, then those of more remote degree take by representation.

(d) If there is no surviving issue, parent, brothers or sisters, or children of deceased brothers and sisters of a decedent, but the decedent is survived by 1 or more grandparents or issue of grandparents, 1/2 of the estate shall pass to the surviving paternal grandparents, or to the issue of the paternal grandparents if both are deceased, the issue to take equally if they are all of the same degree of kinship to the decedent, but if of unequal degree, then those of more remote degree shall be excluded; and the other 1/2 shall pass to the maternal relatives in the same manner; but if there is no surviving grandparents or issue of grandparents on the paternal or maternal side, the entire estate shall pass to the relatives on the other side in the same manner as the 1/2.

(e) If an eligible survivor is not then known or determinable to take under subdivisions (a) to (d), then to the state by escheat.[105]

MINNESOTA

Section 525.13. Estate.

As used in Sections 525.13 to 525.173, the word "estate" includes every right and interest of a decedent in property, real or personal, except such as are terminated or otherwise extinguished by his death.

Section 525.145. Descent of homestead.

(1) Where there is a surviving spouse the homestead, including a manufactured home which is the family residence, shall descend free from any testamentary or other disposition thereof to which the spouse has not consented in writing or by election to take under the will as provided by law, as follows:

(a) If there be no surviving child or issue of any deceased child, to the spouse;

(b) If there be children or issue of deceased children surviving, then to the spouse for the term of the spouse's natural life and the remainder in equal shares to the children and the issue of deceased children by right of representation.

(2) Where there is no surviving spouse and the homestead has not been disposed of by will, it shall descend as other real estate.

(3) Where the homestead passes by descent or will to the spouse or children or issue of deceased children, it shall be exempt from all debts which were not valid charges thereon at the time of decedent's death; except that the homestead shall be subject to a claim filed pursuant to Section 246.53 for state hospital care or 256B.15 for medical assistance benefits. If the homestead passes to a person other than a spouse or child or issue of a deceased child, it shall be subject to the payment of the items mentioned in Section 525.16. No lien or other charge against any homestead which is so exempted shall be enforced in the probate court, but the claimant may enforce the lien or charge by an appropriate action in the district court.

Section 525.15. Allowances to spouse.

When any person dies, testate or intestate,

(1) The surviving spouse shall be allowed from the personal property of which the decedent was possessed or to which he was entitled at the time of his death, the wearing apparel, and, as selected by him, furniture and household goods not exceeding $6,000 in value and other personal property not exceeding $3,000 in value;

(2) When, except for one automobile, all of the personal estate of the decedent is allowed to the surviving spouse by clause (1), the surviving spouse shall also be allowed such automobile;

(3) If there is no surviving spouse, the minor children shall receive the property specified in clause (1) as selected in their behalf;

(4) During administration, but not exceeding 18 months, unless an extension shall have been granted by the court, or, if the estate be insolvent, not exceeding 12 months, the spouse or children, or both, constituting the family of the decedent shall be allowed reasonable maintenance;

(5) In the administration of an estate of a nonresident decedent, the allowances received in the domiciliary administration shall be deducted from the allowances under this section.

Section 525.16. Descent of property.

Except as provided in Sections 525.14 and 525.145, and subject to the allowances provided in Section 525.15 and the payment of the expenses of administration, funeral expenses, expenses of last illness, taxes, and debts, the estate, real and personal, shall descend and be distributed as follows:

(1) Personal property: To the surviving spouse, one-third thereof free from any testamentary disposition thereof to which such survivor shall not have consented in writing or by election to take under the will as provided by law;

(2) Real property: To the surviving spouse, an undivided one-third of all real property of which the decedent at any time while married to such spouse was seized or possessed, to the disposition whereof by will or otherwise such survivor shall not have consented in writing or by election to take under the will as provided by law, except such as has been transferred or sold by judicial partition proceedings or appropriated to the payment of the decedent's debts by execution or judicial sale, by general assignment for the benefit of creditors, or by insolvency or bankruptcy proceedings, and subject to all judgment liens;

(3) If only a spouse, or a spouse and only one child or the issue of a deceased child survive, the share of the spouse under the provisions of clauses (1) and (2) shall be one-half instead of one-third;

(4) Subject to the preceding provisions of this section, the whole estate, real and personal, except as otherwise disposed of by will shall descend and be distributed as follows:

(a) In equal shares to the surviving children and to the issue of deceased children by right of representation;

(b) If there be no surviving child or issue of any deceased child, and if the intestate leave a surviving spouse, then to such spouse;

(c) If there be no surviving issue or spouse, then to the father and mother in equal shares, or if but one survives, then to such survivor;

(d) If there be no surviving issue, spouse, father, or mother, then in equal shares to the surviving brothers and sisters and to the issue of deceased brothers and sisters by right of representation; and if there be no surviving brothers or sisters, then in equal shares to the issue of deceased brothers and sisters if all are of equal degree and, if not, then in equal shares to those in the nearest degree and by right of representation to those in a more remote degree;

(e) If there be no surviving issue, spouse, father, mother, brother, sister, or issue of any deceased brother or sister, then in equal shares to the next of kin in equal degree, except that when there are two or more collateral kindred in equal degree claiming through different ancestors, those who claim through the nearest ancestor shall take to the exclusion of those claiming through an ancestor more remote.

(5) If a minor die leaving no spouse or issue surviving, all of his estate that came to him by inheritance or will from his parent shall descend and be distributed to the other children of the same parent, if any, and to the issue of any deceased child of such parent in equal shares if all are of equal degree and, if not, then in equal shares to those in the nearest degree and by right of representation to those in a more remote degree; failing all such, it shall descend and be distributed by intestate succession as in other cases;

(6) If the intestate leave no spouse or kindred, the estate shall escheat to the state.

Section 525.161. No surviving spouse or kindred; notices to attorney general.

When it appears from the petition or application for administration of the estate, or otherwise, in a proceeding in the court that the intestate left surviving no spouse or kindred, the court shall give notice of such fact and notice of all subsequent proceedings in such estate to the attorney general forthwith; and the attorney general shall protect the interests of the state during the course of administration. The residue which escheats to the state shall be transmitted to the attorney general. All moneys, stocks, bonds, notes, mortgages and other securities, and all other personal property so escheated shall then be given into the custody of the state treasurer, who shall notify the commissioner of finance thereof and immediately credit the moneys received to the general fund. The treasurer shall hold such stocks, bonds, notes, mortgages and other securities, and all other personal property, subject to such investment, sale, or other disposition as the state board of investment may direct pursuant to Section 11A.04(9). The attorney general shall immediately report to the state executive council all real property received in the individual escheat, and any sale or disposition of such real estate shall be made in accordance with Sections 94.09 to 94.16.[106]

MISSISSIPPI

Section 91-1-1. What law to govern.

All personal property situated in this state shall descend and be distributed according to the laws of this state regulating the descent and distribution of such property, regardless of all marital rights which may have accrued in other states, and notwithstanding the domicile of the deceased may have been in another state, and whether the heirs or persons entitled to distribution be in this state or not. The widow of such deceased person shall take her share in the personal estate according to the laws of this state.

Section 91-1-3. Descent of land.

When any person shall die seized of any estate of inheritance in lands, tenements, and hereditaments not devised, the same shall descend to his or her children, and their descendants, in equal parts, the descendants of the deceased child or grandchild to take the share of the deceased parent in equal parts among them. When there shall not be a child or children of the intestate or descendants of such children, then to the brothers and sisters and father and mother of the intestate and the descendants of such brother of the intestate to have in equal parts among them their deceased parent's share. If there shall not be a child or children of the intestate, or descendants of such children, or brothers or sisters, or descendants of them, or father or mother, then such estate shall descend, in equal parts, to the grandparents and uncles and aunts, if any there be; otherwise, such estate shall descend in equal parts to the next of kin of the intestate in equal degree, computing by the rules of the civil law. There shall not be any representation among collaterals, except among the descendants of the brothers and sisters of the intestate.

Section 91-1-7. Descent of property between husband and wife.

If a husband dies intestate and does not leave children or descendants of children, his widow shall be entitled to his entire estate, real and personal, in fee simple, after payment of his debts; but where the deceased husband shall leave a child or children by that or a former marriage, or descendants of such child or children, his widow shall have a child's part of his estate, in either case in fee simple. If a married woman dies owning any real or personal estate not disposed of, it shall descend to her husband and her children or their descendants if she has any surviving her, either by a former husband or by the surviving husband, in equal parts, according to the rules of descent. If she has children and there also be descendants of other children who have died before the mother, the descendants shall inherit the share to which the parent would have been entitled if living, as coheirs with the surviving children. If she has no children or descendants of them, then the husband shall inherit all of her property.

Section 91-1-9. Descent of trust estates.

If any cestui que trust shall die leaving a trust in lands, tenements, or hereditaments in fee simple or in freehold, the trust shall descend as real estate if not disposed of by will, or if not inconsistent with the declaration of the trust.

Section 91-1-11. Personal estate to descend as real estate.

When any person shall die possessed of goods and chattels or personal estate not bequeathed, the same shall descend to and be distributed among his or her heirs in the same manner that real estate not devised descends.

Section 91-1-13. Estate of testator not disposed of by will to descend.

All estate, real and personal, not devised or bequeathed in the last will and testament of any person shall descend and be distributed in the same manner as the estate of an intestate; and the executor or administrator shall administer the same accordingly.[107]

MISSOURI

474.010. General rules of descent.

All property as to which any decedent dies intestate shall descend and be distributed, subject to the payment of claims, as follows:

(1) The surviving spouse shall receive:

(a) The entire intestate if there is no surviving issue or parent of the decedent;

(b) The first twenty thousand dollars in value of the intestate estate, plus one-half of the balance of the intestate estate, if there is no surviving issue, but the decedent is survived by one or both parents;

(c) The first twenty thousand dollars in value of the intestate estate, plus one-half of the balance of the intestate estate, if there are surviving issue, all of whom are also issue of the surviving spouse;

(d) One-half of the intestate estate if there are surviving issue, one or more of whom are not issue of the surviving spouse;

(2) The part not distributable to the surviving spouse, or the entire intestate property, if there is no surviving spouse, shall descend and be distributed as follows:

(a) To his children, or their descendants, in equal parts;

(b) If there are no children, or their descendants, then to his father, mother, brothers and sisters and their descendants in equal parts;

(c) If there are no children, or their descendants, father, mother, brother or sister, or their descendants, then to the grandfathers, grandmothers, uncles and aunts and their descendants in equal parts;

(d) If there are no children or their descendants, father, mother, brother, sister, or their descendants, grandfather, grandmother, uncles, aunts, nor their descendants, then to the great-grandfathers, great-grandmothers, and their descendants, in equal parts; and so on, in other cases without end, passing to the nearest lineal ancestors and their children, and their descendants, in equal parts; provided, however, that collateral relatives, that is, relatives who are neither ancestors nor descendants of the decedent, may not inherit unless they are related to the decedent at least as closely as the ninth degree, the degree of kinship being computed according to the rules of civil law; that is, by counting upward from the decedent to the nearest common ancestor, and then downward to the relative, the degree of kinship being the sum of these two counts, so that brothers are related in the second degree;

(3) If there is no surviving spouse or kindred of the decedent entitled to inherit, the whole shall go to the kindred of the wife or husband of the decedent, in like course as if such wife or husband had survived the decedent and then died entitled to the property;

(4) If no person is entitled to inherit as provided in this section the property shall escheat as provided by law.[108]

MONTANA

72-2-201. Intestate estate.

Any part of the estate of a decedent not effectively disposed of by his will passes to his heirs as prescribed in the following sections of this code.

72-2-202. Share of spouse.

The intestate share of the surviving spouse is:

(1) if there is no surviving issue or if there are surviving issue all of whom are issue of the surviving spouse also, the entire remaining estate;

(2) if there are surviving issue, one or more of whom are not issue of the surviving spouse, as follows:

(a) if there is surviving only one such child or the issue of one such child, one-half of the intestate estate;

(b) if there are surviving more than one such child or one such child and the issue of one or more deceased children, one-third of the intestate estate.

72-2-203. Share of heirs other than surviving spouse.

The part of the intestate estate not passing to the surviving spouse under 72-2-202, or the entire intestate estate if there is no surviving spouse, passes as follows:

(1) to the issue of the decedent; if they are all of the same degree of kinship to the decedent, they take equally, but if of unequal degree, then those of more remote degree take by representation;

(2) if there is no surviving issue, to his parent or parents equally;

(3) if there is no surviving issue or parent, to the brothers and sisters and the children or grandchildren of any deceased brother or sister, by representation;

(4) if there is no surviving issue, parent, brother, sister, or children or grandchildren of a deceased brother or sister, to the next of kin in equal degree, except that where there are two or more collateral kindred in equal degree claiming through different ancestors, those who claim through the nearer ancestors must be preferred to those claiming through an ancestor more remote.

72-2-207. No taker—Escheat to state.

If there is no taker under the provisions of 72-2-202 and 72-2-203, the intestate estate passes to the state of Montana.

72-2-503. Half-bloods, adopted persons, and illegitimates included in class gift terminology.

Half-bloods, adopted persons, and persons born out of wedlock are included in class gift terminology and terms of relationship in accordance with rules for determining relationships for purposes of intestate succession.[109]

NEBRASKA

30-2301. Intestate estate.

Any part of the estate of a decedent not effectively disposed of by his will passes to his heirs as prescribed in the following sections of this code.

30-2302. Share of the spouse.

The intestate share of the surviving spouse is:

(1) if there is no surviving issue or parent of the decedent, the entire intestate estate;

(2) if there is no surviving issue but the decedent is survived by a parent or parents, the first thirty-five thousand dollars, plus one-half of the balance of the intestate estate;

(3) if there are surviving issue all of whom are issue of the surviving spouse also, the first thirty-five thousand dollars, plus one-half of the balance of the intestate estate;

(4) if there are surviving issue one or more of whom are not issue of the surviving spouse, one-half of the intestate estate.

30-2303. Share of heirs other than surviving spouse.

The part of the intestate estate not passing to the surviving spouse under Section 30-2302, or the entire intestate estate if there is no surviving spouse, passes as follows:

(1) to the issue of the decedent; if they are all of the same degree of kinship to the decedent, they take equally, but if of unequal degree, then those of more remote degree take by representation;

(2) if there is no surviving issue, to his parent or parents equally;

(3) if there is no surviving issue or parent, to the issue of the parents or either of them by representation;

(4) if there is no surviving issue, parent, or issue of a parent, but the decedent is survived by one or more grandparents or issue of grandparents, half of the estate passes to the paternal grandparents if both survive, or to the surviving paternal grandparent, or to the issue of the paternal grandparents if both are deceased, the issue taking equally if they are all of the same degree of kinship to the decedent, but if of unequal degree, those of more remote degree take by

representation; and the other half passes to the maternal relatives in the same manner; but if there be no surviving grandparent or issue of grandparent on either the paternal or the maternal side, the entire estate passes to the relatives on the other side in the same manner as the half;

(5) if there is no surviving issue, parent, issue of a parent, grandparent, or issue of a grandparent, the entire estate passes to the next of kin in equal degree, excepting that when there are two or more collateral kindred in equal degree, but claiming through different ancestors, those who claim through the nearest ancestor shall be preferred to those claiming through a more remote ancestor.[110]

NEVADA

123.250. Death of spouse; ownership of survivor; disposal by will of decedent.

1. Upon the death of either husband or wife:

(a) An undivided one-half interest in the community property is the property of the surviving spouse and his or her sole separate property.

(b) The remaining interest is subject to the testamentary disposition of the decedent, in the absence thereof goes to the surviving spouse, and is the only portion subject to administration under the provisions of Title 12 of NRS.

2. The provisions of this section apply to all community property whether acquired prior or subsequent to July 1, 1975.

134.010. Vesting of community property on death of husband or wife.

Upon the death of either the husband or the wife community property shall vest as provided in NRS 123.250.

134.030 Descent and distribution of separate property.

When any person having title to any estate which is his or her separate property, not otherwise limited by contract, shall die intestate as to such estate, it shall descend and be distributed, subject to the payment of his or her debts, in the manner provided in NRS 134.040 to 134.130, inclusive.

134.040. Surviving spouse and issue.

1. If the decedent leaves a surviving husband or wife, and only one child, or the lawful issue of one child, the estate goes one-half to the surviving husband or wife and one-half to such child or issue of such child.

2. If the decedent leaves a surviving husband or wife, and more than one child living, or one child and the lawful issue of one or more deceased children, the estate goes one-third to the surviving husband or wife, and the remainder in equal shares to his or her children and the lawful issue of any deceased child by right of representation.

3. If there be no child of the intestate living at his or her death, the remainder shall go to all of his or her lineal descendants, and if all the lineal descendants are in the same degree of kindred to the intestate, they share equally; otherwise, they shall take according to the right of representation.

134.050. Surviving spouse and no issue.

1. If the decedent shall leave no issue, the estate shall go one-half to the surviving husband or wife, and one-fourth to the intestate's father, and one-fourth to the intestate's mother, if both are living; if not, one-half to either the father or the mother then living.

2. If the decedent shall leave no issue, or father, or mother, one-half of the separate property of the intestate shall go to the surviving husband or wife, and the other one-half thereof shall go in equal shares to the brothers and sisters of the intestate and to the children of any deceased brother or sister by right of representation.

3. If the decedent shall leave no issue, or husband, or wife, the estate shall go one-half to the intestate's father and one-half to the intestate's mother, if both are living; if not, the whole estate shall go to either the father or mother then living.

4. If the decedent shall leave no issue, or husband, or wife, or father, or mother, then the estate goes in equal shares to the brothers and sisters of the intestate and to the children of any deceased brother or sister by right of representation.

134.060. No surviving spouse or issue.

If there be no issue, or husband, or wife, or father, or mother, then the estate goes in equal shares to the brothers and sisters of the intestate and to the children of any deceased brother or sister by right of representation.

134.070. No surviving spouse, no issue or immediate family.

If the intestate shall leave no issue, or husband, or wife, or father, or mother, and no brother or sister living at his or her death, the estate shall go to the next of kin in equal degree, excepting that when there are two or more collateral kindred in equal degree, but claiming through different ancestors, those who claim through the nearest ancestors shall be preferred to those who claim through ancestors more remote; but if any person shall die leaving several children, or leaving one child and issue of one or more children, and any such surviving child shall die under age and not having been married, all of the estate that came to the deceased child by inheritance from the deceased parent shall descend in equal shares to the other children of the same parent, and to the issue of any other children who may have died, by right of representation.

134.090. No surviving spouse but issue.

If the decedent leaves no surviving husband or wife, but there be a child or children, the estate shall, if there be only one child, all go to that child; and if there be more than one child, the estate shall descend and be distributed to all the intestate's children, share and share alike.

134.100. No surviving spouse but issue and children of issue.

If the decedent leaves no surviving husband or wife, but there shall be a child or children and the lawful issue of a child or children, the estate shall descend and be distributed to such child or children and the lawful issue of such child or children by right of representation as follows: To such child or children each a child's part, and to the lawful issue of each deceased child, by right of representation, the same part and proportion that its parent would have received in case the parent had been living at the time of the intestate's death; that is, the lawful issue of any deceased child shall receive the part and proportion that its parent would have received had the parent been living at the time of the intestate's death.

134.110. No surviving spouse or issue but children of issue.

If the decedent leaves no surviving husband or wife, or child or children, but there be the lawful issue of a child or children, all of the estate shall descend and be distributed to the lawful issue of such child or children by right of representation, and this rule shall apply to the lawful issue of all such children, and to the lawful issue ad infinitum.

134.120. Escheat.

If the intestate shall leave no husband, or wife, or kindred, the estate shall escheat to the state for educational purposes.[111]

NEW HAMPSHIRE

561:1. Distribution upon Intestacy.

The real estate and personal estate of every person deceased, not devised or bequeathed, subject to any homestead right, and liable to be sold by license from the court of probate in cases provided by law, and personalty remaining in the hands of the administrator on settlement of his account, shall descend or be distributed by decree of the probate court:

I. If the deceased is survived by a spouse, the spouse shall receive:

(a) If there is no surviving issue or parent of the deceased, the entire intestate estate;

(b) If there is no surviving issue but the decedent is survived by a parent or parents, the first fifty thousand dollars, plus one-half of the balance of the intestate estate;

(c) If there are surviving issue all of whom are issue of the surviving spouse also, the first fifty thousand dollars, plus one-half of the balance of the intestate estate;

(d) If there are surviving issue, one or more of whom are not issue of the surviving spouse, one-half of the intestate estate.

II. The part of the intestate estate not passing to the surviving spouse under paragraph I, or the entire intestate estate if there is no surviving spouse, passes as follows:

(a) To the issue of the decedent; if they are all of the same degree of kinship to the decedent, they take equally, but if of unequal degree, then those of more remote degree take by representation;

(b) If there is no surviving issue, to his parent or parents equally;

(c) If there is no surviving issue or parent, to the brothers and sisters and the issue of each deceased brother or sister by representation; if there is no surviving brother or sister, the issue of brothers and sisters take equally if they are all of the same degree of kinship to the decedent, but if of unequal degree, then those of more remote degree take by representation;

(d) If there is no surviving issue, parent, or issue of a parent but the decedent is survived by one or more grandparents or issue of grandparents, half of the estate passes to the paternal grandparents if both survive, or to the surviving paternal grandparent, or to the issue of the paternal grandparents if both are deceased, the issue taking equally if they are all of the same degree of kinship to the decedent, but if of unequal degree, those of more remote degree take by representation; and the other half passes to the maternal relatives in the same manner; but if there be no surviving grandparent or issue of grandparent on either the paternal or the maternal side, the entire estate passes to the relatives on the other side in the same manner as the half.

561:8 Escheat, etc.

If there be no heir, legatee, or devisee of an estate, the same shall accrue to the widow or widower, and if there be no widow or widower, the same shall accrue to the state. If as herein provided the surviving spouse is entitled to the estate, he or she may certify under oath, recorded in the registry of probate, that to the best of his or her knowledge and belief the deceased was survived by no children, or issue of any deceased children, father or mother, grandfather or grandmother, brother or sister of their representatives, aunt or uncle, or first cousin, and if no heir or next of kin files an appearance in the estate within a period of three years after the date of appointment of the administrator, such certificate shall be a conclusive presumption that no heir or next of kin exists who can affect the right of the surviving spouse to take under this section.

561.9 Payment to state.

If no heir or legatee be ascertained at the expiration of three years from the original grant of administration, the judge shall order the administrator to pay the balance into the state treasury, where it shall be subject to the claims of persons entitled thereto, upon application to the legislature.[112]

NEW JERSEY

3B:5-2. Intestate estate.

Any part of the estate of a decedent not effectively disposed of by his will passes to his heirs as prescribed in N.J.S. 3B:5-3 through N.J.S. 3B:5-14.

3B:5-3. Intestate share of surviving spouse.

The intestate share of the surviving spouse is:

a. If there is no surviving issue or parent of the decedent, the entire intestate estate;

b. If there is no surviving issue but the decedent is survived by a parent or parents, the first $50,000.00, plus one-half of the balance of the intestate estate;

c. If there are surviving issue all of whom are issue of the surviving spouse also, the first $50,000.00, plus one-half of the balance of the intestate estate;

d. If there are surviving issue one one or more of whom are issue of the surviving spouse, one-half of the intestate estate.

3B:5-4. Intestate share of heirs other than surviving spouse.

The part of the intestate estate not passing to the surviving spouse under N.J.S. 3B:5-3, or the entire intestate estate if there is no surviving spouse, passes as follows:

a. To the issue of the decedent; if they are all of the same degree of kinship to the decedent, they take equally, but if of unequal degree, then those of more remote degree take by representation;

b. If there is no surviving issue, to the parent or parents equally;

c. If there is no surviving issue or parent, to the issue of the parents or either of them by representation;

d. If there is no surviving issue, parent, or issue of a parent, but the decedent is survived by one or more grandparents;

(1) Half of the estate passes to the maternal grandparents equally if both survive or to the surviving paternal grandparent; or if both are deceased and the decedent is survived by maternal grandparents or grandparent, then to the issue of the paternal grandparents, the issue taking equally if they are all of the same degree of kinship to the decedent, but if of unequal degree, those of more remote degree take by representation;

(2) The other half passes to the maternal grandparents equally if both survive or to the surviving maternal grandparent; or if both are deceased and the decedent is survived by paternal grandparents or grandparent, then to the issue of the maternal grandparents, the issue taking equally if they are all of the same degree of kinship to the decedent, but if of unequal degree, those more remote take by representation;

(3) If the decedent is survived by a grandparent or grandparents only on the paternal side or only on the maternal side and by no issue of the grandparents on the other side, the entire estate passes to the surviving grandparent or grandparents equally;

e. If there is no surviving issue, parent, issue of a parent, or no surviving grandparent, but the decedent is survived by the issue of grandparents, the issue taking equally if they are all of the same degree of kinship to the decedent, but if of unequal degree those of more remote degree take by representation.

3B:5-5. Escheat to state.

If there are none who may inherit an intestate estate, that estate shall escheat to the state.

3B:5-16. Inheritance by children not provided for in will.

a. If a testator fails to provide in his will for any of his children born or adopted after the execution of his will, the omitted child receives a share in the estate equal in value to that which he would have received if the testator had died intestate unless:

(1) It appears from the will that the omission was intentional;

(2) When the will was executed the testator had one or more children and devised substantially all his estate to the other parent of the omitted child; or

(3) The testator provided for the child by transfer outside the will, and the intent that the transfer be in lieu of a testamentary provision is shown by statements of the testator or from the amount of the transfer or other evidence.

b. If at the time of execution of the will the testator fails to provide in his will for a living child solely because he believes the child to be dead, the child receives a share in the estate equal in value to that which he would have received if the testator had died intestate.

c. The share of the child shall be taken from devisees under the will ratably and in proportion to their respective interests therein.[113]

NEW MEXICO

45-2-101. Intestate estate.

Any part of the estate of a decedent not effectively disposed of by his will passes to his heirs as prescribed in Sections 2-101 through 2-113 [45-2-101 to 45-2-113 NMSA 1978] of the Probate Code.

45-2-102. Share of the spouse.

The intestate share of the surviving spouse is determined as follows:

A. as to separate property:

(1) if there is no surviving issue of the decedent, the entire intestate estate; or

(2) if there is surviving issue of the decedent, one-fourth of the intestate estate; and

B. as to community property, the one-half of the community property as to which the decedent could have exercised the power of testamentary disposition passes to the surviving spouse.

45-2-103. Share of heirs other than surviving spouse.

The part of the intestate estate not passing to the surviving spouse under Section 45-2-101 NMSA 1978, or the entire intestate estate if there is no surviving spouse, passes as follows:

A. to the issue of the decedent; if they are all of the same degree of kinship to the decedent, they take equally, but if of unequal degree, then those of more remote degree take by representation;

B. if there is no surviving issue, to the decedent's parent or parents equally;

C. if there is no surviving issue or parent, to the issue of the parents or either of them by representation; and

D. if there is no surviving issue, parent, or issue of a parent, but the decedent is survived by one or more grandparents or issue of grandparents, half of the estate passes to the paternal grandparents if both survive, or the surviving paternal grandparent, or to the issue of the paternal grandparents if both are deceased, the issue taking equally if they are all of the same degree of kinship to the decedent, but if of unequal degree, those of more remote degree take by representation; and the other half passes to the maternal relatives in the same manner; but if there is no surviving grandparent or issue of grandparent on either the paternal or maternal side, the entire estate passes to the relatives on the other side in the same manner as the half.

45-2-105. No taker.

If there is no taker under the provisions of Sections 2-101 through 2-902 [45-2-101 to 45-2-902 NMSA 1978] of the Probate Code, the intestate passes to the state.[114]

NEW YORK

PART 1. RULES GOVERNING INTESTATE SUCCESSION

Section 4-1.1 Descent and distribution of a decedent's estate.

The property of a decedent not disposed of by will, after payment of administration and funeral expenses, debts, and taxes, shall be distributed as follows:

(a) If a decedent is survived by:

(1) A spouse and children or their issue, money or personal property not exceeding in value four thousand dollars and one-third of the residue to the spouse and the balance thereof to the children or their issue per stirpes.

(2) A spouse and only one child, or a spouse and only the issue of one deceased child, money or personal property not exceeding in value four thousand dollars and one-half of the residue to the spouse and the balance thereof to the child or to his issue per stirpes.

(3) A spouse and both parents, and no issue, twenty-five thousand dollars and one-half of the residue to the spouse and the balance thereof to the parents. If there is no surviving spouse, the whole to the parents.

(4) A spouse and one parent, and no issue, twenty-five thousand dollars and one-half of the residue to the spouse and the balance thereof to the parent. If there is no surviving spouse, the whole to the parent.

(5) A spouse, and no issue or parent, the whole to the spouse.

(6) Issue, and no spouse, the whole to the issue per stirpes.

(7) Brothers or sisters or their issue, and no spouse, issue, or parent, the whole to the brothers or sisters or to their issue per stirpes.

(8) Grandparents only, the whole to the grandparents. If there are no grandparents, the whole to the issue of the grandparents in the nearest degree of kinship to the decedent per capita.

(9) Great-grandparents only, the whole to the great-grandparents. If there are no great-grandparents, the whole to the issue of great-grandparents in the nearest degree of kinship to the decedent per capita. Provided that in the case of a decedent who is survived by great-grandparents only, or the issue of great-grandparents only, such great-grandparents or the issue of such great-grandparents shall not be entitled to inherit from the decedent unless the decedent was at the time of his death an infant or an adjudged incompetent. Provided, further, that this subparagraph nine shall be applicable only to the estates of persons dying on or after its effective date.

(b) If the distributees of the decedent are in equal degree of kinship to him, their shares are equal.

(c) There is no distribution per stirpes except in the case of the decedent's issue, brothers or sisters, and the issue of brothers or sisters.

(d) For all purposes of this section, decedent's relatives of the half blood shall be treated as if they were relatives of the whole blood.

(e) Distributees of the decedent, conceived before his death but born alive thereafter, take as if they were born in his lifetime.

(f) The right of an adopted child to take a distributive share and the right of succession to the estate of an adopted child continue as provided in the domestic relations law.

(g) A distributive share passing to a surviving spouse under this section is in lieu of any right of dower to which such spouse may be entitled.[115]

NORTH CAROLINA

ARTICLE 2: SHARES OF PERSONS WHO TAKE UPON INTESTACY

Section 29-13. Descent and distribution upon intestacy.

All the estate of a person dying intestate shall descend and be distributed, subject to the payment of costs of administration and other lawful claims against the estate, and subject to the payment by the recipient of state inheritance taxes, as provided in this chapter.

Section 29-14. Share of surviving spouse.

(a) Real Property. The share of the surviving spouse in the real property is:

(1) If the intestate is survived by only one child or by any lineal descendant of only one deceased child, a one-half undivided interest in the real property;

(2) If the intestate is survived by two or more children, or by one child and any lineal descendant of one or more deceased children, or by lineal descendants of two or more deceased children, a one-third undivided interest in the real property;

(3) If the intestate is not survived by a child, children, or any lineal de-

scendant of a deceased child or children, but is survived by one or more parents, a one-half undivided interest in the real property;

(4) If the intestate is not survived by a child, children, or any lineal descendant of a deceased child or children, or by a parent, all the real property.

(b) Personal Property. The share of the surviving spouse in the personal property is:

(1) If the intestate is survived by only one child or by any lineal descendant of only one deceased child, and the net personal property does not exceed fifteen thousand dollars ($15,000) in value, all of the personal property; if the net personal property exceeds fifteen thousand dollars ($15,000) in value, the sum of fifteen thousand dollars ($15,000) plus one-half of the balance of the personal property.

(2) If the intestate is survived by two or more children, or by one child and any lineal descendant of one or more deceased children, or by lineal descendants of two or more deceased children, and the net personal property does not exceed fifteen thousand dollars ($15,000) in value, all of the personal property; if the net personal property exceeds fifteen thousand dollars ($15,000) in value, the sum of fifteen thousand dollars ($15,000) plus one-third of the balance of the personal property;

(3) If the intestate is not survived by a child, children, or any lineal descendant of a deceased child or children, but is survived by one or more parents, and the net personal property does not exceed twenty-five thousand dollars ($25,000) in value, all of the personal property; if the net personal property exceeds twenty-five thousand dollars ($25,000) in value, the sum of twenty-five thousand dollars ($25,000) plus one half of the balance of the personal property.

(4) If the intestate is not survived by a child, children, or any lineal descendant of a deceased child or children, or by a parent, all of the personal property.

Section 29-15. Shares of others than surviving spouse.

Those persons surviving the intestate, other than the surviving spouse, shall take that share of the net estate not distributable to the surviving spouse, or the entire net estate if there is no surviving spouse, as follows:

(1) If the intestate is survived by only one child or by only one lineal descendant of only one deceased child, that person shall take the entire net estate or share, but if the intestate is survived by two or more lineal descendants of only one deceased child, they shall take as provided in G.S. 29-16; or

(2) If the intestate is survived by two or more children or by one child and any lineal descendant of one or more deceased children, or by lineal descendants of two or more deceased children, they shall take as provided in G.S. 29-16; or

(3) If the intestate is not survived by a child, children, or any lineal descendant of a deceased child or children, but is survived by both parents, they shall take in equal shares, or if either parent is dead, the surviving parent shall take the entire share; or

(4) If the intestate is not survived by such children or lineal descendants or by a parent, the brothers and sisters of the intestate, and the lineal descendants of any deceased brothers or sisters, shall take as provided in G.S. 29-16; or

(5) If there is no one entitled to take under the preceding subdivisions of this section or under G.S. 29-14,

a. The paternal grandparents shall take one-half of the net estate in equal shares, or, if either is dead, the survivor shall take the entire one-half of the net estate, and if neither paternal grandparent survives, then the paternal uncles and aunts of the intestate and the lineal descendants of deceased paternal uncles and aunts shall take said one-half as provided in G.S. 29-16; and

b. The maternal grandparents shall take the other half in equal shares, or if either is dead, the survivor shall take the entire one-half of the net estate, and if neither maternal grandparent survives, then the maternal uncles and aunts of the intestate and the lineal descendants of deceased maternal uncles and aunts shall take one-half as provided in G.S. 29-16; but

c. If there is no grandparent and no uncle or aunt, or lineal descendant of a deceased uncle or aunt, on the paternal side, then those of the maternal side who otherwise would be entitled to take one-half as hereinbefore provided in this subdivision shall take the whole; or

d. If there is no grandparent and no uncle or aunt, or lineal descendant of a deceased uncle or aunt, on the maternal side, then those on the paternal side who otherwise would be entitled to take one-half as hereinbefore provided in this subdivision shall take the whole.

ARTICLE 3: DISTRIBUTION AMONG CLASSES

Section 29-16. Distribution among classes.

(a) Children and Their Lineal Descendants. If the intestate is survived by lineal descendants, their respective shares in the property which they are entitled to take under G.S. 29-15 of this chapter shall be determined in the following manner:

(1) Children. To determine the share of each surviving child, divide the property by the number of surviving children plus the number of deceased children who have left lineal descendants surviving the intestate.

(2) Grandchildren. To determine the share of each surviving grandchild by a deceased child of the intestate in the property not taken under the preceding subdivision of this subsection, divide that property by the number of such surviving grandchildren plus the number of deceased grandchildren who have left lineal descendants surviving the intestate.

(3) Great-grandchildren. To determine the share of each surviving great-grandchild by a deceased grandchild of the intestate in the property not taken under the preceding subdivisions of this subsection, divide that property by the number of such surviving great-grandchildren who have left lineal descendants surviving the intestate.

(4) Great-great-grandchildren. To determine the share of each surviving

great-great-grandchild by a deceased great-grandchild of the intestate in the property not taken under the preceding subdivisions of this subsection, divide that property by the number of such surviving great-great-grandchildren plus the number of deceased great-great-grandchildren who have left lineal descendants surviving the intestate.

(5) Other lineal descendants of children. Divide, according to the formula established in the preceding subdivisions of this subsection, any property not taken under such preceding subdivisions among the lineal descendants of the children of the intestate not already participating.

(b) Brothers and sisters and their lineal descendants. If the intestate is survived by brothers and sisters or the lineal descendants of deceased brothers and sisters, their respective shares in the property which they are entitled to take under G.S. 29-15 of this chapter shall be determined in the following manner:

(1) Brothers and sisters. To determine the share of each surviving brother and sister, divide the property by the number of surviving brothers and sisters plus the number of deceased brothers and sisters who have left lineal descendants surviving the intestate within the fifth degree of kinship to the intestate.

(2) Nephews and nieces. To determine the share of each surviving nephew or niece by a deceased brother or sister of the intestate in the property not taken under the preceding subdivision of this subsection, divide that property by the number of deceased nephews and nieces who have left lineal descendants surviving the intestate within the fifth degree of kinship to the intestate.

(3) Grandnephews and grandnieces. To determine the share of each surviving grandnephew or grandniece by a deceased nephew or niece of the intestate in the property not taken under the preceding subdivisions of this subsection, divide that property by the number of such surviving grandnephews and grandnieces plus the number of deceased grandnephews and grandnieces who have left children surviving the intestate.

(4) Great-grandnephews and great-grandnieces. To determine the share of each surviving child of a deceased grandnephew or grandniece of the intestate, divide equally among the great-grandnephews and great-grandnieces of the intestate any property not taken under the preceding subdivisions of this subsection.

(5) Grandparents and others. If there is no one within the fifth degree of kinship to the intestate entitled to take the property under the preceding subdivisions of this subsection, then the intestate's property shall go to those entitled to take under G.S. 29-15(5).

(c) Uncles and aunts and their lineal descendants. If the intestate is survived by uncles and aunts or the lineal descendants of deceased uncles and aunts, their respective shares in the property which they are entitled to take under G.S. 29-15 shall be determined in the following manner:

(1) Uncles and aunts. To determine the share of each surviving uncle and aunt, divide the property by the number of surviving uncles and aunts plus the number of deceased uncles and aunts who have left children or grandchildren surviving the intestate.

(2) Children of uncles and aunts. To determine the share of each surviving child of a deceased uncle or aunt of the intestate in the property not taken under the preceding subdivision of this subsection, divide that property by the number of surviving children of deceased uncles and aunts plus the number of deceased children of deceased uncles and aunts who have left children surviving the intestate.

(3) Grandchildren of uncles and aunts. To determine the share of each surviving child of a deceased child of a deceased uncle or aunt of the intestate, divide equally among the grandchildren of uncles or aunts of the intestate any property not taken under the preceding subdivisions of this subsection.[116]

NORTH DAKOTA

30.1-04-01 (2-101). Intestate estate.

Any part of the estate of a decedent not effectively disposed of by his will passes to his heirs as prescribed in the following sections of this title.

30.1-04-02 (2-102). Share of the spouse.

The intestate share of the surviving spouse is:

1. If there is no surviving issue or parent of the decedent, the entire intestate estate.

2. If there is no surviving issue but the decedent is survived by a parent or parents, the first fifty thousand dollars, plus one-half of the balance of the intestate estate.

3. If there are surviving issue all of whom are issue of the surviving spouse also, the first fifty thousand dollars, plus one-half of the balance of the intestate estate.

4. If there are surviving issue, one or more of whom are not issue of the surviving spouse, one-half of the intestate estate.

30.1-04-03 (2-103). Share of heirs other than surviving spouse.

The part of the intestate estate not passing to the surviving spouse under Section 30.1-04-02, or the entire intestate estate if there is no surviving spouse, passes as follows:

1. To the issue of the decedent. If they are all of the same degree of kinship to the decedent they take equally, but if of unequal degree, then those of more remote degree take by representation.

2. If there is no surviving issue, to his parent or parents equally.

3. If there is no surviving issue or parent, to the issue of the parents or either of them by representation.

4. If there is no surviving issue, parent, or issue of a parent, but the decedent is survived by one or more grandparents or issue of grandparents, half of the estate passes to the paternal grandparents if both survive, or to the surviving paternal grandparent, or to the issue of the paternal grandparents if both are deceased, by representation; and the other half passes to the maternal relatives

in the same manner. If there be no surviving grandparent or issue of grandparent on either the paternal or the maternal side, the entire estate passes to the relatives on the other side in the same manner as the half.

30.1-04-05 (2-105). No taker.

If there is no taker under the provisions of this title, the intestate estate passes to the state for the support of the common schools, and an action for the recovery of such property and to reduce it into the possession of the state or for its sale and conveyance may be brought by the attorney general or by the state's attorney in the district court of the county in which the property is situated.

30.1-04-09 (2-109). Meaning of child and related terms.

If, for purposes of intestate succession, a relationship of parent and child must be established to determine succession, by, through, or from a person:

1. An adopted person is the child of an adopting parent and not of the natural parents, except that adoption of a child by the spouse of a natural parent has no effect on the relationship between the child and either natural parent.

2. In cases not covered by subsection 1, a person is the child of its parents regardless of the marital status of its parents and the parent and child relationship may be established under the Uniform Parentage Act.[117]

OHIO

Section 2105.6 Statute of descent and distribution.

When a person dies intestate having title or right to any personal property, or to any real estate or inheritance in this state, the personal property shall be distributed, and the real estate or inheritance shall descend and pass in parcenary, except as otherwise provided by law, in the following course:

(A) If there is no surviving spouse, to the children of the intestate or their lineal descendants, per stirpes;

(B) If there is a spouse and one child or his lineal descendants surviving, the first thirty thousand dollars if the spouse is the natural or adoptive parent of the child, or the first ten thousand dollars if the spouse is not the natural or adoptive parent of the child, plus one-half of the balance of the intestate estate to the spouse and the remainder to the child or his lineal descendants, per stirpes;

(C) If there is a spouse and more than one child or their lineal descendants surviving, the first thirty thousand dollars, if the spouse is the natural or adoptive parent of one of the children, or the first ten thousand dollars if the spouse is the natural or adoptive parent of none of the children, plus one-third of the balance of the intestate estate to the spouse and the remainder to the children equally, or to the lineal descendants of any deceased child, per stirpes;

(D) If there are no children or their lineal descendants, then the whole to the surviving spouse;

(E) If there is no spouse and no children or their lineal descendants, to the parents of the intestate equally, or to the surviving parent;

(F) If there is no spouse, no children or their lineal descendants, and no parent surviving, to the brothers and sisters, whether of the whole or of the half blood of the intestate, or their lineal descendants, per stirpes;

(G) If there are no brothers or sisters or their lineal descendants, one-half to the paternal grandparents of the intestate equally, or to the survivor of them, and one-half to the maternal grandparent of the intestate equally, or to the survivor of them;

(H) If there are no paternal grandparents or no maternal grandparent, one-half to the lineal descendants of the deceased grandparents, per stirpes; if there are no such lineal descendants, then to the surviving grandparents or their lineal descendants, per stirpes; if there are no surviving grandparents or their lineal descendants, then to the next of kin of the intestate, provided there shall be no representation among such next of kin;

(I) If there are no next of kin, to stepchildren or their lineal descendants, per stirpes;

(J) If there are no stepchildren or their lineal descendants, escheat to the state.

Section 2105.14 Posthumous child to inherit.

Descendants of an intestate begotten before his death, but born thereafter, in all cases will inherit as if born in the lifetime of the intestate and surviving him; but in no other case can a person inherit unless living at the time of the death of the intestate.[118]

OKLAHOMA

Section 213. Descent and distribution.

When any person having title to any estate not otherwise limited by marriage contract dies without disposing of the estate by will, it descends and must be distributed in the following manner:

First. If the decedent leave a surviving husband or wife, and only one child, or the lawful issue of one child, in equal shares to the surviving husband, or wife and child, or issue of such child. If the decedent leave a surviving husband or wife, and more than one child living, or one child living and the lawful issue of one or more deceased children, one-third to the surviving husband or wife, and the remainder in equal shares to his children, and to the lawful issue of any deceased child, by right of representation; but if there be no child of the decedent living at his death, the remainder goes to all of his lineal descendants; and if all the descendants are in the same degree of kindred to the decedent they share equally, otherwise they take according to the right of representation: Provided, that if the decedent shall have been married more than once, the spouse at the time of death shall inherit of the property not acquired during coverture with such spouse only an equal part with each of the living children of decedent, and the lawful issue of any deceased child by right of representation. If the decedent leave no surviving husband or wife, but leaves issue, the whole estate goes to such issue, and if such issue consists of one or more deceased children, then the estate goes in equal shares to the children living, or to the child living, and the issue of the deceased child or children by right of representation.

Second. If the decedent leave no issue, the estate goes one-half to the surviving husband or wife, and the remaining one-half to the decedent's father or mother, or, if he leaves both father and mother, to them in equal shares; but if there be no father or mother, then said remaining one-half goes, in equal shares, to the brothers and sisters of the decedent, and to the children of any deceased brother or sister, by right of representation. If decedent leave no issue, nor husband nor wife, the estate must go to the father or mother, or if he leave both father and mother, to them in equal shares: Provided, that in all cases where the property is acquired by the joint industry of husband and wife during coverture, and there is no issue, the whole estate shall go to the survivor, at whose death, if any of the said property remain, one-half of such property shall go to the heirs of the husband and one-half to the heirs of the wife, according to the right of representation.

Third. If there be no issue, nor husband nor wife, nor father, nor mother, then in equal shares to the brothers and sisters of the decedent, and to the children of any deceased brother or sister, by right of representation; if the deceased, being a minor, leave no issue, the estate must go to the parents equally, if living together, if not living together, to the parent having had the care of said deceased minor.

Fourth. If the decedent leave no issue nor husband, nor wife, nor father and no brother or sister is living at the time of his death, the estate goes to his mother to the exclusion of the issue, if any, of deceased brothers or sisters.

Fifth. If the decedent leave a surviving husband or wife, and no issue, and no father, nor mother, nor brother, nor sister, the whole estate goes to the surviving husband or wife.

Sixth. If the decedent leave no issue, nor husband, nor wife, and no father or mother, or brother, or sister, the estate must go to the next of kin in equal degree, excepting that when there are two or more collateral kindred, in equal degree, but claiming through different ancestors, those who claimed through the nearest ancestors must be preferred to those claiming through an ancestor more remote.

Seventh. If the decedent leave several children, or one child and the issue of one or more children, and any such surviving child dies under age, and not having been married, all the estate that came to the deceased child by inheritance from such decedent, descends in equal shares to the other children of the same parent, and to the issue of any such other children who are dead, by right of representation.

Eighth. If, at the death of such child who dies under age, not having been married, all the other children of his parents are also dead, and any of them have left issue, the estate that came to such child by inheritance from his parent descends to the issue of all other children of the same parent; and if all the issue are in the same degree of kindred to the child, they share the estate equally, otherwise, they take according to the right of representation.

Ninth. If the decedent leave no husband, wife, or kindred, the estate escheats to the State for the support of common schools.

CHILDREN

Section 60.16. Effect of final decree.

(1) After the final decree of adoption is entered, the relation of parent and child and all the rights, duties, and other legal consequences of the natural relation of child and parent shall thereafter exist between such adopted child and the adoptive parents adopting such child and the kindred of the adoptive parents. From the date of the final decree of adoption, the child shall be entitled to inherit real and personal property from and through the adoptive parents in accordance with the statutes of descent and distribution, and the adoptive parents shall be entitled to inherit real and personal property from and through the child in accordance with said statutes.

(2) After a final decree of adoption is entered, the natural parents of the adopted child, unless they are the adoptive parents or the spouse of an adoptive parent, shall be relieved of all parental responsibilities for said child and have no rights over such adopted child or to his property by descent and distribution.[119]

OREGON

112.015 Net intestate estate.

Any part of the net estate of a decedent not effectively disposed of by his will shall pass as provided in ORS 112.025 to 112.055.

112.025 Share of surviving spouse if decedent leaves issue.

If the decedent leaves a surviving spouse and issue, the surviving spouse shall have a one-half interest in the net intestate estate.

112.035 Share of surviving spouse if decedent leaves no issue.

If the decedent leaves a surviving spouse and no issue, the surviving spouse shall have all of the net intestate estate.

112.045 Share of others than surviving spouse.

The part of the net intestate estate not passing to the surviving spouse shall pass:

(1) To the issue of the decedent. If the issue are all of the same degree of kinship to the decedent, they shall take equally, but if of unequal degree, then those of more remote degrees take by representation.

(2) If there is no surviving issue, to the surviving parents of the decedent.

(3) If there is no surviving issue or parent, to the brothers and sisters of the decedent and the issue of any deceased brother or sister of the decedent by

representation. If there is no surviving brother or sister, the issue of brothers and sisters take equally if they are all of the same degree of kinship to the decedent, but if of unequal degree, then those of more remote degrees take by representation.

(4) If there is no surviving issue, parent, or issue of a parent, to the grandparent of the decedent and the issue of any deceased grandparent of the decedent by representation. If there is no surviving grandparent, the issue of grandparents take equally if they are all of the same degree of kinship to the decedent, but if of unequal degree, then those of more remote degrees take by representation.

(5) If, at the time of taking, surviving parents or grandparents of the decedent are married to each other, they shall take real property as tenants by the entirety and personal property as joint owners with the right of survivorship.

112.055 Escheat.

If no person takes under ORS 112.025 to 112.045, the net intestate estate shall escheat to the state of Oregon.[120]

PENNSYLVANIA

Section 2101. Intestate descent.

The real and personal estate of a decedent, whether male or female, subject to payment of debts and charges, and not disposed of by will or otherwise, shall descend as hereinafter provided.

Section 2102. Share of surviving spouse.

The surviving spouse shall be entitled to the following share or shares:

(1) More than one child. One-third if the decedent is survived by more than one child, or by one or more children and the issue of a deceased child or children, or by the issue of more than one deceased child; or

(2) One child. One-half if the decedent is survived by one child only, or by no child, but by the issue of one deceased child; or

(3) No issue. The first $20,000 in value and one-half of the balance of the estate, if the decedent is survived by no issue. In case of partial intestacy, any amount received by the surviving spouse under the will shall satisfy pro tanto the $20,000 allowance; or

(4) No issue or other designated person. All of the estate if the decedent is survived by no issue, parent, brother, sister, child of a brother or sister, grandparent, uncle, or aunt.

Section 2103. Shares of others than surviving spouse.

The share of the estate, if any, to which the surviving spouse is not entitled, and the entire estate if there is no surviving spouse, shall descend in the following order:

(1) Issue. To the issue of the decedent.

(2) Parents. If no issue survives the decedent, then to the parents or parent of the decedent.

(3) Brothers, sisters, or their issue. If no parent survives the decedent, then to the issue of each of the decedent's parents.

(4) Grandparents. If no issue of either of the decedent's parents but at least one grandparent survives the decedent, then half to the paternal grandparents or grandparent, or if both are dead, to the children of each of them and the children of the deceased children of each of them, and half to the maternal grandparents or grandparent, or if both are dead to the children of each of them and the children of the deceased children of each of them. If both of the paternal grandparents or both of the maternal grandparents are dead leaving no child or grandchild to survive the decedent, the half which would have passed to them or to their children and grandchildren shall be added to the half passing to the grandparents or grandparent on the other side.

(5) Uncles, aunts, and their children and grandchildren. If no grandparent survives the decedent, then to the uncles and aunts and the children and grandchildren of deceased uncles and aunts as provided in Section 2104(1) of this code (relating to taking in different degrees).

(6) Commonwealth. In default of all persons hereinbefore described, then to the Commonwealth of Pennsylvania.

Section 2104. Rules of descent.

The provisions in this chapter shall be applied to both real and personal estate in accordance with the following rules:

(1) Taking in different degrees. The shares descending under this chapter to the issue of the decedent, to the issue of his parents or grandparents or to his uncles or aunts or to their children or grandchildren shall descend to them as follows: The part of the estate descending to any such persons shall be divided into as many equal shares as there shall be persons in the nearest degree of consanguinity to the decedent living and taking shares therein and persons in that degree who have died before the decedent and have left issue to survive him who take shares therein. One equal share shall descend by representation to the issue of each such deceased person, except that no issue of a child of an uncle or aunt of the decedent shall be entitled to any share of the estate unless there be no relatives as close as a child of an uncle or aunt living and taking a share therein, in which case the grandchildren of uncles and aunts of the decedent shall be entitled to share, but no issue of a grandchild of an uncle or aunt shall be entitled to any share of the estate.

(2) Taking in same degree. When persons entitled to take under this chapter other than as a surviving spouse are all in the same degree of consanguinity to the decedent, they shall take in equal shares.

(3) Whole and half blood. Persons taking under this chapter shall take without distinction between those of the whole and those of the half blood.

(4) Afterborn persons; time of determining relationships. Persons begotten before the decedent's death but born thereafter shall take as if they had been born in his lifetime.

(5) Source of ownership. Real estate shall descend under this chapter without regard to the ancestor or other relation from whom it has come.

(6) Quantity of estate. Any person taking real or personal estate under this chapter shall take such interest as the decedent had therein.

(7) Tenancy in estate. When real or personal estate or shares therein shall descend to two or more persons, they shall take it as tenants in common, except that if it shall descend to a husband and wife they shall take it as tenants by the entireties.

(8) Alienage. Real and personal estate shall descend without regard to whether the decedent or any person otherwise entitled to take under this chapter is or has been an alien.

(9) Person related to decedent through two lines. A person related to the decedent through two lines of relationship shall take one share only which shall be the larger share.

Section 2105. Spouse's rights.

(a) Widow. The shares of the estate to which a widow is entitled shall be in lieu and full satisfaction of her dower at common law, so far as relates to real estate of which the husband dies seised; and her share in real estate aliened by the husband in his lifetime, without her joining in the conveyance shall be the same as her share in real estate of which the husband died seised. The widow shall receive the same share in a future estate owned by the husband as in an estate of which he dies seised, although the particular estate shall not terminate before the death of the husband.

(b) Surviving husband. The shares of the estate to which the surviving husband is entitled shall be in lieu and full satisfaction of his curtesy at common law so far as relates to real estate of which his wife dies seised, and his share in real estate aliened by the wife in her lifetime without his joint in the conveyance shall be the same as his share in real estate of which the wife dies seised. The surviving husband shall receive the same share in a future estate owned by the wife as in an estate of which she dies seised, although the particular estate shall not terminate before the death of the wife.

Section 2110. Spouse's allowance; procedure.

The allowance shall be set aside and awarded in distribution to the surviving spouse, or his successor in interest, in the same manner as other distributive shares of the estate are awarded, without any right in the surviving spouse to choose particular real or personal property in satisfaction thereof. Nothing herein shall be construed as limiting the right of the surviving spouse and other distributees to demand that property, not theretofore sold, be distributed in kind to them.

Section 2111. Procedure to establish title to real property when spouse claims entire estate.

A surviving spouse entitled under the provisions of this chapter to the entire estate of the decedent shall have it awarded to him in the same manner as a lesser share of the estate would be so awarded.

Section 2112. Property distributable to the Commonwealth.

When the estate is distributable to the Commonwealth, as statutory heir under the provisions of this chapter, it shall be reduced to cash in all cases by the personal representative and awarded by the court in distribution to the Commonwealth and paid by the personal representative through the Department of Revenue into the state Treasury.[121]

PUERTO RICO

Section 2591. When legitimate succession takes place.

1. If a person dies without a will or with a void will or (one) which may have lost its validity subsequently.

2. When the will does not contain the designation of heirship to all or part of the property or does not dispose of all that belongs to the testator. In such case legitimate succession shall take place only with regard to the property of which the testator has not disposed.

3. When the condition imposed for the designation of heirship is lacking, or if the heir dies before the testator, or repudiates the inheritance, without having a substitute, and there being no right of accretion.

4. When the heir designated is disqualified to succeed.

Section 2592. Disposition of inheritance in absence of testamentary heirs.

In the absence of testamentary heirs, the law gives the inheritance, according to the rules hereafter set forth, to the legitimate and natural relatives of the deceased, to the widower or widow, and to the Commonwealth of Puerto Rico.

Section 2593. Disqualifications in intestate succession.

The provisions relating to disqualification to succeed by will are also applicable to intestate succession.

Section 2602. Direct and collateral lines.

A series of degrees forms the line, which may be direct or collateral.

A direct line is one constituted by a series of degrees among persons descending one from the other.

A collateral line is that constituted by a series of degrees among persons not descending one from the other but proceeding from a common trunk.

Section 2604. Computation of degrees.

In the lines as many degrees are counted as there are generations or persons, deducting the progenitor.

In the direct line the ascent is made only to the trunk. Thus the son is one degree removed from the father, two from the grandfather, and three from the great-grandfather.

In the collateral line the ascent is made up to the common trunk and then a descent to the person with whom the computation is made. Therefore the brother is two degrees removed from the brother, three from the uncle, brother of his father or mother, four from the first cousins, and so forth.

Section 2605. Application in all matters.

The computation of which the foregoing section treats governs [*sic*] without exception in all matters.

Section 2606. Whole blood relationship.

Whole blood relationship is the relation in the father's and mother's line at the same time.

Section 2607. Nearest relative excludes more remote; relatives in the same degree.

In inheritance the relative nearest in degree excludes the most remote excepting the right of representation in proper cases. Relatives who are in the same degree shall inherit in equal shares, with the exception of what is provided in Section 2674 of this title with regard to whole blood relationship.

Section 2608. Disposition of portion of relative unwilling or unable to succeed.

Should there be several relatives in the same degree, and one or more of them should not wish to or could not succeed, his portion shall accrue to the others of the same degree, reserving the right of representation in a proper case.

Section 2609. Disposition of inheritance repudiated by nearest relative.

If the inheritance is repudiated by the nearest relative should there be one only, or by all the nearest relatives, designated by law, should there be several, those of the following degree shall inherit in their own right, without being able to represent those repudiating the inheritance.

Section 2621. Right of representation defined.

The right which all the legitimate or legally recognized natural relatives of a person have to succeed him in all the rights which he would have if alive, or which he might have inherited, is called the right of representation.

Section 2622. Right in direct descending line; collateral line.

The right of representation shall always take place in the direct descending line but never in the ascending.

In the collateral line it shall take place only in favor of the children of brothers or sisters, whether they be of the whole or half blood.

Section 2623. Division per stirpes.

Whenever the inheritance is taken by representation, the division of the estate shall be made per stirpes; thus the representative or representatives do not inherit any more than that which the person they represent would inherit if alive.

Section 2624. Representation when children of brothers or sisters survive.

When children of one or more brothers and sisters of the deceased survive, they shall succeed the latter by representation, if uncles also survive. But if they alone survive they shall inherit in equal shares.

Section 2625. Representation not lost by renunciation of inheritance.

The right of representing a person is not lost by the renunciation of the inheritance.

Section 2626. Representation of living person.

A living person cannot be represented except in cases of disinheritance or incapacity.

Section 2641. To whom succession pertains in first place.

Succession pertains, in the first place, to the descending direct line.

Section 2642. Sex and age; children of different marriages.

Legitimate and acknowledged illegitimate children and their issue succeed to their fathers and other ancestors without distinction of sex and age and even though they proceed from different marriages.

Section 2643. Rights of children.

The children of the deceased shall always inherit from him in their own right, dividing the inheritance in equal shares.

Section 2644. Grandchildren and other descendants.

The grandchildren and other descendants shall inherit by right of representation, and if one of them should die, leaving several heirs, the portion pertaining to him shall be divided among the latter in equal parts.

Section 2645. Children and descendants of deceased children.

Should any children and descendants of deceased children survive, the former shall inherit in their own right and the latter by right of representation.

Section 2651. When ancestors succeed.

In default of lawful or acknowledged illegitimate issue and their issue, ancestors shall inherit from the decedent to the exclusion of collaterals.

Section 2652. Parents.

The father and the mother as regards their legitimate children, and illegitimate parents as regards their acknowledged natural child, if any, shall inherit in equal shares.

Section 2653. Other ancestors.

In default of father and mother the lawful ancestors nearest in degree shall succeed or natural parents with respect to the illegitimate child recognized by the father or the mother in whose place the ancestor is put by the right of succession.

If there have been different ancestors of the same degree belonging to the same line, the inheritance shall be divided according to the number of ancestors (per capita). If they be of different lines, but of equal degree, one-half shall go to the paternal ancestors and the other half to the maternal ancestors. In each line, the division shall be made according to the number of ancestors (per capita).

Section 2654. Succession of ascendants to things given their descendants.

The provisions of the two preceding sections are understood without prejudice to what is prescribed in Section 2366 of this title, which is applicable to intestate as well as testamentary successions.

Section 2661. Rights of succession of recognized natural children.

In default of legitimate or legitimized descendants or ascendants, the natural children legally recognized shall succeed the deceased in the whole of the inheritance.

If with the natural children there shall concur the descendants of another deceased natural child, the former shall succeed by their own right and the latter by the right of representation.

The rights of inheritance granted to natural children by the two preceding paragraphs shall pass at their death to their descendants, who shall inherit their deceased grandparent.

In case of legitimate children concurring with recognized natural children in the inheritance, the same shall be apportioned to all the children share and share alike.

Should there be legitimate ascendants, the recognized natural descendants shall receive only the portion of the inheritance granted to them in Section 2342 of this title.

A recognized natural child has the right to succeed legitimate children or relatives of the father or mother who has recognized him or her, and they to succeed a recognized natural child.

Should a recognized natural child die, without leaving a legitimate, legitimized, or recognized posterity, the deceased shall be succeeded in his or her entirety by the father or mother who recognized him or her; and if both parents performed the recognition and live, both shall inherit in equal portions.

In default of natural ascendants, the recognized natural child shall be succeeded by his or her natural brothers or sisters, in accordance with the rules established for legitimate brothers and sisters, and if there be no natural brothers or sisters he or she shall be succeeded by the legitimate ascendants and descendants of the father and mother who have recognized him or her.

Section 2671. When collaterals and spouses inherit.

In the absence of the persons included in the three preceding subchapters, the collateral relations and the spouses shall inherit in the order established in the following sections.

Section 2672. Brothers and sisters of whole blood.

Should there be only brothers or sisters of the whole blood, they shall inherit in equal shares.

Section 2673. Brothers and nephews of whole blood.

Should brothers survive with nephews, children of brothers of the whole blood, the former shall inherit per capita and the latter per stirpes.

Section 2674. Brothers of whole blood and brothers of half blood.

Should brothers of the whole blood survive with brothers of half blood, the former shall receive a share in the inheritance double that of the latter.

Section 2675. Brothers of half blood only.

In case there are only brothers of half blood, some on the father's and some on the mother's side, all shall inherit equal shares without distinction of property.

Section 2676. Children of brothers of half blood.

Children of brothers of half blood shall succeed per capita or per stirpes, according to the rules established for brothers or sisters of the whole blood.

Section 2677. Surviving spouse.

In default of brothers and nephews, the surviving spouse shall succeed to all the property of the decedent, whether or not the sisters and nephews be of the whole blood or the half blood.

Section 2678. Other collateral relatives.

Should there be neither brothers nor sisters, nor children of brothers or sisters, nor a surviving spouse, the other collateral relatives shall succeed to the estate of the deceased.

The succession of the latter shall follow without distinction of lines or preference among them by reason of the whole blood.

Section 2691. Right of succession by Commonwealth.

In default of persons who have the right to inherit in accordance with the preceding subchapters, the Commonwealth of Puerto Rico shall take the inheritance and devote the property to the benefit of the University Fund.

Section 2692. Judicial proceeding required for possession of escheated inheritances.

In order that the Commonwealth of Puerto Rico may obtain possession of escheated inheritances, it must be declared entitled by escheat, and the property must be adjudicated to it in default of lawful heirs by means of a judicial proceeding.

Section 2693. Transfer of property of Commonwealth acquired ab intestato to University and Land Authority.

The governor of Puerto Rico is authorized and directed to execute a public instrument or deed ceding to the University of Puerto Rico all the real and personal property that the Commonwealth of Puerto Rico may hereafter acquire by ab intestato inheritance under the provisions of Section 2691, and preceding similar sections of this title, devoted to the Permanent Fund of the University, with the exception of arable lands, which shall be transferred by the governor, in like manner, to the Land Authority of Puerto Rico.[122]

RHODE ISLAND

Section 33-1.1. Real estate descending by intestacy to children or descendants, parents, or brothers and sisters.

Whenever any person having title to any real estate of inheritance shall die intestate as to such estate, it shall descend and pass in equal portions to his kindred in the following course:

First. To his children or their descendant, if any there be.

Second. If there be no children or their descendants, then to the parents in equal shares or to the surviving parent of such intestate.

Third. If there be no parent, then to the brothers and sisters of such intestate, and their descendants, or such of them as there be.

Section 33-1.2. Descent of real estate to paternal or maternal kindred.

If there be no parent, or brother, or sister, or their descendants, the inheritance shall go in equal moieties to the paternal and maternal kindred, each in the following course:

First. To the grandparents, in equal shares, if any there be.

Second. If there be no grandparent, then to the uncles and aunts, or their descendants by representation, or such of them as there be.

Third. If there be no grandparent, or uncle, or aunt, or their descendants, then to the great grandparents in equal shares, if any there be.

Fourth. If there be no great grandparent, then to the great uncles and great aunts of their descendants by representation, or such of them as there be; and so on, in other cases, without end, passing to the nearest lineal ancestors and their descendants or such of them as there be.

Section 33-1-3. Descent when no paternal or maternal kindred survive.

When in this chapter the inheritance is directed to go by moieties to the paternal and maternal kindred, if there be no such kindred on the one part, the whole shall go to the other part; and if there be no kindred either on the one part or the other, the whole shall go to the husband or wife of the intestate, and if the husband or wife be dead, it shall go to his or her kindred in the like course as if such husband or wife had survived the intestate and then died entitled to the estate.

15-7-16. Inheritance by and from adoptive kindred.

A child lawfully adopted shall be deemed, for the purpose of inheritance by such child and his descendants from the parents by adoption and the lineal and collateral kindred of the parents by adoption, and for the purpose of inheritance by the parents by adoption, and the lineal and collateral kindred of the parents by adoption, from such child and his descendants, and for all other legal consequences and incidents of the natural relation of parents and children (except as provided in Sec. 15-7-17), the child of the parents by adoption, the same as if he had been born to them in lawful wedlock. In the construction of any instrument, whether executed before or after the time of the enactment of this chapter, a child so adopted and the descendants of such child shall be deemed within the limitation to the lawful heirs, issue, children, descendants, or the like as the case may be, of the parent or parents by adoption, unless a contrary intention shall appear by the terms thereof or unless the particular estate so limited shall have vested in and as to the person or persons entitled thereto on April 20, 1962; provided that this sentence shall not apply to the construction of any instrument as to any child who is over the age of eighteen (18) years at the time of his adoption and who is adopted after the death of the maker of such instrument.

When a child so adopted is related by blood to the parent or parents by adoption, he and his descendants shall be entitled to inherit from and through such parent or parents only as adopted child or descendants of an adopted child and not by virtue of such blood relationship.[123]

SOUTH CAROLINA

Section 21-3-20. Intestate distribution; presumptions as to missing persons.

(1) If the intestate shall leave a widow and more than one child, the widow shall take one-third of the estate and the remaining two-thirds shall be divided equally among the children; but if the intestate shall leave a widow and only one child, then the widow shall take one-half of the estate and the child shall take the remaining one-half of such estate.

The lineal descendants of the deceased shall represent their respective parents and shall take among them the share or shares to which their parents would have been entitled had such parent survived the intestate.

(2) If the intestate shall leave no child or other lineal descendant but shall leave a widow and a father and mother and brothers and sisters or brother or sister of the whole blood, the estate, real and personal, of such intestate shall be distributed in the following manner, that is to say: The widow shall be entitled to one moiety thereof, and the other moiety shall be equally divided amongst the father and the mother and the brethren of the whole blood, so that such father and mother and each brother and sister shall receive an equal share thereof. The children of a deceased brother or sister of the whole blood shall take among them the share which their parent would have been entitled to had such parent survived the intestate; provided, that there shall be no representation admitted among collaterals after the brothers' and sisters' children. If the intestate leaves no father and mother the provision made in this item for such parents shall go as the rest of the estate is directed to be distributed herein. If the intestate shall not leave a child or other lineal descendant or brothers, or sisters, one or more, of the whole blood, or children of a brother or sister of the whole blood but

shall leave a widow and a father and mother, the widow of the intestate shall be entitled to one moiety of the estate and the father and the mother to the other moiety; and if either father or mother be dead such moiety shall go to the survivor of them.

(3) If the intestate shall not leave a lineal descendant, father or mother, but shall leave a widow and brothers and sisters or a brother or sister of the whole blood, the widow shall be entitled to one moiety of the estate and the brothers and sisters or brother or sister to the other moiety as tenants in common. The children of a deceased brother or sister shall take among them respectively the share which their respective ancestors would have been entitled to had they survived the intestate.

(4) If the intestate shall leave no child or other lineal descendant, father, mother, brother, or sister of the whole blood, but shall leave a widow and brother or sister of the half blood and a child or children of a brother or sister of the whole blood, the widow shall take one moiety of the estate and the other moiety shall be equally divided between the brothers and sisters of the half blood, and the children of the brothers and sisters of the whole blood, the children of every deceased brother and sister of the whole blood taking among them a share equal to the share of a brother or sister of the half blood. If there be no brother or sister of the half blood, then a moiety of the estate shall descend to the child or children of the deceased brother or sister of the whole blood, taking by representation of the parent, and if there be no child of a brother or sister of the whole blood, then said moiety shall descend to the brothers and sisters of the half blood.

(5) If the intestate shall leave no child or other lineal descendant, father, mother, brother, or sister of the whole blood or their children or brother or sister of the half blood, then the widow shall take one moiety and the lineal ancestor, if any there be, the other moiety.

(6) If the intestate shall leave no child or other lineal descendant, father, mother, brother or sister of the whole blood, or child of such brother or sister of the whole blood, or brother or sister of the half blood, or lineal ancestor, the widow shall take the entire estate. If the intestate shall leave no widow the estate shall descend in equal parts to the uncles and aunts, the children of a deceased uncle or aunt to take among them the share to which their parent would have been entitled had such parent survived the intestate. If there be no uncle, aunt, or child of a deceased uncle or aunt, then the estate shall descend to the next of kin.

In reckoning the degree of kindred, the computation shall begin with the intestate and be continued up to the common ancestor and then down to the person claimed kindred inclusively, each step inclusively being reckoned as a degree.

(7) If the intestate shall leave no widow the provision made for her shall go as the rest of the estate is directed to be distributed in the respective clauses in which the widow is provided for.

(8) On the death of a married woman intestate the husband shall be entitled to the same share of her estate as is herein given to the widow out of the estate of the husband and the remainder of her estate shall be distributed among her descendants and relations in the same manner as is directed in case of intestacy of a married man.

If the intestate leaves no husband, the provision herein made for him shall go as the rest of the estate is directed to be distributed in the preceding clauses.

(9) If any married person shall die without leaving any child or other lineal descendant, father, mother, brother or sister of the whole blood or their children, brother or sister of the half blood, lineal ancestor or next of kin, then the wife shall inherit from the husband and the husband from the wife the whole of the real and personal estate of which the other died seized or possessed or was interested in or entitled unto.

(10) If any person shall die without leaving any spouse, child or other lineal descendant, father, mother, brother, or sister of the whole blood, or heir children, brother or sister of the half blood, lineal ancestor or next of kin, but shall leave surviving a stepchild or stepchildren, then such stepchild or stepchildren shall inherit from the decedent the whole of the real and personal estate as tenants in common.

(11) Whenever any person shall be presumed dead by reason of disappearance or long unexplained absence under the common law rule in this state and such person shall have been unmarried at the time of such disappearance and when last heard from, then such person shall further be presumed to have died intestate.[124]

SOUTH DAKOTA

29-1-4. Intestate succession when not otherwise limited.

Subject to debts. When any person having title to any estate not otherwise limited by marriage contract dies without disposing of the estate by will, it is succeeded to and must be distributed, unless otherwise expressly provided in this code, subject to the payment of his debts, in the manner provided by Sections 29-1-5 to 29-1-9, inclusive, or by Section 29-1-24.

29-1-5. Succession when issue survive.

If the decedent leave a surviving husband or wife, and only one child, or the lawful issue of one child, his estate is succeeded to and must be distributed in equal shares to the surviving husband or wife and child or issue of such child. If the decedent leave a surviving husband or wife, and more than one child living, and the lawful issue of one or more deceased children, his estate is succeeded to and must be distributed one-third to the surviving husband or wife and the remainder in equal shares to his children and to the lawful issue of any deceased child, by right of representation; but if there be no child of the decedent living at his death, the remainder goes to all of his lineal descendants; and if all the descendants are in the same degree of kindred to the decedent, they share equally, otherwise they take according to the right of representation. If the decedent leave no surviving husband or wife, but leave issue, the whole estate goes to such issue, and if such issue consists of more than one child living, or one child living and the lawful issue of one or more deceased children, then the estate goes in equal shares to the children living, or to the child living, and the issue of the deceased child or children by right of representation.

29-1-6. Succession when no issue survive but spouse and relatives survive.

Succession by parent when no issue or spouse survives. If the decedent leaves no issue and the estate does not exceed in value one hundred thousand dollars, all the estate goes to the surviving husband or wife; if the estate exceeds one hundred thousand dollars, then the first one hundred thousand dollars goes to the survivor, who shall have the right of selecting the same, and of all property in excess of one hundred thousand dollars in value, one-half goes to the surviving husband or wife, and the other half goes to the decedent's father and mother in equal shares, and if either is dead the whole goes to the other, but if neither survives, then such portion goes in equal shares to the brothers and sisters of the decedent and to the children or grandchildren of any deceased brother or sister by right of representation. If the decedent leaves no issue, or husband or wife, the estate must go to his father and mother in equal shares, or if either is dead, then to the other.

29-1-7. Succession by brothers and sisters and their issue.

If there be no issue, or husband, or wife, or father, or mother, then the estate is succeeded to and must be distributed in equal shares to the brothers and sisters of the decedent and to the children or grandchildren of any deceased brother or sister by right of representation.

29-1-8. Succession by spouse when no issue, parent, brother, or sister survives.

If the decedent leaves a surviving husband or wife, and no issue, and no father, or mother, or brother, or sister, the whole estate goes to the surviving husband or wife.

29-1-9. Succession by collateral kindred.

Preference among kindred. If the decedent leaves no issue, or husband, or wife, and no father, or mother, or brother, or sister, or descendants of a deceased brother or sister, the estate must go to the next of kin, in equal degree, excepting that when there are two or more collateral kindred, in equal degree, but claiming through different ancestors, those claiming through the nearest ancestors must be preferred to those claiming through an ancestor more remote.

29-1-24. Escheat to common school fund in absence of heirs.

Standing of state as heir—charges and trusts against property passing to state. If there is no one capable of succeeding under Sections 29-1-5 to 29-1-9, inclusive, the property of the decedent escheats to the state as the ultimate heir for the support of the common schools. In any such case the state shall be entitled to all the rights of an heir in any county court and shall be deemed included in the words ''heir'' or ''heirs'' and the phrase ''any person interested'' or similar expressions as used in title 30 and shall have the same right as any other claimant to heirship to institute, participate in, and direct probate proceedings, and the circuit courts of this state are invested with jurisdiction to hear and determine any claim of the estate in such cases in the course of probate proceedings, and to adjudge therein that an estate has escheated, and enter final decree accordingly, subject to the provisions of Sections 30-23-18 to 30-23-20, inclusive. When any real property passes to the state under this section, it is subject, in the hands of the state or its grantees, to the same charges and trusts to which it would have been subject if it had passed to other heirs under Sections 29-1-5 to 29-1-9, inclusive.[125]

TENNESSEE

Section 31-110. General rules of descent.

When any person shall die intestate, after the payment of the debts and charges against the estate his or her property, both real and personal shall descend as follows:

(1) To the husband or wife and children, or the descendants of children representing them equally, the husband or wife taking a child's share but never less than one-third (1/3) of the property.

(2) To the husband or wife altogether, if there are no children or the descendants of children.

(3) To the children, or their descendants, in equal parts, if there is no husband or wife, the descendants taking, in equal parts, the shares of their deceased parents.

(4) If no husband, wife, or children, or descendants of children, to the father and mother in equal parts, but if either father or mother be dead, then to the survivor of them, provided, however, that where the father and mother of a person dying intestate have been divorced by valid decree which commits the custody of such person to one (1) of the parents to the exclusion of the other, then the property of such person shall be distributed to that parent to whom such custody has been committed, as sole next of kin, to the exclusion of the other parent.

(5) If no father or mother, to brothers and sisters or the children of such brothers and sisters representing them equally.

(6) If no brother or sister, or their children, to every of the next of kin of the intestate who are in equal degree equally.

(7) There is no representation among collaterals, after intestate's brothers' and sisters' children.

Section 31-111. Descent of homestead.

The homestead exempt in the possession of or belonging to each head of a family shall, upon his death, any provision by will to the contrary notwithstanding, go to the surviving spouse during his natural life, with the products thereof, for his own use and benefit and that of his family who reside with him, and upon his death, any provision by will to the contrary notwithstanding, it shall go to the minor children of the decedent, free from the debts of the father, mother, or said children.

Section 31-201. Intestate estate.

When any person shall die intestate, after the payment of debts and charges against the estate, his property passes to his heirs as prescribed in the following sections of this chapter. Any part of the estate of a decedent not effectively disposed of by his will passes to his heirs in the same manner.

Section 31-202. Share of the surviving spouse.

The intestate share of the surviving spouse is:

(1) If there is no surviving issue of the decedent, the entire intestate estate;

(2) If there is no surviving issue of the decedent, either one-third (1/3) or a child's share of the entire intestate estate, whichever is greater.

(3) If there is no surviving issue or parent, to the brothers and sisters and the issue of each deceased brother and sister by representation; if there is no surviving brother or sister, the issue of brothers and sisters take by representation;

(4) If there is no surviving spouse, parent, or issue of a parent, but the decedent is survived by one or more grandparents or issue of grandparents, half of the estate passes to the paternal grandparents if both survive, or to the surviving paternal grandparent or to the issue of the paternal grandparent or to the issue of the paternal grandparents if both are deceased, the issue taking equally if they are all of the same degree of kinship to the decedent, but if of unequal degree those of more remote degree take by representation; and the other half passes to the maternal relatives in the same manner; but if there be no surviving grandparent or issue of grandparent on either the paternal or maternal side, the entire estate passes to the relatives on the other side in the same manner as the half.[126]

TEXAS

Section 38. Persons who take upon intestacy.

(a) Intestate leaving no husband or wife. Where any person, having title to any estate, real, personal or mixed, shall die intestate, leaving no husband or wife, it shall descend and pass in parcenary to his kindred, male and female, in the following course:

1. To his children and their descendants.

2. If there be no children or their descendants, then to his father and mother, in equal portions. But if only the father or mother survive the intestate, then his estate shall be divided into two equal portions, one of which shall pass to such survivor and the other half shall pass to the brothers and sisters of the deceased

and to their descendants; but if there be none such, then the whole estate shall be inherited by the surviving father or mother.

3. If there be neither father nor mother, then the whole of such estate shall pass to the brothers and sisters of the intestate and to their descendants.

4. If there be none of the kindred aforesaid, then the inheritance shall be divided into two moieties, one of which shall go to the paternal and the other to the maternal kindred, in the following course: To the grandfather and grandmother in equal portions, but if only one of these be living, then the estate shall be divided into two equal parts, one of which shall go to such survivor and the other shall go to the descendant or descendants of such deceased grandfather or grandmother. If there be no such descendants, then the whole estate shall be inherited by the surviving grandfather or grandmother. If there be no surviving grandfather or grandmother, then the whole of such estate shall go to their descendants, and so on without end, passing in like manner to the nearest lineal ancestors and their descendants.

(b) Intestate leaving husband or wife. Where any person having title to any estate, real, personal, or mixed, other than a community estate, shall die intestate as to such estate, and shall leave a surviving husband or wife, such estate of such intestate shall descend and pass as follows:

1. If the deceased have a child or children, or their descendants, the surviving husband or wife shall take one-third of the personal estate, and the balance of such personal estate shall go to the child or children of the deceased and their descendants. The surviving husband or wife shall also be entitled to an estate for life, in one-third of the land of the intestate, with remainder to the child or children of the intestate and their descendants.

2. If the deceased have no child or children, or their descendants, then the surviving husband or wife shall be entitled to all the personal estate, and to one-half of the lands of the intestate, without remainder to any person, and the other half shall pass and be inherited according to the rules of descent and distribution; provided, however, that if the deceased has neither surviving father nor mother nor surviving brothers or sisters, or their descendants, then the surviving husband or wife shall be entitled to the whole of the estate of such intestate.

Section 39. No distinction because of property's source.

There shall be no distinction in regulating the descent and distribution of the estate of a person dying intestate between property which may have been derived by gift, devise, or descent from the father and that which may have been derived by gift, devise, or descent from the mother; and all the estate to which such intestate may have had title at the time of death shall descend and vest in the heirs of such person in the same manner as if he had been the original purchaser thereof.

Section 43. Determination of per capita and per stirpes distribution.

When the intestate's children or brothers, sisters, uncles, and aunts, or any other relatives of the deceased standing in the first or same degree alone come into the distribution upon intestacy, they shall take per capita, namely: by persons; and, when a part of them being dead and a part living, the descendants of those dead shall have right to distribution upon intestacy, such descendants shall inherit only such portion of said property as the parent through whom they inherit would be entitled to if alive.

Section 45. Community estate.

Upon the dissolution of the marriage relation by death, all property belonging to the community estate of the husband and wife shall go to the survivor, if there be no child or children of the deceased or their descendants; but if there be a child or children of the deceased, or descendants of such child or children, then the survivor shall be entitled to one-half of said property, and the other half shall pass to such child or children, or their descendants. But such descendants shall inherit only such portion of said property as the parent through whom they inherit would be entitled to if alive. In every case, the community estate passes charged with the debts against it.

Section 46. Joint tenancies abolished.

(a) Where two (2) or more persons hold an estate, real, personal, or mixed, jointly, and one (1) joint owner dies before severance, his interest in said joint estate shall not survive to the remaining joint owner or joint owners but shall descend to, and be vested in, the heirs or legal representatives of such deceased joint owner in the same manner as if his interest had been severed and ascertained. Provided, however, that by an agreement in writing of joint owners of property the interest of any joint owner who dies may be made to survive to the surviving joint owner or joint owners, but no such agreement shall be inferred from the mere fact that the property is held in joint ownership.

(b) A written agreement between spouse and a bank, savings and loan, credit union, or other financial institution may provide that existing funds or securities on deposit and funds and securities to be deposited in the future and interest and income thereof shall by that agreement be partitioned into separate property and may further provide that the property partitioned by that agreement be held in joint tenancies and pass by right of survivorship.[127]

UTAH

75-2-101: Intestate estate.

Any part of the estate of a decedent not effectively disposed of by his will passes to his heirs as prescribed in the following sections of this code.

75-2-102: Share of the spouse.

1. The intestate share of the surviving spouse is:

(a) If there is no surviving issue or parent of the decedent, the entire intestate estate;

(b) If there is no surviving issue but the decedent is survived by a parent or parents, the first $100,000, plus one-half of the balance of the intestate estate;

(c) If there are surviving issue all of whom are issue of the surviving spouse also, the first $50,000, plus one-half of the balance of the intestate estate;

(d) If there are surviving issue one or more of whom are not issue of the surviving spouse, one-half of the intestate estate.

75-2-103: Share of heirs other than surviving spouse.

1. The part of the intestate estate not passing to the surviving spouse under Section 75-2-102, or the entire intestate estate if there is no surviving spouse, passes as follows:

(a) To the issue of the decedent by representation.

(b) If there is no surviving issue, to his parent or parents equally.

(c) If there is no surviving issue or parent, to the issue of the parents or either of them by representation.

(d) If there is no surviving issue, parent, or issue of a parent, but the decedent is survived by one or more grandparents or issue of grandparents, half of the estate passes to the paternal grandparents if both survive or to the surviving paternal grandparent or to the issue of the paternal grandparents if both are deceased, the issue taking by representation; and the other half passes to the maternal relatives in the same manner; but if there be no surviving grandparent or issue of grandparent on either the paternal or the maternal side, the entire estate passes to the relatives on the other side in the same manner as the half.

(e) If there is no surviving issue, parent or issue of a parent, grandparent or issue of a grandparent, then the entire estate passes to the next kin in equal degree, excepting that when there are two or more collateral kindred in equal degree, but claiming through different ancestors, those who claim through the nearest ancestor must be preferred to those claiming through an ancestor more remote.

75-2-104: Requirement that heir survive decedent for 120 hours.

Any person who fails to survive the decedent by 120 hours is deemed to have predeceased the decedent for purposes of homestead allowance, exempt property, and intestate succession, and the decedent's heirs are determined accordingly. If the time of the death of the decedent or of the person who would otherwise be an heir, or the times of death of both, cannot be determined, and it cannot be established that the person who would otherwise be an heir has survived the decedent by 120 hours, it is deemed that the person failed to survive for the required period. This section is not to be applied where its application would result in a taking of intestate estate by the state under Section 75-2-105.

75-2-105: No taker.

If there is no taker under the provisions of this part, the intestate estate passes to the state for the benefit of the state school fund.[128]

VERMONT

Section 551. General rules of descent.

The real and personal estate of a decedent, not devised or bequeathed and not otherwise appropriated and distributed in pursuance of law, shall descend in the following manner:

(1) In equal shares to the children of such decedent or the legal representatives of deceased children;

(2) If the decedent is married and leaves no issue and the surviving spouse does not elect to take a third in value of the real estate of which the decedent dies seised in his or her own right, or waives the provisions of the will of such decedent, such spouse shall be entitled to the whole of the decedent's estate forever, if it does not exceed $25,000.00 but if it exceeds that sum, then such spouse shall be entitled to $25,000.00 and half the remainder. The remainder of such estate shall descend as the whole would if such spouse did not survive. If the decedent has no kindred who may inherit the estate, such spouse shall be entitled to the whole of such estate;

(3) If the decedent does not leave issue or surviving spouse, the estate shall descend in equal shares to the father and mother of such decedent. If the mother is not living and the father survives, the estate shall descend to the father. If the father is not living and the mother survives, the estate shall descend to the mother;

(4) If the decedent does not leave issue or surviving spouse, or father, or mother, the estate shall descend in equal shares to the brothers and sisters of such decedent and to the legal representatives of deceased brothers and sisters;

(5) If none of the kindred above named survives the decedent, the estate shall descend in equal shares to the next of kin in equal degree; but a person shall not be entitled, by right of representation, to the share of such next of kin who has died.

(6) Notwithstanding the foregoing rules or provisions otherwise made in any case where a person is entitled to inherit, including a devisee or legatee under the last will of the decedent, such person's share in the decedent's estate shall be forfeited and shall pass to the remaining heirs of the decedent if such person stands convicted in any court of the United States or by any of the individual states of the United States of intentionally and unlawfully killing the decedent. In any proceedings to contest the right of a person to inherit, the record of such person's conviction of intentionally and unlawfully killing the decedent shall be admissible evidence and may be taken as sufficient proof that such person did intentionally kill the decedent. This act shall take effect with respect to the estates of decedents who die on or after July 1, 1970.

Section 559. Person absent and unheard of; share of.

If a person entitled to a distributive share of the estate of a decedent is absent and unheard of for fifteen years, five years of which are after the death of such decedent, or is absent and unheard of for a period of twenty-five years, two years of which are after such death, the probate court may order the share of such absent person distributed among his lineal heirs, if it is shown to the probate court that he has any, otherwise among the heirs of such decedent. If such absent person proves to be alive, he shall be entitled to his share of such estate notwithstanding such distribution and may recover in an action of contract on this statute any portion thereof which any one received under such order. Before an order is made for the payment or distribution of any money or estate as herein authorized, the probate court shall cause the same notice to be given as upon the settlement of an administrator's account and such other notice by publication or otherwise, as the court deems proper.

DOMESTIC RELATIONS

Section 448. Rights, duties, obligations.

Upon the issuance of a final adoption decree the same rights, duties, and obligations and the same right of inheritance shall exist between the parties as though the person adopted had been the legitimate child of the person or persons making the adoption, except that the person adopted shall not be capable of taking property expressly limited to the heirs of the body of the persons making such adoption. The same right of inheritance shall exist between the person adopted and his issue on the one hand and natural or adopted children of the person or persons making the adoption and their issue on the other hand as though the person adopted had been the legitimate child of the person or persons making the adoption. However, there shall be no right of inheritance between the person adopted and his issue on the one hand and predecessors in line of descent and collateral kin of the person or persons making the adoption on the other hand. The natural parents of a minor shall be deprived, by the adoption, of all legal right to control of such minor, and such minor shall be freed from all obligations of obedience and maintenance to them. A person adopted shall have the same right of inheritance from and through his natural parents as though the adoption had not occurred, but the natural parents, predecessors in line of descent, and collateral kin of a person adopted shall be deprived of all right of inheritance from or through such person. Notwithstanding the foregoing provisions of this section, when the adoption is made by a spouse of a natural parent, obligations of obedience to and rights of inheritance by and through the natural parent who has inter-married with the adopting parent shall not be affected.[129]

VIRGINIA

Section 64.1-1. Course of descents generally.

When any person having title to any real estate of inheritance shall die intestate as to such estate, it shall descend and pass in parcenary to such of his kindred, male and female, in the following course:

First. To the intestate's children and their descendants subject to the provisions of Section 64.1-19.

Second. If there be no child, nor the descendant of any child, then the whole shall go to the surviving spouse of the intestate.

Third. If there be none such, then to his or her father and mother or the survivor.

Fourth. If there be none such, then to his or her brothers and sisters and their descendants.

Fifth. If there be none such, then one moiety shall go to the paternal, the other to the maternal kindred, of the intestate, in the following course:

Sixth. First to the grandfather and grandmother or the survivor.

Seventh. If there be none, then to the uncles and aunts and their descendants.

Eighth. If there be none such, then to the great-grandfathers or great-grandfather and great-grandmothers or great-grandmother.

Ninth. If there be none, then to the brothers and sisters of the grandfathers and grandmothers and their descendants.

Tenth. And so on, in other cases, without end, passing to the nearest lineal ancestors and the descendants of such ancestors.

Eleventh. If there be no paternal kindred, the whole shall go to the maternal kindred; and if there be no maternal kindred, the whole shall go to the paternal kindred. If there be neither maternal nor paternal kindred, the whole shall go to the kindred of the husband or wife, in the like course as if such husband or wife had died entitled to the estate.

Section 64.1-2. How collaterals of half blood inherit.

Collaterals of the half blood shall inherit only half so much as those of the whole blood; but if all the collaterals be of the half blood, the ascending kindred, if any, shall have double portions.

Section 64.1-3. When parties take per capita and when per stirpes.

Whenever those entitled to partition are all in the same degree of kindred to the intestate, they shall take per capita or by persons; and when, a part of them being dead and a part living, the issue of those dead have right to partition, such issue shall take per stirpes or by stocks, that is to say, the shares of their deceased parents.

Section 64.1-11. Distribution of personal estate.

When any person shall die intestate as to his personal estate or any part thereof, the surplus (subject to the provisions of Title 34) after payment of funeral expenses, charges of administration, and debts shall pass and be distributed to and among the same persons, and in the same proportions, to whom and in which real estate is directed to descend, except that if the intestate was married, the surviving spouse shall be entitled to one-third of such surplus, if the intestate left surviving children or their descendants. If no such children or their descendants survive, the surviving spouse shall be entitled to the whole of such surplus.

Section 64.1-12. Right of state, if no other distributee.

To the Commonwealth shall accrue all the personal estate of every decedent of which there is no other distributee.[130]

VIRGIN ISLANDS

Section 84: Descent and distribution of estate of decedent.

The real property of a deceased person, male or female, not devised, shall descend, and the surplus of his or her personal property, after payment of debts and legacies, and if not bequeathed, shall be distributed to the surviving spouse, children, or next of kin or other persons, in manner following:

1. One-third to the surviving spouse and the residue in equal portions to the children, and such persons as legally represent the children if any of them have died before the deceased.

2. If the deceased leaves a surviving spouse and both parents surviving, and no child or descendant, the surviving spouse shall take five thousand dollars and one-half of the residue, and the parents shall take the balance; if there be no surviving spouse, the surviving parent shall take the whole.

3. If the deceased leaves one parent surviving, and no child or descendant, and a surviving spouse, the surviving spouse shall take five thousand dollars and one-half of the residue, and the parents shall take the balance; if there be no surviving spouse, the surviving parent shall take the whole.

4. If the deceased leaves a surviving spouse, and no descendant, parent, brother or sister, nephew or niece, the surviving spouse shall be entitled to the whole thereof; but if there be a brother or sister, nephew or niece, and no descendant or parent, the surviving spouse shall take ten thousand dollars and one-half of the residue, and the balance shall descend and be distributed to the brothers and sisters and their representatives.

5. If there be no surviving spouse, the whole thereof shall descend and be distributed equally to and among the children and such as legally represent them.

6. If there be no surviving spouse, and no children, and no representatives of a child, and no parent, the whole shall descend and be distributed to the next of kin in equal degrees to the deceased; and if all the brothers and sisters of the intestate be living, the whole shall descend and be distributed to them; if any of them be living and any be dead, per stirpes to the brothers and sisters living, and the descendants in whatever degree of those dead; so that to each living brother or sister shall descend or be distributed such shares as would have descended or been distributed to him or her if all the brothers and sisters of the intestate who shall have died leaving issue had been living, and so that there shall be distributed to such descendants in whatever degree, collectively, the share which their parent would have received if living; and the same rule shall prevail as to all direct lineal descendants of every brother and sister of the intestate whenever such descendants are of unequal degrees.

7. If the deceased was illegitimate and leaves a mother, and no child, or descendant, and no surviving spouse, such mother shall take the whole and shall be entitled to letters of administration in exclusion of all other persons. If the deceased shall leave a surviving spouse, the surviving spouse shall take five thousand dollars and one-half of the residue and the mother shall take the balance.

If the mother of such deceased be dead, the relatives of the deceased on the part of the mother shall take in the same manner as if the deceased had been legitimate and be entitled to letters of administration in the same order.

8. Where the distributees of the deceased, entitled to share in his estate, are all in equal degree to the deceased, their shares shall be equal.

9. When such distributees are of unequal degrees of kindred, the whole shall descend and shall be distributed to those entitled thereto, according to their respective stocks; so that those who take in their own right shall receive equal shares, and those who take by representation shall receive the share to which the parent whom they represent, if living, would have been entitled.

10. No representation shall be admitted among collaterals after brothers' and sisters' descendants.

11. Relatives of the half-blood shall take equally with those of the whole blood in the same degree; and the representatives of such relatives shall take in the same manner as if they had been born in the lifetime of the deceased and had survived him.[131]

WASHINGTON

11.04.015 Descent and distribution of real and personal estate.

The net estate of a person dying intestate, or that portion thereof with respect to which the person shall have died intestate, shall descend subject to the provisions of RCW 11.04.250 and RCW 11.02.070 and shall be distributed as follows:

(1) Share of surviving spouse. The surviving spouse shall receive the following share:

(a) All of the decedent's share of the net community estate; and

(b) One-half of the net separate estate if the intestate is survived by issue; or

(c) Three-quarters of the net separate estate if there is no surviving issue, but the intestate is survived by one or more of his parents, or by one or more of the issue of one or more of his parents; or

(d) All of the net separate estate, if there is no surviving issue or parent or issue of parent.

(2) Shares of others than surviving spouse. The share of the net estate not distributable to the surviving spouse, or the entire net estate if there is no surviving spouse, shall descend and be distributed as follows:

(a) To the issue of the intestate, if they are all in the same degree of kinship to the intestate, they shall take equally, or if of unequal degree, then those of more remote degree shall take by representation.

(b) If the intestate not be survived by issue, then to the parent or parents who survive the intestate.

(c) If the intestate not be survived by issue or by either parent, then to those issue of the parent or parents who survive the intestate; if they are all in the same degree of kinship to the intestate, they shall take equally, or, if of unequal degree, then those of more remote degree shall take by representation.

(d) If the intestate not be survived by issue or by either parent, or by any issue of the parent or parents who survive the decedent, then to the grandparent or grandparents who survive the intestate; if both maternal and paternal grandparents survive the intestate, the maternal grandparent or grandparents shall take one-half and the paternal grandparent or grandparents shall take one-half.

(e) If the intestate not be survived by issue or by either parent, or by any issue of the parent or parents or by any grandparent or grandparents, then to those issue of any grandparent or grandparents who survive the intestate; taken as a group, the issue of the maternal grandparent or grandparents shall share equally with the issue of the paternal grandparent or grandparents, also as a group; within each such group, all members share equally if they are all in the same degree of kinship to the intestate, or, if some be of unequal degree, then those of more remote degree shall take by representation.[132]

WEST VIRGINIA

Section 42-1-1. Course of descent generally.

When any person having title to any real estate of inheritance shall die intestate as to such estate, it shall descend and pass in parcenary to his kindred, male and female, in the following course:

(a) To his children and their descendants;

(b) If there be no child, or descendant of any child, then the whole shall go to the wife or husband, as the case may be;

(c) If there be no child, or descendant of any child, or wife, or husband, then one moiety each to the mother and father; or if there be no child, or descendant of any child, or wife, or husband, or mother, then the whole shall go the father; or if there be no child, or any descendant of any child, or wife, or husband, or father, then the whole shall go to the mother;

(d) If there be no child, or descendant of any child, or wife, or husband, or mother, or father, the whole shall go to the intestate's brothers and sisters and the descendants of brothers and sisters;

(e) And if there be no child, or descendant of any child, or father, or mother, or wife or husband, or brother, or sister, or descendant of any brother or sister, then one moiety shall go to the paternal and the other to the maternal kindred in the following course:

(f) First to the grandfather and grandmother one-half of the moiety each;

(g) If no grandmother, one-half of the moiety to the grandfather, or if no grandfather, one-half of the moiety to the grandmother; and in either case the other one-half of the moiety, or if there be neither grandfather nor grandmother, the whole of the moiety, shall go to the uncles and aunts on the same side and their descendants;

(h) If there be no grandmother, or such uncle, or such aunt, or descendant of any such uncle or aunt, then the whole of the moiety to the grandfather; or if there be no grandfather, or such uncle, or such aunt, or descendant of any such uncle or aunt, then the whole of the moiety to the grandmother;

(i) If there be no grandfather, or grandmother, or such uncle, or such aunt, or descendant of any such uncle or aunt, then to the great-grandfathers and great-grandmothers one-fourth of the moiety each;

(j) If any great-grandfather or great-grandmother be dead, then his or her share, or the whole of the moiety in case all the great-grandfathers and great-grandmothers be dead, shall go to the brothers and sisters of the grandfathers and grandmothers and the descendants of such brothers and sisters of the grandfathers and grandmothers; and if there be no brother or sister of any grandfather or grandmother, or the descendant of any such brother or sister, then the whole of the moiety shall go to such of the great-grandfathers and great-grandmothers as may then be living, in equal shares, or to the survivor of them;

(k) And so on, in like manner, in other cases without end, passing to the nearest lineal ancestors, male and female, and if any of them be dead his or her share, or if all of them be dead, the whole, to the brothers and sisters of the lineal ancestors, male and female, of the degree next nearer the intestate and the descendants of such brothers and sisters; and if there be no brother or sister of any lineal ancestor, male or female, of the degree next nearer the intestate or descendant of any such brother or sister, then to such of the lineal ancestors in this subdivision (k) first mentioned as may then be living, in equal shares, or to the survivor of them;

(1) If there be no paternal kindred the whole shall go to the maternal kindred, and if there be no maternal kindred the whole shall go to the paternal kindred. If there be neither paternal nor maternal kindred, the whole shall go to the kindred of the wife or husband of the intestate in the like course as if such wife or husband had survived the intestate and died entitled to the whole of the estate.

Section 42-1-3. When parties take per capita and when per stirpes.

Whenever the children of the intestate, or the brothers and sisters of the intestate, or the uncles and aunts of the intestate, or the brothers and sisters of any of the intestate's lineal ancestors of the same degree, come into partition, they shall take per capita or by persons; and where, a part of them being dead and a part living, the descendants of those dead have right to partition, such descendants shall take per stirpes, or by stocks, that is to say, the shares of their deceased ancestors; but whenever the persons entitled to partition, other than those whose shares are definitely fixed by the statute of descents, are all in the same degree of kindred to the intestate, they shall take per capita or by persons.

Section 42-1-9. Establishment and recordation of descent.

Where any person having title to an estate of inheritance in real estate within this state has died intestate, or testate, without having devised his real estate, his heirs, or any of them, or any person deriving title from or through such heirs, or any of them, may at any time within twenty years after the death of such person present to the circuit court of the county where such real estate, or any part thereof, is situated, a petition, under oath, describing such real estate, setting forth the interest or share of the petitioner and of each other heir of the decedent in such real estate, and praying for a decree establishing the right of inheritance thereto, and that all the heirs of the decedent, and other parties in interest may be summoned to show cause why the prayer of the petition should not be granted. There shall also be set out in the petition and be made parties, the heirs or devisees of any person who inherited from the decedent but who had died before the proceeding is instituted, and any purchasers or successors in title from such a person, and any holders of liens on the whole property or on the share of any person interested in the property. Upon the presentation of such petition a rule to show cause, returnable within such time as the court shall direct, shall be issued accordingly, except in a case where all the interest parties unite in such petition or appear and waive service of the rule. Guardians ad litem for all infants, convicts in confinement and insane persons, who may be parties to such proceeding, shall be appointed and attend, and nonresident persons may be proceeded against by order of publication, as in other cases. Upon the return of the rule to show cause the circuit court shall hear the allegations and proofs of the parties and determine all the issues raised. The petitioner shall establish the fact of the decedent's death; the place of his residence at the time of his death; his will or intestacy, either generally, or as to the real estate in question; the heirs entitled to inherit the real estate in question; the name, age, residence and relationship to the decedent, of each; and the interest or share of each heir or other person in such real estate. The court, when these facts are established, shall make a decree describing the real estate and declaring that the right of inheritance thereto has been established to the court's satisfaction, in accordance with the facts which shall be recited in the decree, and that at the death of the testator or intestate certain persons, who shall be named in the decree, were entitled to take the property in certain proportions, which shall also be set out in the decree. A certified copy of such decree shall be recorded in the office of the clerk of the county court of the county or counties in which such real estate is situated, in the record of deeds, and indexed in the general index of deeds in the name of the decedent as if grantor, and in the name of each heir as if grantee, and the fees for such recording and indexing shall be the same as for deeds. From the time when such copy is so recorded, the decree, or the record thereof, shall be conclusive evidence of the facts so declared to be established thereby against all parties to such proceeding.

An appeal from such decree shall lie to the supreme court of appeals as in other cases, and any person under disability or proceeded against by publication and not appearing may have the matter reheard as in other cases.[133]

WISCONSIN

Section 852.01 Basic Rules for intestate succession.

(1) Who are heirs. The net estate of a decedent which he has not disposed of

by will, whether he dies without a will, or with a will which does not completely dispose of his estate, passes to his surviving heirs as follows:

(a) To the spouse:

1. If there are no surviving issue of the decedent, the entire estate;

2. If there are surviving issue all of whom are issue of the surviving spouse also, the first $25,000 (reduced, in case of partial intestacy, by any amount given the spouse by the will) plus one-half of the balance if there is only one surviving child and no surviving issue of a deceased child, or if only the issue of one deceased child survives, but one-third of the balance in other cases; property distributed to satisfy the dollar amount under this provision is valued at current fair market value at time of distribution;

3. If there are surviving issue one or more of whom are not issue of the surviving spouse, one-half of the estate if there is only one surviving child and no issue of a deceased child, or if only the issue of one deceased child survives, and in other cases one-third of the estate.

(b) To the issue, the share of the estate not passing to the spouse under par.(a), or the entire estate if there is no surviving spouse; if the issue are all in the same degree of kinship to the decedent they take equally, but if they are of unequal degree, then those of more remote degrees take by representation.

(c) If there is no surviving spouse or issue, to the parents.

(d) If there is no surviving spouse, issue, or parent, to the brothers and sisters and the issue of any deceased brother or sister by representation.

(e) If there is no surviving spouse, issue, parent, or brother or sister, to the issue of brothers and sisters; if such issue are all in the same degree of kinship to the decedent, they take equally, but if they are of unequal degree, then those of more remote degrees take by representation.

(2) Requirement that heir survive decedent for a certain time. If any person who would otherwise be an heir under sub.(1) dies within 72 hours of the time of death of the decedent, the net estate not disposed of by will passes under this section as if that person who would otherwise be an heir, or the times of death of both, cannot be determined, and it cannot be established that the person who would otherwise be an heir has survived the decedent by 72 hours of the decedent's death. In computing time for purposes of this subsection, local standard time at the place of death of the decedent is used.

(2m) Requirement that heir not have intentionally killed the decedent.

(a) If any person who would otherwise be an heir under sub.(1) has feloniously and intentionally killed the decedent, the net estate not disposed of by will passes as if the killer had pre-deceased the decedent.

(b) A final judgment of conviction of felonious and intentional killing is conclusive for purposes of this subsection. In the absence of such a conviction, the court, on the basis of clear and convincing evidence, may determine whether the killing was felonious and intentional for purposes of this subsection.

(c) This subsection does not affect the rights of any person who, before rights under this subsection have been adjudicated, purchases for value and without notice from the killer property that the killer is liable for the amount of the proceeds. No insurance company, bank, or other obligor paying according to the terms of its policy or obligation is liable because of this subsection unless before payment it has received at its home office or principal address written notice of a claim under this subsection.

(3) Escheat. If there are no heirs of the decedent under subs.(1) and (2), the net estate escheats to the state to be added to the capital of the school fund.[134]

Wyoming

Section 24-101. Rule of descent; generally; dower and curtesy abolished.

(a) Whenever any person having title to any real or personal property having the nature or legal character of real estate or personal estate undisposed of, and not otherwise limited by marriage settlement, dies intestate, the estate, shall descend and be distributed in parcenary to his kindred, male and female, subject to the payment of his debts, in the following course and manner:

(i) If the intestate leaves husband or wife and children, or the descendants of any children surviving, one-half (1/2) of the estate shall descend to the surviving husband or wife and the residue thereof to the surviving children and descendants of children, as hereinafter limited;

(ii) If the intestate leaves husband or wife and no child or descendants of any child, then the real and personal estate of the intestate shall descend as follows:

[A] All of the estate up to twenty thousand dollars ($20,000.00), after the payment of the debts of the intestate and the expenses of administration, shall descend and vest in the surviving husband or wife; and

[B] The balance of the estate over twenty thousand dollars ($20,000.00), after payment of the debts and expenses of administration, shall descend three-fourths (3/4) to the surviving husband or wife and one-fourth (1/4) to the father and mother of the intestate, or the survivor of them, or if both parents are dead, to the brothers and sisters and to the descendants of brothers and sisters who are dead, the descendants collectively taking the share which their parents would have taken if living, in equal parts;

(iii) If the intestate leave a husband or wife and no child or descendants of any child, and no parents, and no brothers and sisters or descendants of deceased brothers and sisters, then the whole of the estate irrespective of its value shall descend to and vest in the surviving husband or wife as his or her absolute estate, subject to the payment of the debts.

(b) Dower and the tenancy by the curtesy are abolished and neither husband nor wife shall have any share in the estate of the other dying intestate, save as herein provided.

(c) Except in cases above enumerated, the estate of any intestate shall descend and be distributed as follows:

(i) To his children surviving, and the descendants of his children who are dead, the descendants collectively taking the share which their parents would have taken if living;

(ii) If there are no children, or their descendants, then to his father, mother, brothers, and sisters and to the descendants of brothers and sisters who are dead, the descendants collectively taking the share which their parents would have taken if living;

(iii) If there are no children or their descendants, or father, mother, brothers, sisters, or descendants of deceased brothers and sisters, or husband or wife, living, then to the grandfather, grandmother, uncles, aunts, and their descendants, the descendants taking collectively, the share of their immediate ancestors, in equal parts.[135]

7 Western European Inheritance Laws

Many Western European countries impose a form of inheritance tax on assets that a decedent may have possessed during his or her lifetime. Domicile or residency is often immaterial. However, please note the individual tax treaties entered into between the United States and the particular country for rules governing double taxation and other matters.

BELGIUM

In Belgium an inheritance tax is imposed upon the net value of an individual's (including alien's) worldwide assets at the time of a decedent's death, if the decedent resided in Belgium. A Belgium estate duty is imposed at the time of death on the gross value of real property located in Belgium that is owned by a non-resident alien. Inheritance tax and estate duty rates are both progressive and vary, depending upon the size of the estate to accrue to each heir and the distance in relationship between the deceased and each of the heirs or legatees.

FRANCE

The French estate tax rate varies from 5 to 60 percent of the net estate. The factors considered when calculating the tax include the size of the estate, the number of decedent's children, whether or not decedent was married, the relationship between heirs and decedent, and the number of decedent's children and of children of the heirs or legatees. A tax exemption exists of F. 250,000 for the decedent's surviving spouse, direct descendants (living or represented), or ascendants who are bequeathed or inherit a portion of a decedent's estate. For the most part, a gift tax is levied at the same rate as an estate tax. Gifts made in premarital agreements are allowed a 25 percent reduction. Additionally, if property passes to an heir, legatee, or donee, who due to a permanent physical disability has a diminished ability to earn a livelihood, he or she will be granted an abatement of F. 275,000. Also, single, divorced, or separated brothers and sisters who meet certain age and other requirements and inherit a portion of a decedent's estate will be allowed a tax exemption of F. 75,000.

WEST GERMANY

An inheritance tax is imposed on the heir, since it is a tax on the individual inheritance not on the estate. A gift tax is imposed on lifetime gifts on both donor and donee. The estate will be held jointly liable for both the inheritance and gift tax. For non-resident decedents and donors, only the share devolving upon German beneficiaries is taxable. If the testator, donor, and beneficiary are all non-residents, only real estate or certain business property that is located in Germany is taxable. Realty includes mortgages that are required to be registered in the land register in Grundbuch. The tax rate varies according to the size of the share received and the degree of kinship of beneficiary to decedent or donor. For a surviving spouse of a decedent or child, the rate can range from 3 to 35 percent, and for unrelated beneficiaries, the rate ranges from 20 to 70 percent. The highest tax rate of 70 percent is typically imposed on those who are not related to the decedent or donor and are receiving in excess of 100,000,000 DM. Differences between the United States and German tax systems have led to an incidence of double taxation of U.S. citizens' estates in Germany. The United States tax is based upon citizenship basically, while the German tax is imposed upon the basis of domicile. Accordingly, an estate could be taxed twice, once because a U.S. citizen owned it and second because either the U.S. decedent or beneficiary at the time of death was residing in Germany or if property was situated within the German borders.

ITALY

An inheritance and gift tax is imposed upon all residents' properties, both within state and abroad. Non-residents' property within Italy is also subject to these taxes. The tax has two parts with the first affecting the entire estate. These rates are progressive on estates; the rate starts at 3 percent at 30,000,000 lire and progresses to 31 percent at 1,000,000,000 lire and above. The second part will have to be paid in addition to the first part only when the heir or legatee or donee is not a straight relative or spouse of the deceased and affects single shares devolved. The reasoning behind the rates of this part is that those successors or donees who are closer in kinship to the deceased should be taxed less.

FINLAND

Finland has an inheritance tax and gift tax that is progressive and is based on consanguinity between the decedent and others. (See highlights of the Finnish treaty with the United States in Chapter 4.)

IRELAND

In Ireland there is a capital acquisition tax that comprises a gift tax from February 28, 1974, and inheritance tax on deaths after March 31, 1975. Some tax-free thresholds include spouse and children, £ 150,000; parents, grandparents, and grandchildren, £ 30,000; brother, sister, nephew, niece, £ 20,000; others, £ 10,000.

AUSTRIA

An Austrian inheritance tax may be imposed upon the entire estate of a deceased Austrian citizen, except for real property abroad. An alien's estate will be subject to inheritance tax only for his or her real estate located in Austria regardless of where the person resides. The decedent's debts are considered to be located at the creditor's place of residence, whether the creditor is the deceased or a third party. The inheritance tax is calculated using a progressive scale, which takes into consideration the degree of relationship between the deceased and each heir or legatee. An inheritance tax equivalent may be imposed upon juridical persons and is assessed on an annual basis as a surtax on the property tax.

SWITZERLAND

Most cantons levy inheritance and gift taxes. When the tax is levied, it is done so in the certain canton where the decedent or donor is domiciled and is assessed against the heirs, beneficiaries, or donees, who are jointly liable for its payment. The rate of taxation varies with the degree of relationship to the decedent and the amount involved in most cases.

ENGLAND

The capital transfer tax is chargeable on inter vivos gifts and other gratuitous transfers of value and on property transferred on death and is primarily borne by the donor. The tax is charged on inter vivos gifts as they occur and also on a cumulative basis as per that donor. On death of a decedent, a tax is charged on the property passing on death and on a cumulative basis taking into account inter vivos gifts by a decedent.

8 Revocation of Wills

Revocation of a decedent's Last Will and Testament occurs when a will loses its potential capacity to operate at the testator's death. There are three basic ways in which a will can be revoked, and depending upon the circumstances, either the testator or the operation of law can bring about the revocation.

A revocation will be implied by law if the circumstances of the testator undergo one of many changes that is defined by statute. In some jurisdictions, a man or woman's marriage can act to revoke a will. Birth of issue typically does not revoke a will, but if a will was executed before both the marriage and the birth of issue, may in some cases act as a revocation. Divorce will usually not revoke a will, but if there has been a property settlement, statutes usually dictate that this is a marked change of circumstances, thereby revoking the will. In each instance it is important to review the jurisdiction's statutes and account for any peculiarities or exceptions.

State statutes prescribe certain acts that, if done to the will, constitute a revocation. Typically, if the testator or another in the testator's presence and at his or her request mutilates the will, revocation has occurred. The will does not have to be totally destroyed; the slightest intentional damage is sufficient to bring about a revocation. If a testator destroys one duplicate copy of the will, it gives rise to a presumption of revocation in most cases. For this reason attorneys should be aware of the danger that goes along with making duplicates of a will. Although making a copy may seem to be a safeguard, it can backfire if one copy of the will is unaccounted for at the time of probate. It is also important to note that most states do not allow for a partial revocation by an act. In those jurisdictions that recognize revocation by mutilation, nothing will be given to the beneficiary of the revoked part.

A will can be revoked by a subsequent writing if it either expressly or impliedly revokes the will in the form prescribed by statute. The common statutory requirement for revocation is that the subsequent revoking instrument must meet the formalities required for the execution of a written will. A will can be revoked by implication if a subsequent will disposes of all of the testator's property, because when wills conflict, the latter rules.

ALABAMA

Section 43-8-136. Revocation by writing or by act; when witnesses required.

(a) A will or any part thereof is revoked by a subsequent will which revokes the prior will or part expressly or by inconsistency.

(b) A will is revoked by being burned, torn, canceled, obliterated, or destroyed, with the intent and for the purpose of revoking it by the testator or by another person in his presence by his consent and direction. If the physical act is by someone other than the testator, consent and direction of the testator must be proved by at least two witnesses.

Section 43-8-137. Revocation by divorce or annulment; revival by remarriage; no revocation by other changes or circumstances.

If after executing a will the testator is divorced or his marriage annulled, the divorce or annulment revokes any disposition or appointment of property made by the will to the former spouse, any provision conferring a general or special power of appointment on the former spouse, and any nomination of the former spouse as executor, trustee, or guardian, unless the will expressly provides otherwise. Property prevented from passing to a former spouse because of revocation by divorce or annulment passes as if the former spouse failed to survive the decedent, and other provisions conferring some power or office on the former spouse are interpreted as if the spouse failed to survive the decedent. If provisions are revoked solely by this section, they are revived by testator's remarriage to the former spouse. For purposes of this section, divorce or annulment means any divorce or annulment which would exclude the spouse as a surviving spouse within the meaning of Section 43-8-252(b). A decree of separation which does not terminate the status of husband and wife is not a divorce for purposes of this section. No change of circumstances other than as described in this section revokes a will.[136]

ALASKA

Sec. 13.11.180. Revocation by writing or by act.

A will or any part of one is revoked

(1) by a subsequent will which revokes the prior will or part expressly or by inconsistency; or

(2) by being burned, torn, canceled, obliterated, or destroyed, with the intent and for the purpose of revoking it by the testator or by another person in his presence and by his direction.

Sec.13.11.185. Revocation by divorce; no revocation by other changes of circumstances.

If after executing a will the testator is divorced or his marriage annulled, the divorce or annulment revokes any disposition or appointment of property made by the will to the former spouse, any provision conferring a general or special power of appointment on the former spouse, and any nomination of the former spouse as executor, trustee, conservator, or guardian, unless the will expressly provides otherwise. Property prevented from passing to a former spouse because of revocation by divorce or annulment passes as if the former spouse failed to survive the decedent, and other provisions conferring some power or office on the former spouse are interpreted as if the spouse failed to survive the decedent. If provisions are revoked solely by this section, they are revived by testator's remarriage to the former spouse. For purposes of this section, divorce or annulment means any divorce or annulment which would exclude the spouse as a surviving spouse within the meaning of Sec. 300(b) of this chapter. A decree of separation which does not terminate the status of husband and wife is not a divorce for purposes of this section. No change of circumstances other than as described in this section revokes a will.

Sec. 13.11.190. Revival of revoked will.

(a) If a second will which, had it remained effective at death, would have revoked the first will in whole or in part, is thereafter revoked by acts under Sec. 180 of this chapter, the first will is revoked in whole or in part unless it is evident from the circumstances of the revocation of the second will or from testator's contemporary or subsequent declarations that he intended the first will to take effect as executed.

(b) If a second will which, had it remained effective at death, would have revoked the first will in whole or in part, is thereafter revoked by a third will, the first will is revoked in whole or in part, except to the extent it appears from the terms of the third will that the testator intended the first will to take effect.

Sec.13.11.195. Incorporation by reference.

Any writing in existence when a will is executed may be incorporated by reference if the language of the will manifests this intent and describes the writing sufficiently to permit its identification.[137]

ARIZONA

Section 14-2507. Revocation by writing or by act.

A will or any part thereof is revoked by either:

1. A subsequent will which revokes the prior will or part expressly or by inconsistency.

2. Being burned, torn, canceled, obliterated, or destroyed, with the intent and for the purpose of revoking it by the testator or by another person in his presence and by his direction.

Section 14-2508. Revocation by dissolution of marriage or annulment; no revocation by other changes of circumstances.

If after executing a will the testator is divorced or his marriage is dissolved or annulled, the divorce, dissolution, or annulment revokes any disposition or appointment of property made by the will to the former spouse or to any issue of the former spouse who are not also issue of the testator, any provision conferring a general or special power of appointment on the former spouse or such issue, and any nomination of the former spouse or such issue as executor, trustee, conservator, or guardian, unless the will expressly provides otherwise. Property prevented from passing to a person because of revocation under this section passes as if the person failed to survive the decedent; and other provisions conferring some power or office on the former spouse, or issue of the former spouse who are not also issue of the testator, are interpreted as if the spouse or issue failed to survive the decedent. If provisions are revoked solely by this section, they are revived by testator's remarriage to the former spouse. For purposes of this section, divorce, dissolution of marriage, or annulment means any divorce, dissolution of marriage, or annulment which would exclude the spouse as a surviving spouse within the meaning of Section 14-2802, subsection B. A decree of legal separation which does not terminate the status of husband and wife is not a divorce or dissolution of marriage for purposes of this section. No change of circumstances other than as described in this section revokes a will or any part thereof.[138]

ARKANSAS

60-406. Revocation by written will or by act on document.

Except as provided in Section 23 [Section 60-407], a will, or any part thereof, can be revoked only

a. By subsequent will; or

b. By being burnt, torn, cancelled, obliterated, or destroyed, with the intent and for the purpose of revoking the same, by the testator himself or by another person in his presence and by his direction. If such act is done by any person other than the testator, the direction of the testator and the facts of such injury or destruction must be proved by two [2] witnesses who are not benefited by the revocation of the will.

60—407. Revocation by change in circumstances--Marriage or divorce.

If after making a will the testator is divorced, all provisions in the will in favor of the testator's spouse so divorced are thereby revoked. With this exception, no will or any part thereof shall be revoked by any change in the circumstances, condition, or marital status of the testator; subject, however, to the provisions of Section 33 [Section 60-501].

60-412. Devise of property subject to contract to convey.

A valid agreement made by a testator to convey property devised in a will previously made shall not revoke the previous devise, but such property shall pass by the will subject to the same remedies on the agreement against the devisee as might have been enforced against the decedent if he had survived.

60-414. Devise of encumbered property.

A valid charge or encumbrance upon any property shall not revoke any provision of a previously executed will relating to the same property, but the devisee shall take the property subject to the charge or encumbrance, the discharge of which will be governed by the provisions of Section 167 [Section 562-2908].[139]

CALIFORNIA

Section 70. Subsequent marriage; revocation as to spouse.

If a person marries after making a will, and the spouse survives the maker, the will is revoked as to the spouse, unless provision has been made for the spouse by marriage contract, or unless the spouse is provided for in the will, or in such way mentioned therein as to show an intention not to make such provision; and no other evidence to rebut the presumption of revocation can be received.

Section 71. Subsequent marriage; revocation as to issue.

If a person marries after making a will and has issue of such marriage, and any of the issue survives the maker, or is born after *the death of the maker*, the will is revoked as to such issue, unless provision has been made for such issue by some settlement, or unless such issue are provided for in the will, or in such way mentioned therein as to show an intention not to make such provision; and no other evidence to rebut the presumption of such revocation can be received.

Section 72. Subsequent will; effect.

A prior will is not revoked by a subsequent will, unless the latter contains an express revocation or provisions wholly inconsistent with the terms of the prior will. In other cases the prior will remains effectual so far as consistent with the provisions of the subsequent will; but the mere naming of an executor in the prior will need not be given effect by the court when the subsequent will is otherwise wholly inconsistent with the terms of the prior will, the intention of the testator in this respect being left to the determination of the court.

Section 74. Formal revocation.

Except as hereinabove provided, no written will, or any part thereof, can be revoked or altered otherwise than:

(1) Instrument executed with same formalities. By a written will, or other writing of the testator, declaring such revocation or alteration and executed with the same formalities required for the execution of a will; or,

(2) Cancellation, defacing, destruction, etc. By being burnt, torn, canceled, defaced, obliterated, or destroyed, with the intent and for the purpose of revoking the same, by the testator himself, or by some person in his presence and by his direction. If such act is done by any person other than the testator, the direction

of the testator, and the fact of such injury or destruction, must be proved by two witnesses.

Section 80. Dissolution of marriage or declaration of marriage as nullity; effect of waiver of rights in property settlement agreement.

(a) If after executing a will or any codicil thereto, the testator's marriage is dissolved or declared a nullity by a final judgment of a court of competent jurisdiction, and if the testator and his or her former spouse have executed a property settlement agreement waiving and renouncing all rights to inherit the estate of the other at the other's death, or to receive any property of the other under a will executed prior to the agreement, the former spouse of the testator and the lineal descendants of the former spouse of the testator shall be deemed to have predeceased the testator for the purposes of the will or codicil, unless the will or codicil expressly provides otherwise. For the purpose of this section, "lineal descendants" shall include all lineal descendants of the former spouse of the testator who are not also lineal descendants of the testator.

(b) The provisions of subdivision (a) shall not be applicable if the testator's death occurs during the remarriage to the former spouse.

(c) The provisions of this section shall be applicable only to wills or codicils executed on or after January 1, 1981.[140]

COLORADO

15-11-507. Revocation by writing or by act.

(1) A will or any part thereof is revoked by a subsequent will which revokes the prior will or part thereof expressly or by inconsistency.

(2) A will is revoked by being burned, torn, canceled, obliterated, or destroyed with the intent and for the purpose of revoking it by the testator or by another person in his presence and by his direction. "Cancellation of duplicate original raises presumption that testator intended to cancel original will in possession of another (619 P.2d 91). No partial revocation by physical act (43 Colo.App. 296, 605 P.2d 65)," page 61, 'Colorado Law Digest,' *Martindale-Hubbell Law Directory*, Volume VII, 1984.

15-11-508. Revocation by divorce—No revocation by other changes of circumstances.

If after executing a will a testator is divorced or his marriage annulled, the divorce or annulment revokes any disposition or appointment of property made by the will to the former spouse, any provision conferring a general or special power of appointment on the former spouse, and any nomination of the former spouse as executor, trustee, conservator, or guardian, unless the will expressly provides otherwise. Property prevented from passing to a former spouse because of revocation by divorce or annulment passes as if the former spouse failed to survive the decedent. If provisions are revoked solely by this section, they are revived by testator's remarriage to the former spouse. For purposes of this section, divorce or annulment means any divorce or annulment which would exclude the spouse as a surviving spouse within the meaning of Section 15-11-802(2). A decree of separation which does not terminate the status of husband and wife is not a divorce for purposes of this section. No change of circumstances other than as described in this section revokes a will.

15-11-509. Revival of revoked will.

(1) If a second will which, had it remained effective at death, would have revoked the first will in whole or in part is thereafter revoked by acts under Section 15-11-507, the first will is revoked in whole or in part unless it is evident from the circumstances of the revocation of the second will or from testator's contemporary or subsequent declarations that he intended the first will to take effect as executed.

(2) If a second will which, had it remained effective at death, would have revoked the first will in whole or in part is thereafter revoked by a third will, the first will is revoked in whole or in part, except to the extent it appears from the terms of the third will that the testator had intended the first will to take effect.[141]

CONNECTICUT

Section 45-162. Implied and express revocation of will.

(a) If, after the making of a will, the testator marries or is divorced or his marriage is annulled or dissolved or a child is born to the testator or a minor child is legally adopted by him, or a child is born as a result of A.I.D. as defined in Section 45-69f, to which the testator has consented in accordance with subsection (a) of Section 45-69g, and no provision has been made in such will for such contingency, such marriage, divorce, annulment, dissolution, birth, or adoption of a minor child shall operate as a revocation of such will, provided that such divorce, annulment, or dissolution shall not operate as a revocation of such will if the spouse of the testator was not a beneficiary under such will. The revocation of such will by divorce, annulment, or dissolution of marriage shall be effective only as to wills executed on and after October 1, 1967.

(b) A will or codicil shall not be revoked in any other manner except by burning, cancelling, tearing, or obliterating it by the testator or by some person in his presence by his direction or by a later will or codicil.[142]

DELAWARE

Section 208. Revocation of wills generally.

A last will and testament, or any clause thereof, shall not be altered, or revoked, except by cancelling by the testator, or by some person in his presence and by his express direction, or by a valid last will and testament, or by a writing signed by the testator, or by some person subscribing the testator's name in his presence and by his express direction, and attested and subscribed in his presence by 2 or more credible witnesses; but this clause shall not preclude nor extend to an implied revocation.

Section 209. Revocation by divorce; no revocation by other changes or circumstances.

If after executing a will, the testator is divorced or his marriage annulled, the divorce or annulment revokes any disposition or appointment of property made by the will to the former spouse, any provision conferring a general or special power of appointment on the former spouse and any nomination of the former spouse, as executor, trustee, guardian, or other fiduciary, unless the will expressly provides otherwise. Property prevented from passing to a former spouse because of revocation by divorce or annulment passes as if the former spouse failed to survive the decedent, and other provisions conferring some power or office on the former spouse are interpreted as if the spouse failed to survive the decedent. If provisions are revoked solely by this section, they are revived by testator's remarriage to the former spouse. A decree of separation which does not terminate the status of husband and wife is not a divorce for purposes of this section. No change or circumstances other than as described in this section revokes a will or any part thereof.[143]

DISTRICT OF COLUMBIA

Section 18-109. Revocation of wills; revival.

(a) A will or codicil, or a part thereof, may not be revoked, except by implication of law, otherwise than by

(1) a later will, codicil, or other writing declaring the revocation, executed as provided by Section 18-103 or 18-107; or

(2) burning, tearing, cancelling, or obliterating the will or codicil, or the part thereof, with the intention of revoking it, by the testator himself, or by a person in his presence and by his express direction and consent.

(b) A will or codicil, or a part thereof, after it is revoked, may not be revived otherwise than by its re-execution, or by a codicil executed as provided in the case of wills, and then only to the extent to which an intention to revive is shown. "However, the common law rule that marriage and the birth of a child capable of inheriting revoke a prior will, if both occurred after the execution thereof is in force in the district (79 US App DC 354, 147 F.2d 880). A divorce with property settlement presumptively revokes will in favor of former spouse (435 A.2D 379)," page 31, 'District of Columbia Law Digest,' *Martindale-Hubbell Law Directory*, Volume VII, 1984.[144]

FLORIDA

732.505. Revocation by writing.

A will or codicil, or any part of either, is revoked: (1) By a subsequent inconsistent will or codicil, even though the subsequent inconsistent will or codicil does not expressly revoke all previous wills or codicils, but the revocation extends only so far as the inconsistency exists. (2) By a subsequent written will, codicil, or other writing declaring the revocation, if the same formalities required for the execution of wills are observed in the execution of the will, codicil, or other writing.

732.506. Revocation by act.

A will or codicil is revoked by the testator, or some other person in his presence and at his direction, by burning, tearing, canceling, defacing, obliterating, or destroying it with the intent and for the purpose of revocation.

732.508. Revival by revocation.

(1) The revocation by the testator of a will that revokes a former will shall not revive the former will, even though the former will is in existence at the date of the revocation of the subsequent will. (2) The revocation of a codicil to a will does not revoke the will, and, in the absence of evidence to the contrary, it shall be presumed that in revoking the codicil the testator intended to reinstate the provisions of a will or codicil that were changed or revoked by the revoked codicil, as if the revoked codicil had never been executed.

732.509. Revocation of codicil.

The revocation of a will revokes all codicils to that will.[145]

GEORGIA

53-2-74. Express revocation by destruction or obliteration; presumption of intent to revoke.

An express revocation may be effected by a destruction or obliteration of an original will or a duplicate thereof, done by the testator or by another at his direction with an intention to revoke. Such intention will be presumed from the obliteration or canceling of a material portion of the will. If the part of the will which is canceled is immaterial, such as the seal, no presumption of an intention to revoke shall arise.

53-2-76. Revocation of will by marriage, divorce, or birth of child.

Marriage of a testator, his total divorce, or the birth of a child to him, subsequent to the making of a will in which no provision is made in contemplation of such an event, shall be a revocation of the will. ''Revocation by destruction accomplished only by concurrence of both intent to revoke and effective destruction (213 Ga. 613; 100 S.E.2d 772). Will executed pursuant to valid contract may be revoked by subsequent will, but contract remains binding upon parties (213 Ga. 145, 200 S.E.2d 725),'' page 50, *Georgia Law Digest, Martindale-Hubbell Law Directory*, Volume VII, 1984.[146]

HAWAII

Section 560:2-507. Revocation by writing or by act.

(a) A will or any part thereof is revoked by a subsequent will which revokes the prior will or part expressly or by inconsistency.

(b) A will is also revoked by being burned, torn, canceled, obliterated, or destroyed, with the intent and for the purpose of revoking it by the testator or by another person in his presence and by his direction.

Section 560:2-508. Revocation by divorce; no revocation by other changes of circumstances. If after executing a will the testator is divorced or his marriage annulled, the divorce or annulment revokes any disposition or appointment of property made by the will to the former spouse, any provision conferring a general or special power of appointment on the former spouse, and any nomination of the former spouse as executor, trustee, guardian of the property, or guardian of the person, unless the will expressly provides otherwise. Property prevented from passing to a former spouse because of revocation by divorce or annulment passes as if the former spouse failed to survive the decedent, and other provisions conferring some power or office on the former spouse are interpreted as if the spouse failed to survive the decedent. Remarriage to a former spouse shall not revive any provision previously revoked by operation of this section. For purposes of this section, divorce or annulment means any divorce or annulment which would exclude the spouse as a surviving spouse within the meaning of Section 560:2-802(b). A decree of separation which does not terminate the status of husband and wife is not a divorce for purposes of this section. No change of circumstances other than as described in this section revokes a will.[147]

IDAHO

15-2-507. Revocation by writing or by act.

A will or any part thereof is revoked:

(a) By a subsequent will which revokes the prior will or part expressly or by inconsistency; or

(b) By being burned, torn, canceled, obliterated, or destroyed, with the intent and for the purpose of revoking it by the testator or by another person in his presence and in his direction.

(c) The revocation of a will executed in duplicate may be accomplished by revoking one (1) of the duplicates.

15-2-508. Revocation by divorce—No revocation by other changes of circumstances.

If after executing a will the testator is divorced or his marriage is annulled, the divorce or annulment revokes any disposition or appointment of property made by the will to the former spouse, any provision conferring a general or special power of appointment on the former spouse, and any nomination of the former spouse as executor, trustee, conservator, or guardian, unless the will expressly provides otherwise. Property prevented from passing to a former spouse because of revocation by divorce or annulment passes as if the former spouse failed to survive the decedent, and other provisions conferring some power or office on the former spouse are interpreted as if the spouse failed to survive the decedent. If provisions are revoked solely by this section, they are revived by testator's remarriage to the former spouse. For purposes of this section, divorce or annulment means any divorce or annulment which would exclude the spouse as a surviving spouse within the meaning of subsection (b) of Section 15-2-802 of this code. A decree of separation which does not terminate the status of husband and wife is not a divorce for purposes of this section. No change of circumstances other than as described in this section revokes a will.

15-1-509. Revival of revoked will.

(a) If a second will which, had remained effective at death, would have revoked the first will in whole or in part, is thereafter revoked by acts under Section 15-2-507 of this chapter, the first will is revoked in whole or in part unless it is evident from the circumstances of the revocation of the second will or from testator's contemporary or subsequent declarations that he intended the first will to take effect as executed.

(b) If a second will which, had it remained effective at death, would have revoked the first will in whole or in part, is thereafter revoked by a third will, the first will is revoked in whole or in part, except to the extent it appears from the terms of the third will that the testator intended the first will to take effect.

(c) Republication of a revoked will revives such will.[148]

ILLINOIS

Section 4-7. Revocation—Revival.

(a) A will may be revoked only (1) by burning, cancelling, tearing, or obliterating it by the testator himself or by some person in his presence and by his direction and consent, (2) by the execution of a later will declaring the revocation, (3) by a later will to the extent that it is inconsistent with the prior will, or (4) by the execution of an instrument declaring the revocation and signed and attested in the manner prescribed by this Article for the signing and attestation of a will.

(b) No will or any part thereof is revoked by any change in the circumstances, condition, or marital status of the testator, except that divorce or annulment of the marriage of the testator revokes every legacy or interest or power of appointment given to or nomination to fiduciary office of the testator's former spouse in a will executed before the entry of the judgment of divorce or annulment, and the will takes effect in the same manner as if the former spouse had died before the testator.

(c) A will which is totally revoked in any manner is not revived other than by its re-execution or by an instrument declaring the revival and signed and attested in the manner prescribed by this Article for the signing and attestation of a will. If a will is partially revoked by an instrument which is itself revoked, the revoked part of the will is revived and takes effect as if there had been no revocation.[149]

INDIANA

29-1-5-6. Revocation; revival.

No will in writing, or any part thereof, except as in this act provided, shall be revoked, unless the testator, or some other person in his presence and by his direction, with intent to revoke, shall destroy or mutilate the same; or such testator shall execute other writing for that purpose, signed, subscribed, and attested as required in Section 503 [Section 29-1-5-3]. A will can be revoked in part only by the execution of a writing as herein provided. And if, after the making of any will, the testator shall execute a second, a revocation of the second shall not revive the first will, unless it shall appear by the terms of such revocation to have been his intent to revive it, or, unless, after such revocation, he shall duly republish the previous will.

29-1-5-7. Nuncupative will; revocation.

A nuncupative will or any part thereof can be revoked by another nuncupative will.

29-1-5-8. Revocation, divorce, annulment of marriage, change in circumstances.

If after making a will the testator is divorced, all provisions in the will in favor of the testator's spouse so divorced are thereby revoked. Annulment of the testator's marriage shall have the same effect as a divorce as hereinabove provided. With this exception, no written will, or any part thereof, can be revoked by any change in circumstances or condition of the testator.[150]

IOWA

633.284. Revocation—cancellation—revival.

A will can be revoked in whole or in part only by being canceled or destroyed by the act or direction of the testator, with the intention of revoking it, or by the execution of a subsequent will. When done by cancellation, the revocation must be witnessed in the same manner as the making of a new will. No will, or any part thereof, which shall be in any manner revoked, or which shall be or become invalid, can be revived otherwise than by a re-execution thereof, or by the execution of another will or codicil in which the revoked or invalid will, or part thereof, is incorporated by reference.[151]

KANSAS

59-610. Revocation by marriage, birth, or adoption; divorce.

If after making a will the testator marries and has a child, by birth or adoption, the will is thereby revoked. If after making a will the testator is divorced, all provisions in such will in favor of the testator's spouse so divorced are thereby revoked.

59-611. Manner of revocation.

Except as provided in K.S.A. 59-610, no will in writing shall be revoked or altered otherwise than by some other will in writing; or by some other writing of the testator declaring such revocation or alteration and executed with the same formalities with which the will itself was required by law to be executed; or unless such will be burnt, torn, cancelled, obliterated, or destroyed, with the intent and for the purpose of revoking the same, by the testator himself or herself or by another person in the testator's presence by his or her direction.

59-612. Revocation of second will not revivor of first, when.

If the testator shall make a second will, the revocation of the second will shall not revive the first will, unless it appears by the terms of such revocation that it was the testator's intention to revive the first will, or unless after such revocation the testator shall duly republish his or her first will in the presence of two or more competent witnesses who shall subscribe the same in the presence of the testator.[152]

KENTUCKY

394.080. Revocation of will—How effected.

No will or codicil, or any part thereof, shall be revoked, except:

(1) As provided in KRS 394.090;

(2) By subsequent will or codicil;

(3) By some writing declaring an intention to revoke the will or codicil and executed in the manner in which a will is required to be executed; or

(4) By the person who made the will, or some person in his presence and by his direction, cutting, tearing, burning, obliterating, canceling, or destroying the will or codicil, or the signature thereto, with the intent to revoke.

394.090. Marriage revokes will—Exception.

Every will shall be revoked by the marriage of the person who made the will, except:

(1) A will made in exercise of a power of appointment when the estate thereby appointed would not, in default of such appointment, pass to the heir, personal representative, or next of kin of the person who made the will;

(2) A will that expressly provides that it is intended that a subsequent marriage shall not revoke the will.

394.092. Effect of divorce or annulment of marriage of testator.

(1) If after executing a will the testator is divorced or his marriage annulled, the divorce or annulment revokes any disposition or appointment of property made by the will to the former spouse, any provision conferring a general or special power of appointment on the former spouse, and any nomination of the former spouse as executor, trustee, conservator, or guardian, unless the will expressly provides otherwise. Property prevented from passing to a former spouse because of revocation by divorce or annulment passes as if the former spouse failed to survive the decedent, and other provisions conferring some power or office on the former spouse are interpreted as if the spouse failed to survive the decedent. If provisions are revoked solely by this section, they are revived by the testator's remarriage to the former spouse.

(2) This section shall apply to wills executed on or after July 15, 1982.[153]

LOUISIANA

Art. 1492. Hatred, anger, suggestion, or captation; proof inadmissible.

Proof is not admitted of the dispositions having been made through hatred, anger, suggestion, or captation.

Art. 1690. Testator's right to revoke.

Testaments are revocable at the will of the testator until his decease. The testator can not renounce this right of revocation or obligate himself to exercise it only under certain words and restrictions, and if he does so, such declaration shall be considered as not written.

Art. 1692. Form of revocation.

The act by which a testamentary disposition is revoked must be made in one of the forms prescribed for testaments and clothed with the same formalities.

Art. 1705. Subsequent birth or adoption of children.

A testament is revoked by the subsequent birth of a legitimate child to the testator or by the subsequent adoption or legitimation of a child by the testator, unless the testator has made testamentary provision to the contrary or has made testamentary provision for such child.

Art. 3542. Actions prescribed by five years.

The following actions are prescribed by five years: That for the nullity or rescission of contracts, testaments, or other acts. That for the reduction of excessive donations. That for the rescission of partitions and guarantee of the portions. This prescription only commences against minors after their majority.[154]

MAINE

Section 2-507. Revocation by writing or by act.

A will or any part thereof is revoked:

(1) By a subsequent will which revokes the prior will or part expressly or by inconsistency; or

(2) By being burned, torn, canceled, obliterated, or destroyed, with the intent and for the purpose of revoking it by the testator or by another person in his presence and by his direction.

Section 2-508. Revocation by divorce; no revocation by other changes of circumstances.

If after executing a will the testator is divorced or his marriage annulled, the divorce or annulment revokes any disposition or appointment of property made by the will to the former spouse, any provision conferring a general or special power of appointment on the former spouse, and any nomination of the former spouse as executor, trustee, conservator, or guardian, unless the will expressly provides otherwise. Property prevented from passing to a former spouse because of revocation by divorce or annulment passes as if the former spouse failed to survive the decedent, and other provisions conferring some power or office on the former spouse are interpreted as if the spouse failed to survive the decedent. If provisions are revoked solely by this section, they are revived by testator's remarriage to the former spouse. For purposes of this section, divorce, or annulment means any divorce or annulment which would exclude the spouse as a surviving spouse within the meaning of Section 2-802, subsection (b). A decree of separation which does not terminate the status of husband and wife is not a divorce for purposes of this section. No change of circumstances other than as described in this section revokes a will.[155]

MARYLAND

Section 4-105. Revocation of will.

A will, or any part of it, may not be revoked in a manner other than as provided in this section.

(a) Subsequent will. By provision in a subsequent, validly executed will which (1) revokes any prior will or part of it either expressly or by necessary implication, or (2) expressly republishes an earlier will that had been revoked by an intermediate will but is still in existence;

(b) Destruction. By burning, cancelling, tearing, or obliterating the same, by the testator himself or by some other person in his presence and by his express direction and consent;

(c) Subsequent marriage and issue. By the subsequent marriage of the testator followed by the birth, adoption, or legitimation of a child by him, provided such child or his descendant survives the testator; and all wills executed prior to such marriage shall be revoked; or

(d) Divorce or annulment. By a divorce a vinculo matrimonii of a testator to his spouse or the annulment of the marriage, either of which occurs subsequent to the execution of the testator's will; and all provisions in the will relating to the spouse, and only those provisions, shall be revoked unless otherwise provided in the will or decree. "Woman's will not revoked simply by subsequent marriage (76 Md. 369, 25 Atl. 307)," page 59, "Maryland Law Digest," *Martindale-Hubbell Law Directory*, Volume VII, 1984.[156]

MASSACHUSETTS

Section 8. Means of revocation.

No will shall be revoked except by burning, tearing, cancelling, or obliterating it with the intention of revoking it, by the testator himself or by a person in his presence and by his direction; or by some other writing signed, attested, and subscribed in the same manner as a will; or by subsequent changes in the condition or circumstances of the testator from which a revocation is implied by law.

Section 9. Effect of marriage.

The marriage of a person shall act as a revocation of a will made by him previous to such marriage, unless it appears from the will that it was made in contemplation thereof. If the will is made in the exercise of a power of appointment and the real and personal property subject to the appointment would not, without the appointment, pass to the persons who would have been entitled to it if it had been the estate and property of the testator making the appointment and he had died intestate, so much of the will as makes the appointment shall not be revoked by the marriage.[157]

MICHIGAN

700.124. Revocation of will in whole or part.

(1) A will or any part thereof is revoked by either of the following actions:

(a) A subsequent will which revokes the prior will or part expressly or by inconsistency.

(b) Being burned, torn, canceled, obliterated, or destroyed by the testator or by another person in his presence and by his direction, with the intent and for the purpose of revocation.

(2) If after executing a will the testator is divorced or his marriage annulled, the divorce or annulment revokes any disposition or appointment of property made by the will to the former spouse, any provision conferring a general or special power of appointment on the former spouse, and any nomination of the former spouse as a personal representative, unless the will expressly provides otherwise. Property prevented from passing to a former spouse because of revocation by divorce passes as if the former spouse failed to survive the decedent and other provisions conferring some power or office on the former spouse are interpreted as if the spouse failed to survive the decedent. Provisions not revoked by any means except the operation of this subsection are revived by testator's remarriage to the former spouse. A decree of separation which does not terminate

the status of husband and wife is not a divorce for purposes of this section. Any other change of circumstances does not revoke a will.

(3) For purposes of subsection (2), divorce or annulment means either of the following:

(a) A valid divorce or annulment.

(b) A divorce or annulment judgment or decree which is not recognized as valid by the laws of this state for other purposes if it was obtained by the decedent and acknowledged as valid by the surviving spouse by entering into a marriage ceremony with a third person or if it was obtained by the surviving spouse.[158]

MINNESOTA

524.2-507. Revocation by writing or by act.

A will or any part thereof is revoked (1) by a subsequent will which revokes the prior will or part expressly or by inconsistency; or (2) by being burned, torn, canceled, obliterated, or destroyed, with the intent and for the purpose of revoking it by the testator or by another person in his presence and by his direction.

524.2-508. Revocation by dissolution of marriage; no revocation by other changes of circumstances.

If after executing a will the testator's marriage is dissolved or annulled, the dissolution or annulment revokes any disposition or appointment of property made by the will to the former spouse, any provision conferring a general or special power of appointment on the former spouse, and any nomination of the former spouse as executor, trustee, conservator, or guardian, unless the will expressly provides otherwise. Property prevented from passing to a former spouse because of revocation by dissolution of marriage or annulment passes as if the former spouse failed to survive the decedent, and other provisions conferring some power or office on the former spouse are interpreted as if the spouse failed to survive the decedent. If provisions are revoked solely by this section, they are revived by testator's remarriage to the former spouse. For purposes of Chapters 524 and 525, dissolution of marriage includes divorce. A decree of separation which does not terminate the status of husband and wife is not a dissolution of marriage for purposes of this section. No change of circumstances other than as described in this section revokes a will.[159]

MISSISSIPPI

Section 91-5-3. Revocations.

A devise so made, or any clause thereof, shall not be revocable but by the testator or testatrix destroying, canceling, or obliterating the same, or causing it to be done in his or her presence, or by subsequent will, codicil, or declaration, in writing, made and executed. Every last will and testament made when the testator or testatrix had no child living, wherein any child he or she might have is not provided for or not mentioned, if at the time of his or her death he or she have a child, or if the testator leaves his wife enceinte of a child who shall be born, shall have no effect during the life of any such after-born child and shall be void unless the child dies without having been married, or without leaving issue capable of inheriting, and before he or she shall have attained twenty-one years. The estate, both real and personal, so devised shall descend to such child in the same manner as if the testator or testatrix had died intestate, subject, nevertheless, to the bequests made in the last will and testament in case of the death of such child before marriage, or without issue capable of inheriting, and under the age of twenty-one years. When a testator shall leave children born and his wife enceinte, the posthumous child or children, if unprovided for by settlement and neither provided for nor disinherited, but only pretermitted, by the last will and testament, shall succeed to the same portion of the father's estate as such child or children would have been entitled to if the father had died intestate, towards raising which portion the devisees and legatees shall contribute proportionably out of the parts devised and bequeathed to them by the same will and testament.[160]

MISSOURI

474.400. Revocation of wills.

No will in writing, except in the cases herein mentioned, or any part thereof, shall be revoked, except by a subsequent will in writing, or by burning, canceling, tearing, or obliterating the same, by the testator, or in his presence, and by his consent and direction.

474.420. Change in circumstances; divorce.

If after making a will the testator is divorced, all provisions in the will in favor of the testator's spouse so divorced are thereby revoked but the effect of the revocation shall be the same as if the divorced spouse had died at the time of the divorce. With this exception, no written will, or any part thereof, can be revoked by any change in the circumstances or condition of the testator.[161]

MONTANA

72-2-321. Revocation by writing or by act.

A will or any part thereof is revoked:

(1) by a subsequent will which revokes the prior will or part expressly or by inconsistency; or

(2) by being burned, torn, canceled, obliterated, or destroyed with the intent and for the purpose of revoking it by the testator or by another person in his presence and by his direction.

72-2-322. Revocation by divorce or annulment—No revocation by other change in circumstances.

(1) If after executing a will the testator is divorced or his marriage annulled, the divorce or annulment revokes any disposition or appointment of property made by the will to the former spouse, any provision conferring a general or special power of appointment on the former spouse, and any nomination of the former spouse as executor, trustee, conservator, or guardian unless the will expressly provides otherwise.

(2) Property prevented from passing to a former spouse because of revocation by divorce or annulment passes as if the former spouse failed to survive the decedent, and other provisions conferring some power or office on the former spouse are interpreted as if the spouse failed to survive the decedent.

(3) If provisions are revoked solely by this section, they are revived by testator's remarriage to the former spouse.

(4) For purposes of this section, divorce or annulment means any divorce or annulment which would exclude the spouse as a surviving spouse within the meaning of 72-2-103(2). A decree of separation which does not terminate the status of husband and wife is not a divorce for purposes of this section.

(5) No change of circumstances other than as described in this section revokes a will.

72-2-323. Revival of revoked will.

(1) If a second will which, had it remained effective at death, would have revoked the first will in whole or in part is thereafter revoked by acts under 72-2-321, the first will is revoked in whole or in part unless it is evident from the circumstances of the revocation of the second will or from testator's contemporary or subsequent declarations that he intended the first will to take effect as executed.

(2) If a second will which, had it remained effective at death, would have revoked the first will in whole or in part is thereafter revoked by a third will, the first will is revoked in whole or in part, except to the extent it appears from the terms of the third will that the testator intended the first will to take effect.[162]

NEBRASKA

30-2332. Revocation by writing or by act.

A will or any part thereof is revoked:

(1) by a subsequent will which, as is evident either from its terms or from competent evidence of its terms, revokes the prior will or part expressly or by inconsistency; or

(2) by being burned, torn, canceled, obliterated, or destroyed, with the intent and for the purpose of revoking it by the testator or by another person in the presence of and by the direction of the testator.

30-2333. Revocation by divorce; no revocation by other changes of circumstances.

If after executing a will the testator is divorced or his marriage dissolved or annulled, the divorce, dissolution, or annulment revokes any disposition or appointment of property made by the will to the former spouse, any provision conferring a general or special power of appointment on the former spouse, and any nomination of the former spouse as executor, trustee, conservator, or guardian, unless the will expressly provides otherwise. Property prevented from passing to the former spouse because of revocation by divorce, dissolution, or annulment passes as if the former spouse failed to survive the decedent, and other provisions conferring some power or office on the former spouse are interpreted as if the spouse failed to survive the decedent. If provisions are revoked solely by this section, they are revived by testator's remarriage to the former spouse. For purposes of this section, divorce, dissolution, or annulment means any divorce, dissolution, or annulment which would exclude the spouse as a surviving spouse within the meaning of Section 30-2353. A decree of separation which does not terminate the status of husband and wife is not a divorce for purposes of this section. No change of circumstances other than as described in this section revokes a will.[163]

NEVADA

133.110. Revocation by marriage: As to the spouse.

If a person marries after making a will and the spouse survives the maker, the will is revoked as to the spouse, unless provision has been made for the spouse by marriage contract, or unless the spouse is provided for in the will, or in such a way mentioned therein as to show an intention not to make such provision; and no other evidence to rebut the presumption of revocation shall be received.

133.115. Revocation of provisions of will in favor of former spouse on divorce, annulment; exceptions.

Divorce or annulment of the marriage of the testator revokes every beneficial devise, legacy or interest given to the testator's former spouse in a will executed before the entry of the decree of divorce or annulment unless otherwise:

1. Provided in a property or separation agreement which is approved by the court in the divorce or annulment proceedings and not merged in the decree; or
2. Ordered by the court in the divorce or annulment proceedings, and the will shall take effect in the same manner as if the former spouse had died before the testator.

133.120. Other means of revocation.

1. No will in writing shall be revoked unless:

(a) By burning, tearing, canceling, or obliterating the same, with the intention of revoking it, by the testator, or by some person in his presence, or by his direction; or

(b) by some other will or codicil in writing, executed as prescribed in this chapter.

2. Nothing contained in this section shall prevent the revocation implied by law from subsequent changes in the condition or circumstances of the testator.

133.130. Effect of revocation of subsequent will.

If, after the making of any will, the testator shall duly make and execute a second will, the destruction, cancellation, or revocation of the second will shall not revive the first will, unless it appears by the terms of such revocation that it was the intention to revive and give effect to the first will, or unless, after such destruction, cancellation, or revocation, the first will shall be duly reexecuted.[164]

NEW HAMPSHIRE

551:13. Revocation.

No will or clause thereof shall be revoked unless by some other valid will or codicil, or by some writing executed in the same manner, or by canceling, tearing, obliterating, or otherwise destroying the same by the testator, or by some person by his consent and in his presence.

551:14. Implied.

The preceding section shall not control or affect any revocation of a will, implied by law, from any change in the circumstances of the testator, or his family, devisees, legatees, or estate, occurring between the time of making the will and the death of the testator. ''Marriage and birth of a child would seem such a change of circumstances as to revoke a will executed before the marriage (see 63 N.H. 507, 3 A.H. 636),'' page 37, New Hampshire Digest,' *Martindale-Hubbell Law Directory,* Volume VII, 1984.[165]

NEW JERSEY

3B:3-13. Revocation by acts of testator.

A will or any part thereof is revoked:

a. By a subsequent will which revokes the former will or part expressly or by inconsistency; or

b. By being burned, torn, canceled, obliterated, or destroyed with the intent and for the purpose of revoking by the testator or by another person in his presence and by his direction.

3B:3-14. Revocation by divorce or annulment; revival by remarriage to former spouse.

If after having executed a will the testator is divorced or his marriage annulled, the divorce or annulment revokes any dispositions or appointment of property made by the will to the former spouse, any provision conferring a general or special power of appointment on the former spouse, and any nomination of the former spouse as executor, trustee, or guardian, unless the will expressly provides otherwise. Property prevented from passing to a former spouse because of revocation by divorce or annulment passes as if the former spouse failed to survive the decedent, and other provisions conferring some power or office on the former spouse are interpreted as if the spouse failed to survive the decedent. A judgment from bed and board is a divorce for the purpose of this section. If provisions are revoked solely by this section, they are revived by testator's remarriage to the former spouse or by the revocation or suspension of a judgment of divorce from bed and board. No change of circumstances other than as described in this section revokes a will.[166]

NEW MEXICO

45-2-507. Revocation by writing or by act.

A will or any part thereof is revoked by:

A. an instrument in writing, executed and attested in the same manner as is required by law for the execution and attestation of a will, by which instrument the maker distinctly refers to the will and declares that he revokes it;

B. a subsequent will which revokes the prior will or part thereof, expressly or by inconsistency; or

C. being burned, torn, canceled, obliterated, or destroyed, with the intent and for the purpose of revoking it by the testator or by another person in his presence and by his direction.

45-2-508. Revocation by divorce; no revocation by other changes of circumstances.

A. If after executing a will the testator is divorced or his marriage annulled, the divorce or annulment revokes any disposition or appointment of property made by the will to the former spouse, any provision conferring a general or special power or appointment on the former spouse, and any nomination of the former spouse as personal representative, trustee, conservator, or guardian, unless the will expressly provides otherwise.

B. Property prevented from passing to a former spouse because of revocation by divorce or annulment passes as if the former spouse failed to survive the decedent, and other provisions conferring some power or office on the former spouse are interpreted as if the spouse failed to survive the decedent.

C. If provisions are revoked solely by this section, they are revived by testator's remarriage to the former spouse.

D. For purposes of this section, divorce or annulment means any divorce or annulment which would exclude the spouse as a surviving spouse within the meaning of subsection B of Section 2-802 [45-2-802 NMSA 1978]. A decree of separation which does not terminate the status of husband and wife is not a divorce for purposes of this section.

E. No change of circumstances other than as described in this section revokes a will.

45-2-509. Revival of revoked will.

If a person having made a will makes a subsequent will, revoking the prior will, and afterwards revokes the subsequent will, the prior will is not thereby made valid, unless the validity of the prior will is acknowledged in writing.[167]

NEW YORK

Section 3-4.1. Revocation of wills; effect on codicils.

(a) Except as otherwise provided in this chapter, a revocation or alteration, if intended by the testator, may be effected in the following manner only:

(1) A will or any part thereof may be revoked or altered by:

(A) Another will.

(B) A writing of the testator clearly indicating an intention to effect such revocation or alteration, executed with the formalities prescribed by this article for the execution and attestation of a will.

(2) A will may be revoked by:

(A) An act of burning, tearing, cutting, cancellation, obliteration, or other mutilation of destruction performed by:

(i) The testator.

(ii) Another person, in the presence and by the direction of the testator; in which case, the fact that the will was so revoked in the presence and by the direction of the testator shall be proved by at least two witnesses, neither of whom shall be the person who performed the act of revocation.

(B) In addition to the methods set forth in paragraph (A), a will may be revoked or altered by a nuncupative or holographic declaration of revocation or alteration made in the circumstances described by 3-2.2 by any person therein authorized to make a nuncupative or holographic will. Any such nuncupative declaration of revocation or alteration must be clearly established by at least two witnesses; any such holographic declaration, by an instrument written entirely in the handwriting of the testator, although not executed and attested in accordance with the formalities prescribed by this article for the execution and attestation of a will.

(C) The revocation of a will, as provided in this section, revokes all codicils thereto.

Section 3-4.2. Agreement to convey property previously disposed of by will not a revocation.

An agreement made by a testator to convey any property does not revoke a prior testamentary disposition of such property; but such property passes under the will to the beneficiaries, subject to whatever rights were created by such agreement.

Section 5-1.3. Revocatory effect of marriage after execution of will.

(a) If the testator leaves a will executed prior to September 1, 1930 and marries at any time after such will was executed, the spouse who survives such testator is entitled to succeed to the same portion of the testator's estate as would have passed to such spouse had the testator died intestate, unless provision was made for the surviving spouse by ante nuptial agreement in writing. No evidence shall be admissible to impair or defeat the rights of a surviving spouse hereunder except to establish the existence of such ante nuptial agreement.

(b) A surviving spouse may recover the portion of the testator's estate to which he is entitled under this section from the beneficiaries, ratably, out of the portions of the estate passing to such persons under the will. In abating the interests of the beneficiaries the character of the testamentary plan adopted by the testator shall be preserved to the maximum extent possible.

(c) A surviving spouse may waive his right under this section to an intestate share of the testator's estate and may accept in lieu thereof any benefits he may have received, in whatever status, under the will.[168]

NORTH CAROLINA

Section 31-5.1 Revocation of written will.

A written will, or any part thereof, may be revoked only

(1) By a subsequent written will or codicil or other revocatory writing executed in the manner provided herein for the execution of written wills, or

(2) By being burnt, torn, canceled, obliterated, or destroyed, with the intent and for the purpose of revoking it, by the testator himself or by another person in his presence and by his direction.

Section 31-5.3. Will not revoked by marriage; dissent from will made prior to marriage.

A will is not revoked by a subsequent marriage of the maker; and the surviving spouse may dissent from such will made prior to the marriage in the same manner, upon the same conditions, and to the same extent, as a surviving spouse may dissent from a will made subsequent to marriage.

Section 31-5.4. Revocation by divorce.

Dissolution of marriage by absolute divorce after making a will does not revoke the will of any testator but is revokes all provisions in the will in favor of the testator's spouse so divorced, including but not by way of limitation, the appointment of such spouse as executor or executrix.[169]

NORTH DAKOTA

30.1.-08-07 (2-507). Revocation by writing or by act.

A will or any part thereof is revoked: 1. By a subsequent will which revokes the prior will or part expressly or by inconsistency; or 2. By being burned, torn, canceled, obliterated, or destroyed, with the intent and for the purpose of revoking it by the testator or by another person in his presence and by his direction.

30.1-08-08 (2-508). Revocation by divorce—No revocation by other changes of circumstances.

If after executing a will the testator is divorced or his marriage annulled, the divorce or annulment revokes any disposition or appointment of property made by the will to the former spouse, any provision conferring a general or special power of appointment on the former spouse, and any nomination of the former spouse as executor, trustee, conservator, or guardian, unless the will expressly provides otherwise. Property prevented from passing to a former spouse because of revocation by divorce or annulment passes as if the former spouse failed to survive the decedent, and other provisions conferring some power or office on the former spouse are interpreted as if the spouse failed to survive the decedent. If provisions are revoked solely by this section, they are revived by testator's remarriage to the former spouse. For purposes of this section, divorce or annulment means any divorce or annulment which would exclude the spouse as a surviving spouse within the meaning of Sec. 30.1-10-02. A decree of separation which does not terminate the status of husband and wife is not a divorce for purposes of this section. No change of circumstances other than as described in this section revokes a will.[170]

OHIO

Section 2107.33. Revocation of will.

(A) A will shall be revoked by the testator by tearing, canceling, obliterating, or destroying it with the intention of revoking it, or by some person in the testator's presence, or by the testator's express written direction, or by some other written will or codicil, executed as prescribed by Sections 2107.01 to 2107.62 of the Revised Code, or by some other writing that is signed, attested, and subscribed in the manner provided by those sections. A will that has been declared valid and is in the possession of a probate judge may also be revoked according to division (C) of section 2107.084 [2107.08.4] of the Revised Code.

(B) If a testator removes a will that has been declared valid and is in the possession of a probate judge pursuant to Section 2107.084 [2107.08.4] of the Revised Code from the possession of the judge, the declaration of validity that was rendered no longer has any effect.

(C) If after executing a will, a testator is divorced, obtains a dissolution of marriage, or has his marriage annulled, or upon actual separation from his spouse, enters into a separation agreement whereby the parties intend to fully and finally settle their prospective property rights in the property of the other, whether by expected inheritance or otherwise, any disposition or appointment of property made by the will to the former spouse, any provision in the will conferring a general or special power of appointment on the former spouse, and any nomination in the will of the former spouse as executor, trustee, or guardian, shall be revoked unless the will expressly provides otherwise.

(D) Property prevented from passing to a former spouse because of revocation by this section shall pass as if the former spouse failed to survive the decedent, and other provisions conferring some power or office on the former spouse shall be interpreted as if the spouse failed to survive the decedent. If provisions are revoked solely by this section, they shall be deemed to be revived by testator's remarriage with the former spouse or upon the termination of a separation agreement executed by them.

(E) A bond, agreement, or covenant made by a testator, for a valuable consideration, to convey property previously devised or bequeathed in a will, does not revoke the devise or bequest. The property passes by the devise or bequest, subject to the remedies on the bond, agreement, or covenant, for a specific performance or otherwise, against the devisees or legatees, that might be had by law against the heirs of the testator, or his next of kin, if the property had descended to them.

Section 2107.37. Subsequent marriage.

A will executed by an unmarried person is not revoked by a subsequent marriage.[171]

OKLAHOMA

Section 101. Revocation of wills.

Except in the cases in this article mentioned no written will, or any part thereof, can be revoked or altered otherwise than:

1. By a written will or other writing of the testator, declaring such revocation or alteration, and executed with the same formalities with which a will should be executed by such testator; or,

2. By being burnt, torn, canceled, obliterated, or destroyed, with intent and for the purpose of revoking the same, by the testator himself, or by some person in his person and by his direction.

Section 114. Divorce or annulment as revoking will.

If, after making a will, the testator is divorced, all provisions in such will in favor of the testator's spouse so divorced are thereby revoked. Annulment of the testator's marriage shall have the same effect as a divorce. Provided, however, this section shall not apply if the decree of divorce or of annulment is vacated or if the testator remarries his former spouse.[172]

OREGON

112.275. Manner of revocation or alteration exclusive.

A will may be revoked or altered only as provided in ORS 112.285 to 112.315.

112.285. Express revocation or alteration.

(1) A will may be revoked or altered by another will.

(2) A will may be revoked by being burned, torn, canceled, obliterated, or destroyed, with the intent and purpose of the testator of revoking the will, by the testator, or by another person at the direction of the testator and in the presence of the testator. The injury or destruction by a person other than the testator at the direction and in the presence of the testator shall be proved by at least two witnesses.

112.305. Revocation by marriage.

A will is revoked by the subsequent marriage of the testator if the testator is survived by his spouse, unless:

(1) The will evidences an intent that it not be revoked by the subsequent marriage or was drafted under circumstances establishing that it was in contemplation of the marriage; or

(2) The testator and his spouse entered into a written contract before the marriage that either makes provision for the spouse or provides that the spouse is to have no rights in the estate of the testator.

112.315. Revocation by divorce or annulment.

Unless a will evidences a different intent of the testator, the divorce or annulment of the marriage of the testator after the execution of the will revokes all provisions in the will in favor of the former spouse of the testator and any provision therein naming the former spouse as executor, and the effect of the will is the same as though the former spouse did not survive the testator.[173]

PENNSYLVANIA

Section 2505. Revocation of a will.

No will or codicil in writing, or any part thereof, can be revoked or altered otherwise than:

(1) Will or codicil. By some other will or codicil in writing;

(2) Other writing. By some other writing declaring the same, executed and proved in the manner required of wills; or

(3) Act to the document. By being burnt, torn, canceled, obliterated, or destroyed, with the intent to and for the purpose of revocation, by the testator himself or by another person in his presence and by his express direction. If such act is done by any person other than the testator, the direction of the testator must be proved by the oaths or affirmations of two competent witnesses.

Section 2507. Modification by circumstances.

Wills shall be modified upon the occurrence of any of the following circumstances, among others:

(1) Death within 30 days; religious and charitable gifts. Any bequest or devise for religious or charitable purposes included in a will or codicil executed within 30 days of the death of the testator shall be invalid to the extent that someone who would benefit by its invalidity objects: Provided, That the Commonwealth shall not have the right to so object. No such objection shall be valid unless it is in writing signed by the objector and unless a copy thereof shall be filed with the clerk of the court having jurisdiction within six months of the probate of the will. Each person so objecting shall receive the share he would have received if the entire bequest or devise shall be valid. The 30-day period shall be so computed as to include the day on which the will or codicil is written and to exclude the day of death. Unless the testator directs otherwise, if such a will or

codicil could revoke or supersede a prior will or codicil executed at least 30 days before the testator's death, and not theretofore revoked or superseded and the original of which can be produced in legible condition, and if each instrument shall contain an identical gift for substantially the same religious or charitable purpose, the gift in the later will or codicil shall not be subject to objection; or if each instrument shall give for substantially the same religious or charitable purpose a cash legacy or a share of the residuary estate or a share of the same asset, payable immediately or subject to identical prior estates and conditions, the later gift shall not be subject to objection to the extent to which it shall not exceed the prior gift. If a bequest or devise is revoked within 30 days of death and the revocation has the effect of increasing the religious or charitable bequest or devise, such increase shall not be considered a new or additional bequest or devise for religious or charitable purposes within the meaning of this act.

(2) Divorce. If the testator is divorced from the bonds of matrimony after making a will, all provisions in the will in favor of or relating to his spouse so divorced thereby become ineffective for all purposes.

(3) Marriage. If the testator marries after making a will, the surviving spouse shall receive the share of the estate to which he would have been entitled had the testator died intestate, unless the will shall give him a greater share.

(4) Birth or adoption. If the testator fails to provide in his will for his child born or adopted after making his will, unless it appears from the will that the failure was intentional, such child shall receive out of the testator's property not passing to a surviving spouse, such share as he would have received if the testator had died unmarried and intestate owning only that portion of his estate not passing to a surviving spouse.

(5) Slaying. Any person who participates either as a principal or as an accessory before the fact in the willful and unlawful killing of any person shall not in any way acquire property or receive any benefits as the result of the willful and unlawful killing but such property or benefits shall be distributed as provided by Chapter 88 of this code (relating to slayers).[174]

RHODE ISLAND

33-5-9. Revocation of will by marriage.

The marriage of a person shall act as a revocation of a will made by him previous to such marriage unless it appears from the will that it was made in contemplation thereof; but if the will exercises a power of appointment and the real and personal property thereby appointed would not, in default of such appointment, pass to the persons who would have been entitled to it had it been the property and estate of the testator making such appointment and had he died intestate, so much of the will as makes such appointment shall not be revoked by such marriage.

33-5-10. Methods of revoking will.

No will or codicil or any part thereof shall be revoked otherwise than as provided in Sec. 33-5-9, or by another will or codicil executed in manner hereinbefore required, or by some writing declaring an intention to revoke the same and executed in the manner in which a will is hereinbefore required to be executed, or by burning, tearing, or otherwise destroying the same by the testator, or by some person in his presence and by his direction, with the intention of revoking the same.

33-5-11. Alteration of circumstances.

No will shall be revoked by any presumption of intention on the ground of an alteration in circumstances.[175]

SOUTH CAROLINA

Section 21-7-210. Revocation of will generally.

No wills or testament in writing of any real or personal property or any clause thereof shall be revocable but by some other will or codicil in writing, or other writing declaring the same, attested and subscribed by three witnesses as required by Section 21-7-50, or by destroying or obliterating the same by the testator himself, or some other person in his presence, and by his direction and consent.

Section 21-7-220. Revocation by marriage.

If any person making a will shall afterwards marry and die leaving his widow or leaving issue of such marriage, unless the will shall have been made in contemplation of marriage expressed on its face and shall contain provision for future wife and children, if any, such marriage shall be deemed and taken to be a revocation of such will to all intents and purposes.

Section 21-7-230. Revocation by divorce a vinculo.

Any will offered for and admitted to probate, subsequent to April 22, 1966, made by husband and wife who have been divorced, a vinculo matrimonii, from each other subsequent to the date of the will shall be made null and void by means of the divorce insofar as the will affects the surviving divorced spouse as beneficiary, trustee, executor, or any other capacity, unless the will shall have been made in contemplation of such divorce expressed on its face.[176]

SOUTH DAKOTA

29-3-1. Primary means of revoking will.

Except in the cases in this chapter mentioned, no written will, or any part thereof, can be revoked or altered, otherwise than:

(1) By a written will or other writing of the testator, declaring such revocation or alteration, and executed with the same formalities with which a will should be executed by such testator; or

(2) By being burned, torn, canceled, obliterated, or destroyed, with the intent and for the purpose of revoking the same, by the testator himself, or by some person in his presence and by his direction.

29-3-2. Prior will not revoked by subsequent will unless express or inconsistent.

A prior will is not revoked by a subsequent will unless the latter contains an express revocation, or provisions wholly inconsistent with the terms of the former will; but in other cases the prior will remains effectual so far as consistent with the provisions of the subsequent will.

29-3-3. Revocation by obliteration.

A revocation by obliteration on the face of the will may be partial or total and is complete if the material part is so obliterated as to show an intention to revoke; but where, in order to effect a new disposition the testator attempts to revoke a provision of the will by altering or obliterating it on the fact thereof, such revocation is not valid unless the new disposition is legally effected.

29-3-4. Proof of testator's direction to destroy will.

When a will is canceled or destroyed by any other person than the testator, the direction of the testator and the fact of such injury or destruction must be proved by two witnesses.

29-3-5. Revocation of duplicate will.

The revocation of a will, executed in duplicate, may be made by revoking one of the duplicates.

29-3-6. Prior will not revived by revocation of subsequent will.

If after making a will, the testator duly makes and executes a subsequent will, the destruction, canceling, or revocation of the latter does not revive the former, unless it appears by the terms of such revocation that it was his intention to revive the former will, or unless after such destruction, canceling, or revocation he duly republishes the prior will.

29-3-7. Revocation of will by subsequent marriage where spouse survives—Evidence rebutting presumption of revocation.

If a person, after making a will, marries, and the spouse survives such testator or testatrix, the will is revoked, unless provision has been made for the surviving spouse by marriage contract, or unless the surviving spouse is provided for in the will, or in such way mentioned therein as to show an intention not to make such provision; and no other evidence to rebut the presumption of revocation can be received.

29-3-8. Revocation of will by subsequent marriage where issue survives—Evidence rebutting presumption of revocation.

If a person, after having made a will, marries and has issue of such marriage, born either in the lifetime or after the death of such person, and the issue survives such person, the will is revoked unless provision has been made for such issue by some settlement, or unless such issue is provided for in the will, or in such way mentioned therein as to show an intention not to make such provision; and no other evidence to rebut the presumption of such revocation can be received.

29-3-9. Codicils revoked by revocation of will.
The revocation of a will revokes all its codicils.[177]

TENNESSEE

"A will is not revoked by subsequent marriage of testator without issue of such marriage, nor is the will of a married person revoked by subsequent birth of a child; but a will is revoked by testator's subsequent marriage and the birth of a child to such marriage."[178]

TEXAS

Section 63. Revocation of wills.
No will in writing, and no clause thereof or devise therein, shall be revoked, except by a subsequent will, codicil, or declaration in writing, executed with like formalities, or by the testator destroying or canceling the same, or causing it to be done in his presence.

Section 69. Voidness arising from divorce.
(a) If the testator is divorced after making a will, all provisions in the will in favor of the testator's spouse so divorced, or appointing such spouse to any fiduciary capacity under the will or with respect to the testate or person of the testator's children, shall be null and void and of no effect.
(b) A person who is divorced from the decedent or whose marriage to the decedent has been annulled is not a surviving spouse unless, by virtue of a subsequent marriage, the person is married to the decedent at the time of death.[179]

UTAH

75-2-507. Revocation by writing or by act.
(1) A will or any part thereof is revoked:
(a) By a subsequent will which revokes the prior will or part expressly or by inconsistency; or
(b) By being burned, torn, canceled, obliterated, or destroyed, with the intent and for the purpose of revoking it by the testator or by another person in his presence and by his direction.
(2) The revocation of a will executed in duplicate may be accomplished by revoking one of the duplicates.

75-2-508. Revocation by divorce—No revocation by other changes of circumstances.
If after executing a will the testator is divorced or his marriage annulled, the divorce or annulment revokes any disposition or appointment of property made by the will to the former spouse or to any issue of the former spouse who are not also issue of the testator, any provision conferring a general or special power

of appointment on the former spouse or such issue, and any nomination of the former spouse or such issue as executor, trustee, conservator, or guardian, unless the will expressly provides otherwise. Property prevented from passing to a former spouse or such issue because of revocation under this section passes as if the former spouse and such issue failed to survive the decedent, and other provisions conferring some power or office on the former spouse or such issue are interpreted as if the spouse or issue failed to survive the decedent. If provisions are revoked solely by this section, they are revived by testator's remarriage to the former spouse. For purposes of this section, divorce or annulment has reference to the interlocutory decree entered by the court and also means any divorce or annulment which would exclude the spouse as a surviving spouse within the meaning of subsection 75-2-803(2). A decree of separation which does not terminate the status of husband and wife is not a divorce for purposes of this section. No change of circumstances other than as described in this section revokes a will or any part thereof.[180]

VERMONT

Section 11. How revoked.

A will shall not be revoked, except by implication of law, otherwise than by some will, codicil, or other writing, executed as provided in case of wills; or by burning, tearing, canceling, or obliterating the same, with the intention of revoking it, by the testator himself, or by some person in his presence and by his express direction.

''A will is not revoked by subsequent marriage or birth of a child (45 Vt. 145),'' page 21, Vermont Law Digest,' *Martindale-Hubbell Law Directory,* Volume VII, 1984.[181]

VIRGINIA

Section 64.1-58. Revocation of wills generally.

No will or codicil, or any part thereof, shall be revoked, unless by a subsequent will or codicil, or by some writing declaring an intention to revoke the same, executed in the manner in which a will is required to be executed, or by the testator, or some person in his presence and by his direction, cutting, tearing, burning, obliterating, canceling, or destroying the same, or the signature thereto, with the intent to revoke. The subsequent marriage of the testator or birth of a child to the testator, or both, shall not operate to revoke a will previously executed by the testator.

''When executed copy of will is traced to testator's custody and cannot be found at his death, presumption arises that it was destroyed by him with intent to revoke (216 Va. 716, 222 SE 2d 543),'' page 41, Virginia Law Digest,' *Martindale-Hubbell Law Directory,* Volume VII, 1984.

Section 64.1-59. Partial revocation by divorce.

If, after making a will, the testator is divorced a vinculo matrimonii, all provisions in the will in favor of the testator's divorced spouse are thereby revoked.

Section 64.1-60. Revival of wills after revocation.

No will or codicil, or any part thereof, which shall be in any manner revoked, shall, after being revoked, be revived otherwise than by the reexecution thereof, or by a codicil executed in the manner hereinbefore required, and then only to the extent to which an intention to revive the same is shown.

Section 64.1-61. Effect of subsequent conveyance on will.

No conveyance or other act, subsequent to the execution of a will, shall, unless it be an act by which the will is revoked as aforesaid, prevent its operation with respect to such interest in the state comprised in the will as the testator may have power to dispose of by will at the time of his death.

Section 64.1.96. Same; later will.

The title of a bona fide purchaser without notice for valuable consideration from the devisee, or from the personal representative with power to sell, encumber, lease, or exchange, under the will of a person who has died heretofore, or may die hereafter, having title to any real estate of inheritance in this Commonwealth, shall not be affected by any other devise of such real estate made by the testator in another will, unless within one year after the testator's death such other will or, if such other will has been probated, shall be filed for probate before the court or clerk having jurisdiction for that purpose and shall afterwards be admitted to probate and recorded in the proper court or clerk's office as a will of real estate.[182]

WASHINGTON

11.12.040. Revocation of will, how effected.

A will, or any part thereof, can be revoked

(1) By a written will; or

(2) By being burnt, torn, canceled, obliterated, or destroyed, with the intent and for the purpose of revoking the same, by the testator himself or by another person in his presence and by his direction. If such act is done by any person other than the testator, the direction of the testator and the facts of such injury or destruction must be proved by two witnesses.

11.12.050. Subsequent marriage of testator—Divorce.

If, after making any will, the testator shall marry and the spouse shall be living at the time of the death of the testator, such will shall be deemed revoked as to such spouse, unless provision shall have been made for such survivor by marriage settlement, or unless such survivor be provided for in the will or in such way mentioned therein as to show an intention not to make such provision, and no other evidence to rebut the presumption of revocation shall be received. A divorce, subsequent to the making of a will, shall revoke the will as to the divorced spouse.[183]

WEST VIRGINIA

Section 41-1-6. When marriage, annulment, or divorce revokes will; certain exceptions.

Every will made by a man or woman shall be revoked by his or her marriage, annulment, or divorce, except a will which makes provision therein for such contingency, or a will which, though not making provision for such contingency, is made in exercise of a power of appointment, when the estate thereby appointed would not, in default of such appointment, pass to his or her heirs, personal representative, or next of kin: Provided, that even when the estate thereby appointed would, in default of such appointment, pass to his or her heirs, personal representative, or next of kin, such will shall, nevertheless, not be revoked (a) by such marriage if such marriage is between the person appointed in the exercise of such power of appointment and the person exercising such power of appointment, or (b) by such annulment or divorce, unless the person appointed in the exercise of such power of appointment is the person whose marriage to the person exercising such power of appointment was terminated by such annulment or divorce.

Section 41-1-7. Revocation generally.

No will or codicil, or any part thereof, shall be revoked, unless under the preceding section [41-1-6], or by a subsequent will or codicil, or by some writing declaring an intention to revoke the same, and executed in the manner in which a will is required to be executed, or by the testator, or some person in his presence and by his direction, cutting, tearing, burning, obliterating, canceling, or destroying the same, or the signature thereto, with the intent to revoke.[184]

WISCONSIN

853.11. Revocation.

(1) Subsequent writing or physical act. A will is revoked in whole or in part by:

(a) A subsequent will, codicil, or other instrument which is executed in compliance with s. 853.03 or 853.05 and which revokes the prior will or a part thereof expressly or inconsistency; or

(b) Burning, tearing, canceling, or obliterating the will or part, with the intent to revoke, by the testator or by some person in the testator's presence and by his direction.

(2) Subsequent marriage. A will is revoked by the subsequent marriage of the testator if the testator is survived by his spouse, unless:

(a) The will indicates an intent that it not be revoked by subsequent marriage or was drafted under circumstances indicating that it was in contemplation of the marriage or makes provision for issue of the decedent; or

(b) Testator and the spouse have entered into a contract before or after marriage, which makes provision for the spouse or provides that the spouse is to have no rights in the estate of the testator.

(3) Annulment or divorce. Any provision in a will in favor of the testator's spouse is revoked by an annulment of the marriage to such spouse or by absolute divorce.

(4) Other methods of revocation. A will is revoked only as provided in this section.

(5) Dependent relative revocation. Except as modified by sub. (6) of this section is not intended to change in any manner the doctrine of dependent relative revocation.

(6) Revival. When a will, codicil, or part thereof has been revoked by a subsequent will, codicil, or other instrument under sub. (1)(a), the later revocation of the revoking instrument by act under sub. (1)(b) revives the prior will or codicil or part thereof: (a) if there is clear and convincing evidence that the testator intended to revive the prior will, codicil, or part; or (b) if the revoking instrument is a codicil which revoked only a part of the will by inconsistency and not expressly, and the evidence is insufficient to provide that the testator intended no revival. Proof of testator's statement at or after the act of revocation is admissible to establish intent. A will, codicil, or part cannot be revived under this subsection unless the original will or codicil is produced in court.[185]

Notes

1. Henry Campbell Black, *Black's Law Dictionary*, St. Paul, Minn.: West, 1979, p. 737.

2. *Id.* at 1433.

3. *See* MASS. GEN. LAWS ANN., Ch. 191. S 5; and Joseph H. Beale, *Conflict of Laws*, Cambridge, Mass.: Harvard University Press, 1935.

4. Fair and Wright, *An Estate Planner's Handbook*, 4th ed., Boston: Little, Brown and Co., 1979.

5. William J. Bowe and Douglas H. Parker, *1 Page on the Law of Wills*, Cincinnati: W. H. Anderson Co., 1960.

6. "What You Should Know about Wills," *Consumer Reports* 434 (July 1980).

7. George W. Shumberg, *Principles of Conflict of Laws*, Chicago: Foundation Press, 1937, p. 6.

8. Walter Wheeler Cook, "Recognition of Massachusetts Rights," 33 *Yale Law Journal* 457 (1918).

9. *Michigan Trust Company v. Ferry*, 228 US 346, 33 Sup. Ct. 550, 57 L. Ed. 867 (1912).

10. Shumberg, Supra note 7, at 414.

11. *Id.* at 416.

12. *Id.* at 422.

13. *In re Handredday's Estate*, 176 Wis. 570, 186 N.W. 744 (1977).

14. *Id.* at 746.

15. Stumberg, Supra note 7, at 428.

16. *See* INTERNAL REVENUE CODE, S 2001.

17. [1 Belgium Estate Tax Treaty] TAX TREATIES (CCH), S 701-11 (1969).

18. [1 French Estate and Gift Tax Treaty] TAX TREATIES (CCH), S 2987-89 (1979).

19. [1 German Estate Tax Treaty] TAX TREATIES (CCH), S 3066-67Q (1981).

20. [1 Italian Estate Tax Treaty] TAX TREATIES (CCH), S 4354-66 (1970).

21. [1 Finnish Estate Tax Treaty] TAX TREATIES (CCH), S 2762-75 (1968).

22. [1 Irish Estate Tax Treaty] TAX TREATIES (CCH), S 4162-71 (1968).

23. [1 Austrian Estate and Gift Tax Treaty] TAX TREATIES (CCH), S 564-69 (1983).

24. [2 Norwegian Estate Tax Treaty] TAX TREATIES (CCH), S 7481-91 (1970).

25. [2 Swiss Estate Tax Treaty] TAX TREATIES (CCH) S 7481-91 (1970).

26. [2 United Kingdom Estate and Gift Tax Treaty] TAX TREATIES (CCH), S 8228-30 (1979).

27. 2 AM.JUR.2D (1964) at 946.

28. *See* George W. Thompson, *Thompson on Wills*, Indianapolis: Bobbs-Merrill, 1936.

29. "Case Comments; Illegitimacy and Intestate Succession: White v. Randolph," 41 *Ohio State Law Journal* (1980) at 1037.

30. Thompson, Supra note 28, at 38-39.

31. ALA. CODE, Vol. 22, 43-4-3, 43-8-48, 43-8-91 (Michie, 1982).

32. ALASKA STAT., Ch. 11, S 13.11.020, 13.11.045, 13.11.115 (Michie, 1982).

33. ARIZ. REV. STAT. ANN., Vol. 6, Tit. 14, S14-2109, 14-2302, 14-2601 (West, 1975).

34. ARK. STAT. ANN., Vol. 5A, S 61-141, 61-142, 61-147 (Bobbs-Merrill, 1971).

35. CAL. [Probate] CODE, Vol. 52, S 90, 250, 255, 256, 257 (West, 1956).

36. COLO. GEN. STAT. ANN., Vol. 6, S 15-11-107, 15-11-108, 15-11-109 (Bradford-Robinson Printing Co., 1973).

37. CONN. GEN. STAT. ANN., Vol. 214, Tit. 45 S 45-277, 45-287, 45-64a (West, 1981).

38. DEL. CODE ANN., Vol. 7, S 310 (1974), 505, 508 (Michie, 1979).

39. D.C. CODE ANN., Vol. 5, S 19-314, 19-316, 16-312, 16-313 (Michie, 1981).

40. FLA. STAT. ANN., Vol. 20B, S 732.101, 732.106, 732.302 (West, 1976).

41. GA. CODE ANN., Vol. 40, S 53-44 (Michie, 1982).

42. HAWAII REV. STAT., Vol. 7, Tit. 28-33, Ch. 501-825, S 532-6, 532-7, 532-9, 578-16 (Authority, 1976).

43. IDAHO CODE, Vol. 3, S 15-2-109, 15-2-302 (Bobbs-Merrill, 1979).

44. ILL. ANN. STAT., Ch. 110 1/2, S 2-2, 2-4, 4-10 (Smith-Hurd, 1978).

45. IND. CODE ANN., Tit. 29, 30, S 29-1-2-6, 7, 8, 29-1-17-3 (Burns, 1979).

46. IOWA CODE ANN., Vol. 47, S 633.220, 21, 22, 23, 633.267 (West, 1964).

47. KAN. STAT. ANN., Vol. 4, S 59-2103, 59-501 (Ensley, 1983).

48. KY. REV. STAT., Vol. 14, S 391.070, 394.090, 394.079, 199.520 (West, 1972 and Michie, 1982).

49. LA. REV. STAT., Vol. 4, Art. 214, S 917, 918, 919, 920 (West, 1982).

50. ME. REV. STAT. ANN., Vol. 10, Tit. 18-A, S 2-109, 2-302 (West, 1981).

51. MD. [Gen. Prov.] CODE ANN., S 3-107, 8, 3-301, 2, 3 (1983), [Estates & Trusts], S 1-207, 8 (Michie, 1974).

52. MASS. GEN. LAWS ANN., Vol. 31, Ch. 190-200A, S 5, 8, 7.

53. MICH. COMP. LAWS ANN., Vol. 36, S 700.108, 700.110, 11, 700.124, 700.127 (West, 1980).

54. MINN. STAT. ANN., Vol. 31, S 525.171, 2 (West, 1975).

55. MISS. CODE ANN., Vol. 20, S 91-1-15, 91-1-29, 91-5-5, 93-17-3 (Lawyer's Co-operative Publishing, 1973).

56. MO. ANN. STAT., Vol. 28, S 474.060, 474.050, 453.090 (Vernon, 1956).

57. MONT. CODE ANN., S 72-2-205, 72-2-212, 13, 72-2-602 (1981) (Montana Legislative Council, 1981).

58. NEB. REV. STAT., Vol. 11A, S 30-2308, 9, 30-2321 (Revisor of Statutes, 1979).

59. NEV. REV. STAT. ANN., Vol. 6, Tit. 13, S 127.160, 133.160 (Legislative Council Bureau, 1983).

60. N.H. REV. STAT. ANN., Vol. 5, Ch. 514-567, S 551:10 (Equity, 1974).

61. N.J. STAT. ANN., Tit. 38, S 3B:5-8, 9, 10 (West, 1983).

62. N.M. STAT. ANN., Vol. 7, Ch. 40-49, S 45-2-107, 8, 9, 45-2-301, (Michie, 1978).

63. N.Y. [EPTL] LAW, Vol. 17B, Art. 4, S 4-1.2, 5-3.2, 6-5.7 (McKinney, 1981).

64. N.C. GEN. STAT., Vol. 2A, S 29-17, 29-19, 28A-22-2 (Michie, 1976).

65. N.D. CENT. CODE, Vol. 6, S 30.1-04-08 (Allen Smith, 1976).

66. OHIO REV. CODE ANN., S 2105.27 (Anderson, 1976).

67. OKLA. STAT. ANN., Tit. 83-84, S 215, 216, 218, 219, 220, 221, 222, 228 (West, 1970).

68. OR. REV. STAT., Vol. 1, S 112.075, 112.095, 112.105, 109.060, 112.175, 112.185, 112.405 (Legislative Counsel Committee, 1981).

69. PA. CONS. STAT. ANN., Tit. 20, S 2107, 2108 (West, 1982).

70. R.I. GEN. LAWS, Vol. 6, S 33-1-8, 33-6-23 (Michie, 1969).

71. S.C. CODE ANN., Vol. 9, Tit. 21-25, S 21-1-30, 21-3-30, 15-45-130 (Lawyers Co-operative Publishing, 1976).

72. S.D. CODIFIED LAWS ANN., Vol. 9, Tit. 25-30, S 2-104, 2-108, 9, 2-302, 2-611 (Allen Smith, 1979).

73. TENN. CODE ANN., Vol. 6, S 31-114, 15, 16, (Michie, 1977).

74. TEX. [Probate] CODE ANN., Vol. 17a, s 40, 67 (Vernon, 1980).

75. UTAH CODE ANN., Vol. 8A, S 75-2-108, 9 (Allen-Smith, 1978).

76. VT. STAT. ANN., Tit. 14-16, S 553, 557 (Equity, 1974).

77. VA. CODE ANN., Vol. 9A, S 64.1-5.1, 5.2, 64.1-70, 64.1-7.1, 64.1-8.1 (Michie, 1980).

78. V.I. CODE ANN., Vol. 3, Tit. 14-16, S 84 (Equity, 1964).

79. WASH. REV. CODE ANN., Tit., II, S 11.04.081, 11.04.085, 11.12.090 (West, 1967).

80. W. VA. CODE ANN., Vol. 12, S 42-1-5, 42-1-8, 48-4-5 (Michie, 1982).

81. WIS. STAT. ANN., Vol. 110H, S 851.51, 852.05, 853.25 (West, 1971).

82. WYO. STAT., Tit. 2, S 2-4-103, 2-4-107 (Michie, 1977).

83. ALA. CODE, Vol. 22, S 43-8-40, 43-4-41, 43-8-42, 43-8-44 (West, 1975).

84. ALASKA STAT., Ch. 11, S 13.11.005, 13.11.010, 13.11.015, 13.11.025 (West, 1982).

85. ARIZ. REV. STAT. ANN., Vol. 6, Tit. 14, S 14-2101, 2, 3, 14-2105 (West, 1975).

86. ARK. STAT. ANN., Vol. 5A, S 61-132, 61-149, 50 (Bobbs-Merrill, 1971).

87. CAL. (Probate] CODE, Vol. 52, S 201, 201.5, 202, 203, 221, 222, 223, 224, 225, 226, 228, 229, 230, 231 (West, 1956).

88. COLO. REV. STAT. ANN., Vol. 6, S 15-11-101, 2, 3, (West, 1973).

89. CONN. GEN. STAT. ANN., Vol. 21A, Tit. 45, S 45-273, 73a, 45-276 (West, 1981).

90. DEL. CODE ANN., Vol. 7, S 501, 502 (West, 1979).

91. D.C. CODE ANN., S 19-301, 2, 3, 4, 5, 6, 7, 8, 9, 10, 11, 12, 13 (West, 1981).

92. FLA. STAT. ANN., Vol. 20B, Tit. XLI, S 732.101, 2, 3, (West, 1976).

93. GA. CODE ANN., Vol. 40, S 53-4-2, 3, 19-8-14 (West, 1982).

94. HAWAII REV., Vol. 7, Tit. 28-33, STAT. S 532-3, 532-4 (West, 1976).

95. IDAHO CODE ANN., VOL. 3, S 15-2-101, 2, 3, 4, 5, (West, 1979).

96. ILL. ANN. STAT., Ch. 110 1/2, S 2-1 (Smith-Hurd, 1978).

97. IND. CODE ANN., Tit. 29-30, S 29-1-2-1 [6-201], 2 (6-202], 3 (6-203], 4 [6-204] (Burns, 1972).

98. IOWA CODE ANN., Vol. 46, S. 633.210, 11, 12, 633.218, 19 (West, 1964).

99. KAN. STAT. ANN., Vol. 4, S 59-502, 59-504, 5, 6, 7, 8, 59-514 (West, 1976).

100. KY. REV. STAT., Vol. 14, S 391.010, 020, 030 (Bobbs-Merrill, 1972).

101. LA. REV. STAT., Vol. 4, Art. 886, 887, 888, 890, 891, 892, 895, 896, 897, 898, 900, 901, 902, 903, 904, 905, 906, 908, 909, 910, 911, 912, 913, 915, 916 (West, 1952).

102. ME. REV. STAT. ANN., Vol. 10, Tit. 18, 18-A, S 2-101, 2, 3, 2-106 (West, 1981).

103. MD. [Estates and Trusts] CODE ANN., S 3-101, 2, 3, 4, 5, 3-110, 3-210, 3-203, 4, 5, 3-208 (Michie, 1974).

104. MASS. GEN. LAWS ANN., Vol. 31, Ch. 190-200A, S 1, 2, 3.

105. MICH. COMP. LAWS ANN., Vol. 36, S 104, 105, 106 (West, 1980).

106. MINN. STAT. ANN., Vol. 31B, S 525.13, 525.145, 525.15, 16, 525.161 (West, 1975).

107. MISS. CODE ANN., Vol. 20, S 91-1-1, 91-1-3, 91-1-7, 91-1-9, 91-1-11, 91-1-13 (West, 1973).

108. MO. ANN. STAT., Vol. 26, S 474.010 (Vernon, 1956).

109. MONT. CODE ANN., S 72-2-201, 2, 3, 72-2-207, 72-2-503 (West, 1981).

110. NEB. REV. STAT., Vol. 11A S 30-2301, 2, 3 (West, 1979).

111. NEV. REV. STAT. ANN., Vol. 6, S 123.250, 134.010, 134.030, 134.040, 34.050, 134.060, 134.070, 134.090, 134.100, 134.110, 134.120 (1979).

112. N.H. REV. STAT. ANN., Vol. 5, S 561:1, 561:8, 9 (Equity, 1974).

113. N.J. STAT. ANN., Tit. 3B, S 3B:5-2, 3, 4, 5, 3B:5-16 (West, 1983).

114. N.M. STAT. ANN., Ch. 45, Pamph. 67, S 45-2-101, 2, 3, 45-2.105 (West, 1978).

115. N.Y. [EPTL] LAW, Book 17B, Art. 4, S 4-1.1 (McKinney, 1981).

116. N.C. GEN. Stat., Vol. 2A, S 29-13, 14, 29-16 (Michie, 1976).

117. N.D CENT. CODE, Vol. 6, S 30.1-04-01 (2-101), 2 (2-102), (2-103), 30.1-04-05 (2-105), 30.1-04-99 (2-109) (Allen Smith, 1976).

118. OHIO REV. CODE ANN., S 2105.6, 2105.14 (Page, 1976).

119. OKLA. STAT. ANN., Tit. 83-84, S 211, 212, 213, 60.16 (West, 1970).

120. OR. REV. STAT., Vol. 1, S 112.015, 112.025, 112.035, 112.045, 112.055 (West, 1981).

121. PA. CONS. STAT. ANN., Tit. 20, S 2101, 2102, 2103, 2104, 2105, 2110, 2111, 2112 (Purdon's 0000).

122. LAWS OF PUERTO RICO ANN., Vol. 7A, Ch. 223, Tit. 31, S 2591, 2592, 2593, 2602, 2604, 2605, 2606, 2607, 2608, 2609, 2621, 2622, 2623, 2624, 2625, 2626, 2641, 2642, 2643, 2644, 2645, 2651, 2652, 2653, 2654, 2661, 2671, 2672, 2673, 2674, 2675, 2676, 2677, 2678, 2691, 2692, 2693 (West, 1967).

123. R.I. GEN. LAWS, Vol. 6, Ch. 43, S 33-1.1, 2, 3, 15-7-16 (West, 1969).

124. S.C. CODE ANN., Vol. 9, S 21-3-20 (West, 1976).

125. S.D. CODIFIED LAWS ANN., Vol., 9, Tit. 25, S 29-1-4, 5, 6, 7, 8, 9, 29-1-24 (West, 1976).

126. TENN. CODE ANN., Vol. 6, S 31-110, 11, 31-201, 2 (West, 1977).

127. TEX. [Probate] CODE ANN., Vol. 17A, S 38, 39, 43, 45, 46 (Vernon, 1980).

128. UTAH CODE ANN., Vol. 8A, S 75-2-101, 2, 3, 4, 5 (West, 1978).
129. VT. STAT. ANN., Tit. 14-16, S 551, 559, 448 (West, 1974).
130. VA. CODE, Vol. 9A, S 64.1-1, 2, 3, 64.1-11, 12 (West, 1980).
131. V.I. CODE ANN., Vol. 3, Tit. 14-16, S 84 (West, 1964).
132. WASH. REV. CODE ANN., Title. II, S 11.04.015, 11.04.250 (West, 1967).
133. W.VA. CODE ANN., Vol. 12, S 42-1-1, 42-1-3, 42-1-9 (West, 1982).
134. WIS. STAT. ANN., Vol. 40H, S 852.01 (West, 1971).
135. WYO. STAT., Tit. 2, S 2-4-101 (West, 1977).
136. ALA. CODE, Vol. 27, 43-8-136, 37 (West, 1975).
137. ALASKA STAT., Ch. 11, S 13.11.180, 13.11.185, 13.11.190, 13.11.195 (West, 1962).
138. ARIZ. REV. STAT. ANN., Vol. 6, Tit. 14, S 14-2507, 8 (West, 1975).
139. ARK. STAT. ANN., Vol. 5A, S 60-406, 7, 60-412, 60-414 (West, 1971).
140. CAL. [Probate] CODE, Vol. 52, S 70, 71, 72, 74, 80 (West, 1956).
141. COLO. REV. STAT., Vol. 6, S 15-11-507, 8, 9 (West, 1973).
142. CONN. GEN. STAT. ANN., Vol. 21A, Tit. 45, S 45-162 (West, 1962).
143. DEL. CODE ANN., Vol. 7, S 208, 209 (West, 1979).
144. D.C. CODE ANN., Vol. 5, S 18-109 (West, 1981).
145. FLA. STAT. ANN., Vol. 20B, Tit. XLI, S 732.505, 6, 732.508, 9 (West, 1976).
146. GA. CODE ANN., Vol. 40, S 53-2-74, 53-2-76 (West, 1982).
147. HAWAII REV. STAT., Vol. 7, Tit. 28-33, S 560:2-507, 8 (West, 1976).
148. IDAHO CODE, Vol. 3, S 15-2-507, 8, 9 (West, 1979).
149. ILL. ANN. STAT., Ch. 110 1/2, S 4-7 (Smith-Hurd, 1978).
150. IND. CODE ANN., Tit. 24, 30, S 29-1-5-6, 7, 8 (West, 1972).
151. IOWA CODE ANN., Vol. 47, S 633.284 (West, 1964).
152. KAN. STAT. ANN., Vol. 4, S 59-610, 11, 12 (West, 1976).
153. KY. REV. STAT., Vol. 14, S 394.080, 394.090, 394.092 (West, 1972).
154. LA. REV. STAT., Vol. 4, Art. 1492, 1690, 1692, 1705, 3542 (West, 1952).
155. ME. REV. STAT. ANN., Vol. 10, Tit. 18-A, S 2-507, 8 (West, 1981).
156. MD. [Gen. Prov.] CODE ANN., S 4-105 (West, 1983).
157. MASS. GEN. LAWS ANN., Vol. 31, Ch. 190-200A, S 8, 9.
158. MICH. COMP. LAWS ANN., Vol. 36, S 700.124 (West, 1980).
159. MINN. STAT. ANN., Vol. 31B, S 524.2-507, 8 (West, 1975).
160. MISS. CODE ANN., Vol. 20, S 91-5-3 (West, 1973).
161. MO. ANN. STAT., Vol. 28, S 474.400, 474.420 (Vernon, 1956).
162. MONT. CODE ANN., S 72-2-321, 22, 23 (West, 1981).
163. NEB. REV. STAT., Vol. 11A, S 30-2332, 33 (West, 1979).
164. NEV. REV. STAT. ANN., Vol. 6, Tit. 13, S 133.110, 133.115, 133.120, 133.130 (West, 1983).
165. N.H. REV. STAT. ANN., Ch. 514-567, S 551:13, 14 (West, 1974).
166. N.J. STAT. ANN., Vol. 7, Ch. 40-49, S 45-2-507, 8, 9, (West, 1978).
167. N.M. STAT ANN., Vol. 7, Ch. 40-49, S 45-2-507, 8, 9 (West, 1978).
168. N.Y. [EPTL] LAW, Vol. 17B, S 3-4.1, 2, 3 (McKinney, 1981).
169. N.C. GEN. STAT., Vol. 2A, S 31-5.1, 31.5.3, 4 (West, 1976).
170. N.D. CENT. CODE, Vol. 6, S 30.1-08-07 (2-507) (2-508) (West, 1976).
171. OHIO REV. CODE ANN., S 2107.33, 2107.37 (Page, 1976).
172. OKLA. STAT. ANN., Tit. 83-84, S 101, 114 (West, 1970).
173. OR. REV. STAT., Vol. 1, S 112.275, 112.285, 112.305, 112, 315 (West, 1981).

174. PA. CONS. STAT. ANN., Tit. 20, S 2505, 2507.

175. R.I. GEN. LAWS, Vol. 6, Ch. 31, S 33-5-9, 10, 11 (West, 1969).

176. S.C. CODE ANN., Vol. 9, Tit. 21-25, S 21-7-210, 21-7-220, 21-7-230 (West, 1976).

177. S.D. CODIFIED LAWS ANN., S 29-3-1, 2, 3, 4, 5, 6, 7, 8, 9 (West, 1979).

178. 27 TENN. APP., 496, 182 S.W. 2d 127, at 41; *Martindale-Hubbell Law Directory* Vol. VII (1984).

179. TEX. [Probate] CODE ANN., Vol. 17A, S 63, 69 (Vernon, 1980).

180. UTAH CODE ANN., Vol. 8A S 75-2-507, 8, (West, 1978).

181. VT. STAT. ANN., Tit. 14-16, S 11 (West, 1974).

182. VA. CODE ANN., Vol. 9A, S 64.1-58, 59, 60, 61, 64.1-96 (West, 1980).

183. WASH. REV. CODE ANN., Tit. II, S 11.12.040, 11.12.050 (West, 1967).

184. W.VA. CODE ANN., Vol. 12, S 41-1-6, 41-7-7 (West, 1982).

185. WIS. STAT. ANN., Vol. 40H, S 853.11 (West, 1971).

Bibliography

ALA. CODE S 43-4-3, 43-8-48, 43-8-91 (Michie, 1982).

ALA. CODE S 43-4-41, 43-8-40-41, 42, 43-8-44, 43-8-136-37 (West, 1975).

ALASKA STAT. S. 13.11.005, 13.11.010, 13.11.015, 13.11.020, 13.11.025, 13.11.045, 13.11.115 (Michie, 1982).

ALASKA STAT. S. 13.11.180, 13.11.185, 13.11.190, 13.11.195 (West, 1962).

2 AM.JUR.2D (1964).

Analysis of the Tax Reform Act of 1984. New York: Mathew Bender, 1984.

ARIZ. REV. STAT. ANN. S 14.2101-3, 14-2105, 14-2109, 14-2302, 14-2507-8, 14-2601 (West, 1975).

ARK. STAT. ANN. S 60-406-7, 60-412, 60-414, 61-132, 61-141-42, 61-147, 61-149-50 (Bobbs-Merrill, 1971).

[1 Austrian Estate and Gift Tax Treaty] TAX TREATIES (CCH) S 564-69 (1983). Beale, Joseph H. *Conflict of Laws*. Cambridge, Mass.: Harvard University Press, 1935.

[1 Belgium Estate Tax Treaty] TAX TREATIES (CCH) S 701-11 (1969).

Black, Henry Campbell. *Black's Law Dictionary*. St. Paul, Minn.: West, 1979.

Bogert, George Gleason, and George Taylor. *The Law of Trusts and Trustees*. St. Paul, Minn.: West, 1965.

Bowe, William J. and Douglas H. Parker, *1 Page on the Law of Wills*, Cincinnati: W.H. Anderson Co., 1960.

Bureau of the Census Catalog of Publications, 1790-1972. Washington, D.C.: U.S. Government Printing Office, 1974.

CAL. [Probate] CODE S 70-72, 74, 80, 90, 201, 201.5, 202-3, 221-26, 228-31, 250, 255-57 (West, 1956).

Carmody-Wait 2d, Volumes 26-30. Rochester, N.Y.: Lawyer's Co-operative Publishing, 1980.

''Case Comments; Illegitimacy and Intestate Succession: White v. Randolph'' 41 *Ohio State Law Journal* 1037 (1980).

COLO. REV. STAT. ANN. S 15-11-101-3, 15-11-107-9, 15-11-507-9 (1973).

CONN. GEN. STAT. ANN. S 45-64a, 45-273-74, 45-276-77, 45-287 (West, 1981).

CONN. GEN. STAT. ANN. S 45-162 (West, 1962).

Cook, Walter Wheeler. ''Recognition of Massachusetts Rights.'' 33 *Yale Law Journal* 457 (1918).

Davis, Allen F., and Jim Watts. *Generations: Your Family in American History*. New York: Knopf, 1974.
D.C. CODE ANN. S 16-312-13, 18-109, 19-301-13, 19-314, 19-316 (Michie, 1981).
DEL. CODE ANN. S 208-9, 501-3, 505, 508 (Michie, 1979).
DEL. CODE ANN. S 310 (West, 1979).
Fair and Wright. *An Estate Planner's Handbook*. Boston: Little, Brown and Co., 1979.
[1 Finnish Estate Tax Treaty] TAX TREATIES (CCH) S 2762-75 (1968).
Fiore, Friedlich, McInerney, and Chevat. *Modern Estate Planning*. New York: Matthew Bender, 1984.
FLA. STAT. ANN. S 732.101-3, 732.106. 732.302, 732.505-9 (West, 1976).
[1 French Estate and Gift Tax Treaty] TAX TREATIES (CCH) S 2987-89 (1979).
GA. CODE ANN. S 19-8-14, 53-2-74, 53-2-76, 53-4-2-4 (Michie, 1982).
[1 German Estate Tax Treaty] TAX TREATIES (CCH) S 3066-7Q (1981).
In re Hanredday's Estate 176 Wis. 570, 186 N.W. 744 (1977).
HAWAII REV. STAT. S 532-2, 532-2-74, 532-2-76, 532-4, 532-6-7, 532-9, 560:2-507-8, 578-16 (Authority, 1976).
Herould, Winfred. *American Newspapers, 1821-1936: A List Available in the United States and Canada*.
IDAHO CODE S 15-2-101-5, 15-2-109, 15-2-302, 15-2-507-9 (Bobbs-Merrill, 1979).
ILL. ANN. STAT., Ch. 110 1/2, S 2-1, 2-2, 2-4, 4-7, 4-10 (Smith-Hurd, 1978).
IND. CODE ANN. S 29-1-2-6-8, 29-1-17-3 (Burns, 1979).
IND. CODE ANN. S 6-201-4, 29-1-5-6-8 (West, 1972).
IOWA CODE ANN. S 633.210.12, 633.218-19, 633.220-23, 633.267, 633.284 (West, 1964).
[1 Irish Estate Tax Treaty] TAX TREATIES (CCH) S 4162-71 (1968).
[1 Italian Estate Tax Treaty] TAX TREATIES (CCH) S 4354-66 (1970).
KAN. STAT. ANN. S 59-501, 59-2103 (Ensley, 1983).
KAN. STAT. ANN. S. 59-502, 59-504-8, 59-514, 59-610-12 (West, 1976).
KY. REV. STAT. S 199.520, 391.070 (Michie, 1982).
KY. REV. STAT. S. 391.010, 391.020, 391.030, 394.079-80, 394.090, 394.092 (West, 1972).
LA. REV. STAT. S 214, 917-20, 917-20 (West, 1982).
LA. REV. STAT. S 886-88, 890-92, 895-98, 900-6, 908-13, 915-16, Art. 1492, 1690, 1705, 3542 (West, 1952).
LAWS OF PUERTO RICO ANN., Tit. 31, S 2591-93, 2602, 2604-9, 2621-26, 2641-45, 2651-54, 2661, 2671-78, 2691-93 (1967).
MASS. GEN. LAWS ANN. Ch. 190-200A, S 1-3, 5, 7-8, 9.
7 Martindale-Hubbell Law Directory (1984).
ME. REV. STAT. ANN., Tit. 18-A, S 2-101-3, 2-106, 2-109, 2-302, 2-507-8 (West, 1981).
MD. [Gen. Prov.] CODE ANN. SS 3-107-8, 3-301-3, 4-105 (West, 1983).
MD. [Estates & Trusts] CODE ANN. S 1-207-8, 3-101-5, 3-110, 3-201, 3-203, 3-204-5, 3-208 (Michie, 1974).
MICH. COMP. LAWS ANN. S 104-6, 700.108, 700.110-11, 700.124, 700-127 (West, 1980).
Michigan Trust Company v. Ferry 228 US 346, 33 Sup. Ct. 550, 57 L.Ed. 867 (1912).
MINN. STAT. ANN. S 507-8, 524.2, 524.2-507-8, 525.13, 525.145, 525.15-16, 525.161, 525.171-2 (West, 1975).

MISS. CODE ANN. S 91-1-1, 91-1-3, 91-1-7, 91-1-9, 91-1-11, 91-1-13, 91-1-15, 91-1-29, 91-5-3, 91-5-5, 93-17-3 (Lawyer's Co-operative Publishing, 1973).

MO. ANN. STAT. S 453.090, 474.010, 474.050, 474.060, 474.400, 474.420 (Vernon, 1956).

MONT. CODE ANN. S 72-2-201-3, 72-2-205, 72-2-207, 72-2-212-13, 72-2-321-23, 72-2-503, 72-2-602 (Montana Legislative Council, 1981).

N.C. GEN. STAT. S 28A-22-2, 29-13-16, 29-17, 29-19, 31-5.1, 31-5.3-4 (Michie, 1976).

N.D. CENT. CODE S 30.1-04-01 (2-101), (2-102), (2-103), 30.1-04-05 (2-105), 30.1-04-09 (2-109), 30.1-04-08, 30.1-08-07 (2-507), (2-508) (Allen Smith, 1976).

Neagles, James and Lila. *Locating Your Immigrant Ancestor*. Logan, Utah: Everton Publishers, 1975.

NEB. REV. STAT. S 30-2301-3, 30-2308-9, 30-2321, 30-2332-33 (Revisor of Statutes, 1979).

NEV. REV. STAT. ANN. S 127.160, 133.110, 133.115, 133.120, 133.130, 133.160 (Legislative Council Bureau, 1983).

NEV. REV. STAT. ANN. S 123.250, 134.010, 134.030, 134.040, 134.050, 134.060, 134.070, 134.090, 134.100, 134.110, 134.120 (West, 1979).

New York Times Obituary Index (1858-1966).

N.H. REV. STAT. ANN. S 551:10, 551:13-14, 561:1, 561:8-9 (Equity, 1974).

N.J. STAT. ANN. S 3B:5-8-10, 3B5-2-5, 3B:5-16, 3B:3-13-14 (West, 1983).

N.M. STAT. ANN. S 45-2-101-3, 45-2-105, 45-2-107-9, 45-2-301-2, 45-2-507-9 (West, 1978).

[2 Norwegian Estate Tax Treaty] TAX TREATIES (CCH) S 6161-76 (1952).

N.Y. [EPT L] LAW S 3-4.1, 2, 4-1.1-2, 5-1.3, 5-3.2, 6-5.7 (McKinney, 1981).

OHIO REV. CODE ANN. S. 2105.6, 2105.14, 2105.17, 2105.27, 2107.33, 2107.37 (Page, 1976).

OKLA. STAT. ANN., Tit. 60.16, 83-84, S 60.16, 101, 114, 211-13, 215-22, 228 (West, 1970).

OR. REV. STAT. S 109.060, 112.015, 112.025, 112.035, 112.045, 112.055, 112.075, 112.095, 112.105, 112.175, 112.185, 112.275, 112.285, 112.305, 112.315, 112.405 (West, 1981).

PA. CONS. STAT. ANN. S 2101-5, 2107-8, 2110-12, 2505, 2507 (West, 1982).

R.I. GEN. LAWS S 15-7-16, 33-1.1-3, 33-1-8, 33-5-9-11, 33-6-23 (West, 1969).

Rottenberg, Dan. *Finding Our Fathers*. New York: Random House, 1977.

Rubincam, Milton, and Jean Stephenson. *Genealogical Research: Methods and Sources*. Washington, D.C.: American Society of Genealogists, 1966.

S.C. CODE ANN. S 15-45-130, 21-1-30, 21-3-20, 21-3-30, 21-7-210, 21-7-220, 21-7-230 (West, 1976).

Schlesinger, Edward S. *Checklist to Guide Client in Establishing Trustees' Discretionary Powers for an Adult Child's Benefit*. Englewood Cliffs, N.J.: Prentice-Hall, 1982.

Schlesinger Edward S., and Julian S. Bush, *Ascertaining the facts,-An Estate Planner's Questionnaire*. Englewood Cliffs, N.J.: Prentice Hall, 1983.

S.D. CODIFIED LAWS ANN. S 2-104-5, 2-108-9, 2-302, 2-611, 29-3-1-9 (Allen Smith, 1979).

S.D. CODIFIED LAWS ANN. S 29-1-4-9, 29-1-24 (West, 1976).

Shumberg, George W. *Principles of Conflict of Laws*. Chicago: Foundation Press, 1937.

[2 Swiss Estate Tax Treaty] TAX TREATIES (CCH) S 7481-91 (1970).

TENN. APP. 496, 182 S.W. 2d 127, at 41.

TENN. CODE ANN. S 31-110-11, 31-114-16, 31-201-2 (Michie, 1977).

TEX. [Probate] CODE ANN. S 38-40, 43, 45-46, 63, 67, 69 (Vernon, 1980).

Thompson, George W. *Thompson on Wills*. Indianapolis: Bobbs-Merrill, 1936.

[2 United Kingdom Estate and Gift Tax Treaty] TAX TREATIES (CCH) S 8228-30 (1979).

UTAH CODE ANN. S 75-2-101-5, 75-2-108-9, 75-2-507-8 (Allen Smith, 1978).

VA. CODE S 64.1-1-3, 64.1-25.1-2, 64.1-7.1, 64.1-11-12, 64.1-5, 64.1-2, 64.1-70-1, 64.1-8.1, 64.1-58-61, 64.1-96 (Michie, 1980) and 216 Va. 716, 222 SE 2d 543 at 41.

VT. STAT. ANN., Tit. 14-16, S 11, 448, 551, 553, 557, 559 (Equity, 1974).

V.I. CODE ANN. Tit. 14-16, S 84 (Equity, 1964).

WASH. REV. CODE ANN. S 11.04.015, 11.04.081, 11.04.085, 11.12.040, 11.12.090, 11.12.050 (West, 1967).

W.VA. CODE ANN. S 41-1-6-7, 42-1.1, 42-1.3, 42-1.9, 42-1-5-7, 42-1-8-9, 48-4-5 (Michie, 1982).

"What You Should Know about Wills," *Consumer Reports* 434 (July, 1980).

WIS. STAT. ANN. S 851.001-879, 851.51, 852.01, 852.05, 853.11, 853.25 (West, 1971).

WYO. STAT. S 2-4-101, 2-4-103, 2-4-107 (Michie, 1977).

Index

About the Author

M. HENNER is presently practicing law with the firm of M. Henner, P.C. & Associates in Hicksville, New York, and is Adjunct Associate Professor at the College of Insurance. He is the author of *The Laws of Wills and Intestate Distribution.*